BUILDING BRANDS

Grace Ong Yan

BUILDING BRANDS

Corporations and
Modern Architecture

LUND
HUMPHRIES

First published in 2020 by Lund Humphries

Lund Humphries
Office 3, Book House
261A City Road
London EC1V 1JX
UK

www.lundhumphries.com

Building Brands: Corporations and Modern Architecture
© Grace Ong Yan, 2020
All rights reserved

ISBN: 978–1–84822–407–0

A Cataloguing-in-Publication record for this book is available from the British Library.

Front cover: PSFS Building.
Photo: Philadelphia Saving Fund Society and Western Savings Bank photograph collection (Accession 1993.302), Hagley Museum and Library, Wilmington, DE (Image: 93302_box6_062).

Copyedited by Pamela Bertram
Designed by Jacqui Cornish
Proofread by Patrick Cole
Set in Circular Std, Champion and Berthold Akzidenz Grotesk
Printed in China

CONTENTS

1   Undulating 'Wave' architectural element that draws customers into the store, Prada Epicenter New York (completed 2001), designed by Rem Koolhaas/OMA.

1 INTRODUCTION

Communicating Messages through Business and Architecture

Today, almost everything we encounter in our man-made environment, from what we eat, wear, and drive to where we live, work, vacation, and otherwise spend our time, has been consciously branded. By definition, a brand is a name, term, design, symbol, or any other feature that identifies one seller's good or service as distinct from those of another.[1] Brands possess a precisely defined personality that elicit human emotions, and trigger 'a person's gut feeling about a product, service, or company'.[2] Strong brands consist of objects, places, individuals, or experiences that create and build on relationships between consumers and companies.[3]

It seems that everyone is in the business of brand management: not only corporations but also other entities such as universities, museums, cities, and nations, as well as individual politicians, celebrities, and artists – even architects. In fact, architects and designers are doubly implicated in the pervasiveness of branding, as not only do they cultivate emotion around their own work as professionals but, when employed by others, they contribute to their client's branding efforts through a multiplicity of design media. Architectural branding literally builds brands as constructions and environments offering rich human experiences. Consistency of architecture and design through buildings, interiors, furniture, objects, graphics, and typography have the potential to establish powerful emotional connections with the consumer.

Many corporations have utilised architecture and design as branding to powerfully connect their products with their consumers. For example, Apple Inc.'s showrooms, encased in perfect glass cubes, function as architectural icons that contribute to and intensify the Apple brand. Prada Epicenter's

Wave, designed by the high-profile Dutch architect Rem Koolhaas, creates a spectacular architectural moment that draws customers to the store and by extension, to the brand (Fig.1). In both of these cases, architecture lends more than an image; it supplies a visceral, three-dimensional spatial expression of the client and amplifies the brand. Exterior form, interior spaces, and discrete, palpable architectural elements aggregate to form an overall experience that inhabitants come to associate with a company.

Because public perception and emotion define a brand, architecture's ability to engage the public experientially and emotionally renders it a particularly compelling medium for branding. Borrowing a term from Marxist philosopher Walter Benjamin, Koolhaas refers to this as creating an 'aura' around experience through the stimulation of desire. Whereas the mass production of commodities – even those of such rarefied brands as Apple and Prada – may compromise their 'aura,' architectural design as a whole, which resists mass production, retains it. At its most successful level, brand identity and brand expansion functions as a creative enterprise delivering mystery, surprise, and delight, rather than as a financial enterprise projecting consistency, predictability, and competence.[4]

While architectural branding is thought of as a phenomenon beginning in the 1990s, this book will show that its formative period of development actually spans the late 1920s to the early 1960s, a period that coincides with the rise of the large corporation in America. During this time, the corporate headquarters emerged as an important building typology. The home of the corporation, its headquarters, became removed from manufacturing sites and, eventually, conceived as instrumental in establishing the company's brand. Commissions called upon architects to synchronise corporate image with architectural form, offering expressions of corporate ideals. The responses to this call were as numerous and varied as the clients and architects that produced them.

In this book, I examine the design of four important corporate headquarters during the mid-20th-century era, each by a noteworthy architect for an American company: the Philadelphia Saving Fund Society, in Philadelphia, Pennsylvania, of 1929–1932, by the partnership of George Howe and William Lescaze; the S.C. Johnson & Son Administration Building, in Racine, Wisconsin, of 1936–1938, by Frank Lloyd Wright; Lever House, in New York City, of 1948–1952, by Skidmore, Owings & Merrill; and the Röhm and Haas Corporate Headquarters, in Philadelphia, of 1962–1964, by Pietro Belluschi. The case studies are examined in chronological order, from the late 1920s to the early 1960s, to study the evolution of architecture as branding. While these four buildings have been previously studied as examples of corporate modernism, they have not been examined as architectural branding – a new and important revelation that this book offers. The following chapters will reveal how architectural branding developed in various ways over the years and reached a paramount expression by the 1960s.

Each corporate headquarters building was chosen in a consecutive decade to tell a different story about how exactly architecture served as branding in its specific historical context, and finally how those strategies continue to persist today. Each of the companies produced products or services that were emblematic of modern society: the Philadelphia Saving Fund Society launched the first savings fund on American soil; S.C. Johnson & Son and Lever Brothers promoted the modern virtue of cleanliness through products like floor cleaners and soap; and Röhm and Haas invented new materials for modern living, including Plexiglas. These corporations' products defined modern life in the 20th century.[5]

Whereas the first three case studies examine well-known buildings, the fourth, the Röhm and Haas headquarters, is far less studied. Architectural historian Meredith Clausen has provided rich and substantive analysis on Pietro Belluschi, which I built upon with my focus on this specific commission. I seized the opportunity to analyse this fascinating building and contribute new knowledge to the field. Because the building itself lacked substantial study, the Röhm and Haas case study was the perfect canvas onto which I could bring my own interpretations and explicate its status as a mature example of architectural branding.

Another consideration in the choice of case studies was the urban nature of the sites. Each of these companies considered building on suburban sites but ultimately made a deliberate decision to place their headquarters in an urban environment. By examining these headquarters and their siting, this book considers the trajectory of corporate modernism in an urban context – an aspect frequently overlooked by other studies.[6] Along with the consideration of urban context, I chose to expand the corporate headquarters form beyond skyscrapers. Although others have chosen to focus on this one typology, I sought to also examine the role played by a variety of building massings, low- and mid-rise, in the development of corporate architecture and branding.[7]

Corporate branding in the architecture of headquarters office buildings – the focus of this book – stands apart from other types of institutional branding and building programming. To be sure, this is not a book about the branding of the company's products, but instead explores architectural branding – how architecture and design contributed to brand identity and expanded corporate brands. Certainly, the notion of using buildings as a form of identity is hardly new. Architecture has long served as promoting its patron or client with extravagant projects like Emperor Chengzu's Forbidden City, Louis XIV's Versailles, and François Mitterrand's Grand Projects.[8]

In this study, I focus on the branding of corporations through headquarters buildings in mid-20th-century America, when both big business and modernism developed and matured. Thus, my study takes the historical context of mid-century America into account, as well as the interaction of the disciplines of business and architectural histories. Studying the corporate headquarters office building allowed an examination of the building type's close relationship to its client, or owner, and in turn, the brand. The building type is emblematic of the corporation itself, from its architecture and interior design to its furniture and graphic design. As the environment where employees work, the company's brand identity has the potential to effectively infuse the workforce. My book mines the client's connection with design, which I believe extended well beyond the pecuniary. What better way to examine an institution's branding than in the commissioning of its own headquarters, its metaphorical home?

Corporate branding philosophy represents a specific covenant between an organisation and its key stakeholder groups, including but not restricted to its customers. This covenant is clearly articulated through multiple channels of communication – from an organisation's products and services all the way down to corporate structure and staff behaviour. The result of a well-executed corporate branding strategy can be measured in its high degree of pervasiveness: it consistently infuses our lives in a way that the branding of other institutions like hotels, department stores, or universities may not.

The works profiled in this book consist exclusively of modern architecture. I chose to focus on this period because of the shared qualities of modern architecture and branding. Both developed out of the historical moment of industrialisation and mass production, both sought to reach mass audiences, and both aimed for the essential and simplified in design and messaging, respectively. As the following chapters will reveal, modern architecture as branding yielded astonishing results.

After World War II especially, examples of American corporate modernism offered an incredible coherence of design, from architecture to interior design and furniture. The experience of such consistency of design has strong effects on building occupants, and as such, was ripe for study. In addition, I sought to follow on from the insightful and excellent publications of architectural historians on corporate skyscrapers of the preceding era, the late 19th and early 20th centuries.[9] Standing on their sturdy shoulders, I set out to explore the succeeding period – the era of modern architecture – as it came to define the corporate headquarters and evolve as agents of branding. Embraced by American corporations, modern architecture became their mouthpiece.[10]

The period under consideration coincides not only with the rise of corporations in America but also with the development of the modern movement, both here and in Europe. In the literature accompanying modern architecture's appearance, the emotional and the rational were frequently depicted as at odds with each other, with the latter establishing dominance over the former. Modern architects' love affair with the rational is well documented, from Jean-Nicolas Durand's systematic, grid-based pedagogy to Le Corbusier's obsessive glorification of the steamship, aeroplane, and automobile. By the late 20th century, the functionalist language of modern architecture posed serious representational problems for the discipline, as it was seen as a self-contained exercise in form-making, decontextualised from its surrounding environment and signifying little outside of itself.[11] Influential historians who analysed modern architecture reinforced this notion that buildings built in the modern idiom lacked communicative qualities. For the headquarters as a building type, the exterior envelope carries the burden of expression. Thus, the curtain wall served as the face of the building and thus became the hallmark of corporate modernism.[12]

As the feature most commonly identified with corporate modernism, the curtain wall also became the feature most vilified – overly determinist, dull, and expressionless, it was identified as a source of societal alienation.[13] But alongside the rational, stood the emotional. While it is perhaps surprising, the architecture of the modern corporate headquarters is as emotional as it is rational. The case studies presented in this book examine corporate modernism through its role as brand-builder. And in doing so, they reveal that these iconic modern corporate headquarters defined powerful brand identities for their corporations – ones that fostered intimate connections between their clients and the American public through architecture and design. Their examination reveals a new perspective on corporate modernism and modern architecture to be a highly communicative and engaging medium of expression. Through the lens of branding, this book demonstrates an alternate perspective on modern architecture that champions its emotional and humanistic qualities.

Instrumental to accepting this historiographical shift in perspective on corporate modernism is the rejection of a once-pervasive belief in the architect as hero: that is, in the notion of the architect as the solitary genius, curing the ills of society through his or her own skilful resolution of the architectural 'problem'. In this study, I dispute the veracity of the hero-architect phenomenon by demonstrating how the collaboration among corporate clients and architects led to the success of American modernism. Information culled from my extensive research in corporate archives supports the claim that brand-conscious corporate executives exerted influence not only on their building projects' finances, but also on key design issues, thus affecting the design in profound ways.

If corporate clients played an expanded role in shaping the modern corporate headquarters, architects also went beyond the traditional scope of their work to define the modern typology of the corporate headquarters. As the case studies make clear, architect and client together developed a variety of ways to give expression to corporate identity: by incorporating signs, by trading on the fame of the architect, by developing trademark form, and by creatively incorporating company materials and products into the architectural design. How they arrived at these particular modes of communication is chronicled in the book's chapters.

As a practising architect and interior designer myself, I have designed environments and buildings that served as architectural branding for business clients. In the early 2000s, I collaborated as a designer within the interdisciplinary branding studio of Gensler in New York. There, I was part of a team that designed brand identities for a number of clients, including Toys "R" Us, the International Center of Photography, and Bally.

At the beginning of the 21st century, architectural branding was an important niche field that lacked substantial research. Invigorated by the practice of architectural branding, I engaged the topic historically through extensive primary research into the archives of business clients as well as architects. My approach, and in turn the perspective of this book, looks beyond architectural branding as merely a propaganda tool for advancing a capitalist agenda, and offers new and important models of interdisciplinary practice and designing for human engagement.

Part of a growing body of scholarship that complicates and enriches the accounts of modern architecture, *Building Brands* traces the emergence of architectural branding in corporate modernism and reveals a humanist focus. It also overturns a number of long-standing misconceptions of modern architecture: that only its rationalist models are most worthy of study, that it was primarily architect-driven, that it lacked emotional or expressive capabilities. This book tells a new story about modern architecture in America, which necessarily weaves interdisciplinary and professional considerations together with industrial, social, and economic ones. The historical backdrops of American business culture and architecture that would entwine through branding are worth examining here, as they form the background against which this critical reappraisal of corporate modernism takes place.

Branding in American Business

By the close of the Civil War, the nature of business in America that had prevailed for almost a century was in transition. In the last decades of the 19th century, the small, family-owned shops that had characterised the early Republic persisted, but they were also giving way to the large, industrialised corporations of the Gilded Age.[14] Prior to the 1880s, few companies mass-produced branded consumer products. Now, industry began producing everything from soap to cigarettes as a standardised product. As production capabilities rose, so too did the pressure to find consumers for goods, now produced in unprecedented quantities. This altered the role of – and need for – advertising.

Early advertising efforts, which had been simple and straightforward, proved inadequate in selling these goods, as more competing products emerged. More direct messaging would be needed if corporations were to secure a market for their goods and distinguish their products from similar ones. The public had to be not only educated about the use of an unfamiliar, factory-made good but also convinced of its effectiveness and superiority in order to change its buying habits. This further heightened the importance of advertising and sales.[15] Thus, in the 1880s with the rise of mass-produced goods, brands were born. To promote strong brand identification, corporations replaced earlier person-to-person relationships between consumers and local merchants with merchandising, or the sale of goods through display. Brands and branding defined the new relationship between consumers and merchandising which created the basis for consumer culture as we know it today.[16]

National advertising of mass-produced, branded goods became one of the most important developments of the post-Civil War era. While advertising is a paid announcement to the public that aims to persuade consumers to buy a product or service, branding refers to the name, logo, symbol, or design that creates a relationship between the consumer and company. Meanwhile, marketing entails business activities to bring together buyers and sellers. Businesses use all three to convince consumers to buy their products. Advertising specific products made them so appealing that consumers would accept no substitutes. A new breed of merchandisers emerged in rapidly growing American cities, creating downtown department stores such as Wanamaker's in Philadelphia, Bamberger's in Newark, Filene's in Boston, Robinson's in Los Angeles, and Marshall Field's in Chicago.[17] Meanwhile Sears Roebuck, Montgomery Ward, and other mail-order outfits advertised directly to consumers through catalogues in order to reach the rest of the US population, the majority of which, until 1920, lived in rural areas. Total advertising volume in the United States grew from about $200 million in 1880 to nearly $3 billion in 1920.

American advertising acquired a new centrality during the 1920s, with an exponential growth fuelled by the creation of new industries, economic prosperity of the post-World War I period, and the increased availability of consumer credit. Nearly all of the 'glamour' products of the era – automobiles, radios, chemicals, movies, pharmaceuticals, and electric refrigerators – established a mediated relationship with the consuming public.[18] Mass-circulation magazines and radio broadcasting provided new media through which advertisements reached consumers. Advertising came of age and modern advertisement creators became specialised facilitators of a high 'velocity of flow' in the purchase of goods.[19]

When, in October 1929, the stock market plummeted and sent the country into a devastating economic depression, public confidence in big business gave way to anxiety and mistrust. From 1929 to 1933, manufacturing output decreased by one third. As the country went into economic recovery mode, a paradox emerged. While Americans were struggling financially, they were increasingly being viewed as a vital part of the marketplace – as the purchasers of goods.[20] This consumerist view developed alongside a marked change in advertising and the subsequent emergence of branding (first product-based, later corporation-based) as an economic engine.

Depression-era advertising was loud, direct, and undignified. Many advertisers of the period cast themselves in the role of hardboiled salesmen needing to pry money out of the hands of a thrifty public.[21] Founded in 1923, the Philadelphia advertising agency Young & Rubicam pitched their services to industry in a 1931 issue of *Fortune* magazine, and their advertisement gave this tendency visual expression with a photograph of a hand tightly clutching paper currency. Underneath, a sentence printed in all capital letters declared 'America has closed its fist' (Fig.2).[22] The advertisement copy stated, 'From a nation that spent money like a drunken sailor, we have become a people who think twice before we spend at all. . . . As a result, advertising today must not only move money in the direction of specific merchandise – it must first overcome the reluctance to part with that money.'[23] The clean, aesthetically pleasing layouts that characterised the 1920s gave way to bold graphics and cluttered pages. White space dwindled as copywriters made use of every square inch of advertisement space. As business historian Roland Marchand points out, advertisers empathised with the public about economic insecurities while attempting to motivate the public to buy their clients' products.[24]

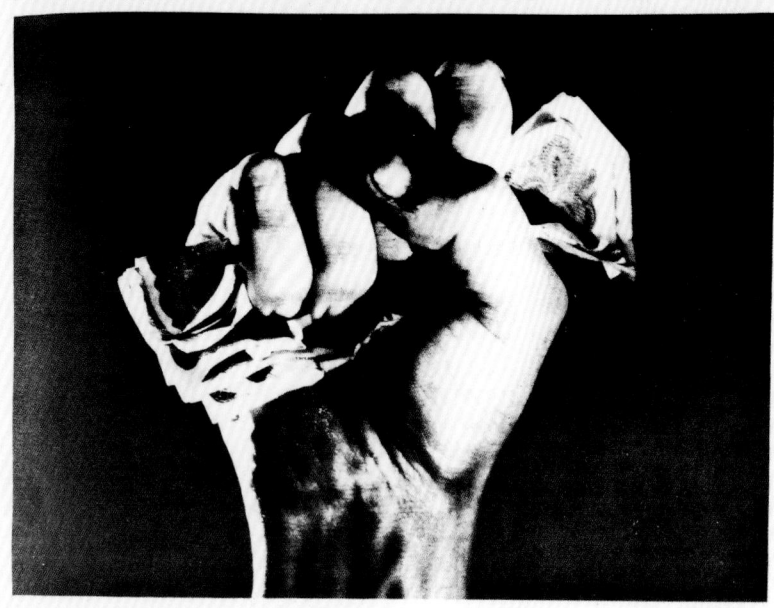

AMERICA HAS CLOSED ITS FIST

From a nation that spent money like a drunken sailor, we have become a people who think twice before we spend at all. ● As a result, advertising to-day must not only move money in the direction of specific merchandise—it must first overcome the reluctance to part with that money. ● This puts an added obligation on advertising. ● It puts an added obligation on those who create advertising.

● It makes the choice of the right advertising agency more important than ever before.

YOUNG & RUBICAM, INCORPORATED · ADVERTISING
NEW YORK · PHILADELPHIA · CHICAGO
· 85 ·

This advertisement appears in September, 1931, issue of Fortune.

2   Young & Rubicam advertising agency ad aimed at potential clients. Advertising agencies portrayed depression consumers as hoarders who resisted spending their money. *Fortune*, September 1931, p.85.

Advertising agencies in the 1920s and 1930s were made up of a number of creative professionals including illustrators, graphic designers, package designers, window-display specialists, and theatre designers. In the booming economy of the 1920s, manufacturers turned to advertising agencies to re-design their goods in order to provide greater appeal to consumers. The first industrial designers emerged during this time, forging a new profession out of existing ones to meet the specific needs of clients. Tasked with the responsibility of stimulating sales, the first industrial designers repackaged their clients' products with success, earning their newly defined profession a degree of authority.

Among these early industrial designers who shaped the new profession in the late 1920s were Norman Bel Geddes, Henry Dreyfuss, Walter Dorwin Teague, and Raymond Loewy. Forging partnerships with corporations – for example,

Dorwin Teague with Ford and Eastman Kodak, and Loewy with Sears, Roebuck and Company and the Pennsylvania Railroad – industrial designers defined their clients' identity through distinctive and innovative design. Industrial designers chronicled their work for corporate clients in books like Roy Sheldon and Egmont Arens's 1932 *Consumer Engineering: A New Technique for Prosperity* and Harold Van Doren's 1940 textbook, *Industrial Design.* Both emphasised the role of design in creating consumer desire.[25] In the rise of industrial design were the seeds of what would later develop as branding.

When the United States entered World War II in 1941, wartime production boosted the economy, returning it to levels not seen since the 1920s. Advertisement agencies focused on maintaining demand throughout the war, but once the conflict ended, advertising expenditures increased. Consumer savings and pent-up demand, together with the development of new technologies and products during wartime, made for a robust postwar economy. American corporations grew larger as the Baby Boom and the Cold War propelled consumerism to new heights in the 1950s.[26] By the end of the decade, one third of the US population had traded in city living for the suburbs, and the car became the most heavily advertised product of the era.

At the same time, the corporate way of life became pervasive. Having suffered the uncertainty of the Great Depression, 'Organization Men' now sought out and relished the security and material prosperity afforded by corporate jobs. The corporatisation of work in America, critics argued, led to a kind a homogenisation of society. Evidence of this can be found in bestsellers like William Whyte Jr's sociological study *The Organization Man* (1956) and Sloan Wilson's novel *The Man in the Gray Flannel Suit* (1955), period social commentaries that portrayed the struggle for individuality over passive support of the collective will as framed by corporate enterprise. Ad men themselves became the target of critiques: Vance Packard's book *The Hidden Persuaders* (1957), for example, exposes the world of 'motivation research' – the psychological technique advertisers use to control the actions of consumers.[27] Such critiques protested against advertising but at the same time revealed just how effective the postwar advertising strategies had become.

With the shift toward audience segmentation came the practice of shaping corporate identity, which defined the look and feel of a company. Corporate identity and branding are closely related as both seek to define the company visually. However, branding's definition is more nuanced: it addresses the emotional relationship between a company and its customers. British graphic designer F.H.K. Henrion, a pioneer of branding, defined corporate identity in 1967:

> A corporation has many points of contact with various groups of people. It has premises, works, products, packaging, station, forms, vehicles, publication and uniforms, as well as the usual kind of promotional activities. These things are seen by customers, agents, suppliers, financiers, shareholders, competitors, the press, and the general public, as well as its own staff. The people in these groups build up their idea of the corporation from what they see and experience of it. An image is therefore an intangible and essentially complicated thing, involving the effect of many and varied factors on many and varied people with many and varied interests.[28]

Corporate identity packages communicated the personality of the business, ensuring that the company's visual identity was consistent throughout the various mediums of graphic communication and design. This consistency differentiated it from traditional advertising and product branding – discrete communications addressed to potential consumers asserting what a specific product has to offer. Brand consultancies – as they were called – offering this comprehensive design service included Lippincott Margulies in New York (est. 1943) and Wolff Olins in London (est. 1965).[29] By the early 1980s, British architectural critic and historian Reyner Banham would define corporate identity, or 'house style,' as 'the practice in all large industrial concerns to inculcate into the minds of the public a recognisable style to identify their products and services . . . undertaken as part of an advertising campaign. It was called "fixing the brand image"'.[30] From the 1960s to the 1980s, the terms corporate identity and branding were often used interchangeably. As mentioned previously, branding implies an emotional connection between the brand and the consumer, which distinguishes it from corporate identity. Not until the 1990s would the practice of corporate identity be replaced by branding.

An emphasis on corporate identity proliferated in the post-1945 era. Its intersection with architecture formed the nexus of development for corporate modernism. Architecture necessarily engages many scales of design: the building structure and envelope, the interior design and finishes, the industrial design of furnishing and fittings, and the graphic design of signage. From the early 20th century onwards, architects and industrial designers have worked across this variety of scales to form corporate identity. They include, in addition to the industrial designers of the 1930s, Peter Behrens's work for the German electric company,

Allgemeine Elektricitäts-Gesellschaft (AEG) in the first decades of the 20th century; former Bauhaus tutors László Moholy-Nagy, Herbert Bayer, and György Kepes's work for Container Corporation of America in the 1930s; Eliot Noyes's design management at International Business Machines (IBM) in 1956; and Ettore Sottsass Jr and Mario Bellini's projects for the Italian office equipment company Olivetti in the late 1960s (Fig.3). These collaborations provide well-documented examples of design consistency across all scales of production – the hallmark of a powerful and effective corporate identity package.

Resistance to corporate conformity marked the 1960s, a time of social and political change, with the consumer movement of protections against corporations gaining force, fuelled in part by social critiques of advertising ethics.[31] Consumer advocates attacked advertisers and

3   Herbert Bayer-designed advertisement for Container Corporation of America, c.1939.

corporations not only for promoting materialism but for perpetrating outright deceptions, such as presenting actors as doctors and portraying cigarettes as if they were not unhealthy. They sought new rights and protections for buyers. As a result, a creative revolution transformed the advertising industry. With a mastery of the medium of television, advertisers produced work from instinct rather than from research. New advertising directions were irreverent, humorous, self-deprecating, and ironic. Innovative campaigns such as Pepsi Cola's 'Think young' and Volkswagen's 'Think small' reflected advertisers' efforts to adjust their approach, appeal to the emotions, and engage in a new relationship with smaller, more clearly defined audiences.[32]

Considering branding beyond the mid-20th-century timeframe of the case studies of this book is important, relevant to current and future branding. From the 1970s to the 1990s, as globalisation and corporate competition intensified, advertising and branding evolved dramatically. No longer seeing consumers as passive recipients of information, industry leaders began to view consumers as active participants, and they began to incorporate consumer opinions into the products they made and sold. By the 1990s, a corporation's brand, while defined as an intangible asset, had become its most valuable one, and the practice of corporate identity evolved into branding. Beginning in the 1990s, relational marketing, which branding is a form of, emerged as a new chapter in the field. The goal of relational marketing was to foster long-term relationships between consumers and companies based on trust and commitment. The key to connecting with consumers was successful 'brand-building' – that is, creating an entity with a lasting personality based on a special combination of physical, functional, and psychological values.[33] Design and architecture were intrinsic to brand-building – so much so that in 1999, the concept of an 'experience economy' emerged: goods and services were no longer enough and events or experiences were needed to engage the attention of audiences in order to make the brand effective.[34] Business professionals B. Joseph Pine II and James H. Gilmore describe how companies wrapped goods and services in unique experiences as a way to more effectively engage their customers. They put forth the concept that experience constituted a distinct economy.[35]

From the mid-19th century onward, product advertising and branding increased radically in their power to shape consumer thinking. Whereas the earliest advertising and sales attempts connected with consumers through personal contact, printed circulars, and modest newspaper ads, the 20th century witnessed the emergence of mass media, in the form of radio, television, and finally the Internet. These media allowed corporations to simultaneously appeal to millions of prospective consumers. But it was the emergence of corporate branding from the 1930s onward that catalysed communication with consumers through design and architecture.

The Architecture of Corporate Modernism

As the history of advertising and branding demonstrates how media developed as a communication tool, the history of corporate office buildings is also worth examining to explore the motivations of business clients as they looked to architecture and design in disseminating their brands. In the decades following the Civil War, the great technological advances that propelled American industry to new heights also deeply affected the architecture that housed American business. In rural locales, vast complexes containing manufacturing plants and warehouse buildings appeared as modes of industrial production began to modernise. Companies migrated their administrative functions away from industrial facilities to urban administrative centres, which offered access to other companies and distributors, as well as potential consumers and employees. Thus, the corporate headquarters was born. The office building became the most innovative new building type of the 19th century, civically important and comparable in prestige to churches and palaces of earlier periods.[36]

The first two decades of the 20th century defined an era of the great industrialist tycoon and, not coincidentally, witnessed the construction of such well-known office buildings as the Fuller ('Flatiron') Building (1901–1902), Singer Building (1906–1908), Metropolitan Life Insurance Company Tower (1907–1909), Bankers Trust Company (1910–1912), and Woolworth Building (1910–1913), all in New York City. These designs provided their corporate clients with headquarters that exerted a strong civic presence and a heightened national presence through the media of advertising.[37] These buildings boldly demonstrated how architecture served as corporate identity, cultivated by their image-conscious clients.

The Metropolitan Life Insurance Company Building, for instance, became the central character of the company's advertising campaign. Between 1907 and 1909, the company's new building, the Metropolitan Tower, designed by Napoleon LeBrun & Sons, was built on 24th and Madison Avenue. The Metropolitan Tower was a tall, slender building, with a gilded cupola whose design was based on the well-known civic monument, the Campanile of San Marco in Venice, Italy. A beacon that emanated from the highly visible tower was christened 'The Light that Never Fails' by company president Haley Fiske (Fig.4).[38] All company publications bore this slogan, which celebrated the power, prosperity, and stability of the company as implied by its palatial tower and guiding light.

The building and its image rapidly became Met Life's corporate symbol, known to staff, policyholders, and the public. The historicist architecture communicated ideas that resonated with the public and thus served as an important advertising tool. It functioned as architecture and, as urban historian Roberta Moudry notes, as 'an iconographic billboard that featured overlapping religious, civic, and familial themes'.[39] The company used the tower image on everything from colouring books to fly swatters. Company Vice-President George Gaston was convinced that the tower made the Metropolitan 'the best-advertised company in the world'.[40] Fiske put it another way: 'We do not have to advertise, for the tower advertises itself.'[41] Indeed, his assertion was the result of six months of worldwide newspaper coverage that garnered over $440,000 of free advertising.[42]

The Woolworth Building, which began construction in 1910 and was completed and opened in 1913, provides another example that business clients recognised architecture as advertising. Frank Woolworth, founder of F.W. Woolworth Company in New York, viewed his Cass Gilbert-designed skyscraper as a 'giant signboard to advertise around the world'.[43] Architectural historian Gail Fenske argues that the Woolworth Building was designed for the sake of conspicuous architectural display.[44] Woolworth took cues from the Singer Tower, completed in 1908, which gave him the idea that the crowns of such towers functioned like trademarks on the skyline.[45] In turn, the Woolworth Building was topped with similar crowns. As a memorable trademark for the company, the Woolworth Building maintained a relationship with millions of customers and, thus, helped to build customer loyalty.

In the mid-19th century, *gesamtkunstwerk*, or 'total work of art,' the comprehensive design of buildings and interiors, emerged and can be understood as related to architectural and design branding. Historically, gesamtkunstwerk was a pre-industrial idea in which many scales of design from exterior architecture to interior design, furniture, graphics, signage, decorative arts, and accessories were cohesively designed with visual unity. The concept began in the mid-19th century with architects of Britain's Arts and Crafts movement, and Belgium's and France's Art Nouveau.

As the modernising forces of mass production and consumption took hold between 1850 and 1914, the notion of gesamtkunstwerk persisted into the industrial and modern eras with mass-produced furniture and accessories. Important examples in the first two decades of the 20th century can be seen in the work of the Bauhaus and by the German architect Peter Behrens for the Berlin-based electric company, AEG. Both examples addressed gesamtkunstwerk at telescoping scales from typography and industrial design to furniture and architecture. As such, gesamtkunstwerk is an important aspect of architectural branding. The client's brand identity will not only reach the public through design strategies, but the total work of art will amplify the message.

European modern architecture arrived in the United States in the 1920s, thus clarifying the difference between American (Louis Sullivan, Chicago School, Frank Lloyd Wright) and European modernism (Walter Gropius, Mies van

4   The headquarters of the Metropolitan Life Insurance Company served as the central character of the company's advertising campaign. Here, it is depicted with company slogan, 'The Light that Never Fails,' on a promotional button created for the building opening, c.1909.

der Rohe, Le Corbusier). In 1929, the stock market crashed, sending the nation into economic crisis for years. Three years after the crash, the Museum of Modern Art in New York (MoMA) opened *Modern Architecture – International Exhibition*, displaying models and photographs of modern architecture from Europe and America as viable examples guiding the future development of architecture. Modern architecture's hallmarks of simplicity and a machine-made aesthetic did not appeal to many Americans. As a result, the modern ethos in American design during the 1930s was not the so-called International Style but streamlined Art Deco and modern classicism.

MoMA director Alfred Barr Jr criticised what he considered historicising and superficial versions of modernism, like modern classicism and Art Deco, which had quickly gained the support of real estate developers and their profit-driven associates. In his preface to *The International Style: Architecture since 1922*, Barr vented: 'We are asked to take seriously the architectural tastes of real estate speculators, renting agents, and mortgage brokers!' He concluded with a warning: 'It is, then, from the commercially successful modernistic architects, that we may expect the strongest opposition to the [International] Style.'[46] Barr condemned other evolving strains of modernism as cheap approximations of the preferred International Style. His denigration of business clients, however, would prove somewhat ironic, as they would later become important patrons of modern architecture.

It was not until after World War II that the American public accepted European modern architecture. In the 1940s and 1950s, corporate offices and headquarters proliferated, and modern architecture came to increasingly define the personality of the corporation. A number of quintessential examples of corporate modernism appeared: the Equitable Building (1944–1948) in Portland, Oregon, designed by Pietro Belluschi; Lever House (1949–1952) in New York, designed by Skidmore, Owings & Merrill; the Alcoa Building (1951–1953) in Pittsburgh, Pennsylvania, designed by Harrison & Abramowitz; and the Seagram Building (1954–1958) in New York, designed by Ludwig Mies van der Rohe. These buildings displayed the abstract language of modern architecture that would become a hallmark of corporate modernism.

By the time the Seagram headquarters was complete, the advertising value of corporate headquarters architecture was well established. So patently obvious was the promotional value of Mies's building, which had been built intentionally to increase the company's prestige, that the City of New York deemed its construction costs a taxable expenditure: it imposed a tax that was 50 per cent higher than was typical for office space at the time. Indeed, Seagram benefited from the lofty image its headquarters offered to the public. The company promoted its headquarters with tours that highlighted information about its esteemed architect and the building's distinctive features, such as its luxurious tinted windows set into bronze mullions.[47]

While a strong postwar economy bolstered the growth of corporate modernism, an instrumental force in its development was the corporate client – a little-studied phenomenon in the rise of modern architecture. There would, though, be some recognition of the role of corporate clients, as seen in the 1957 MoMA-organised *Buildings for Business and Government* exhibition that highlighted the significance of 'informed, cooperative, and increasingly perceptive clients'.[48] Arthur Drexler, curator and director of MoMA's Department of Architecture and Design, praised business organisations that were 'deliberately exceeding strict utilitarian limits' in their patronage of International Style Modernism and were now 'concerned with social and aesthetic value' of their architecture.[49] Also significant was the failure of modernism to take hold in the housing sector, which influenced MoMA's interest in courting corporate patrons for modern architecture. The great change in attitude, from the disparagement of business clients in the 1930s to their high praise in the post-World War II era, occurred within the context of a booming US economy and the exponential rise of a moneyed middle class. As a result, corporate image grew increasingly important, and businesses considered, for the first time, modern architecture as a potent medium for advertising.

A New Perspective

Considering the development of branding and architecture in parallel reveals an intimate relationship between the two realms. In the business history of this period of 40 years, the field of advertising shifted toward appealing to emotions and branding, focusing increasingly on specific audiences and on identifying the company as a whole, in addition to the individual products themselves. At the same time, architecture and design as a medium for communicating corporate messages shifted towards a modern ethos. As corporations evolved to brand themselves by evoking deliberate emotions, so too did architecture. The timeframe of the case studies presented in this book span the late 1920s to the 1960s – crucial years in corporate modernism's development. During this time, collaboration between the fields of business and architecture advanced to the point of integration. Making use of previously unpublished company correspondence, architects' archives, and photographs of key buildings, this book tells an insider's view of the debates, resolutions, and dramas of these buildings' design and construction, as well as their crucial role in the history of modern architecture.[50]

In the early decades of the 21st century, the trend is once again to locate administrative centres in downtown areas. Analogously, the case studies of this book demonstrate the importance of urban centres in the 1930s through the 1960s, as corporations established and maintained crucial business relationships with suppliers, customers, and employees within the city. Today, we find ourselves constantly barraged with digital information and data – a virtual world more vast and complex than we can possibly comprehend. And yet, what we find ourselves craving are environments and things that make us feel – places that engender a sense of empathy. It is this sense-driven quality that architectural branding provides. By uncovering how architecture engaged with and advanced the growth of branding, I suggest a new way of thinking about architecture's past relationship with business. Understanding this overlooked and often misrepresented past will better arm architects and designers going forward, as they and their clients create new environments and construct new relationships within the current milieu.

Building Brands examines the evolution of corporate modernism through a new lens – that of the development of architectural branding. *Building Brands* is not an endorsement of capitalism and corporate politics, nor is it a theoretical and political critique. It does not purport to survey corporate modernism of the 20th century in an exhaustive manner.[51] Instead, by presenting a chronological series of fine-grained analyses, it aims to illuminate in historical terms what the architects and corporations were avowing to achieve at the time of their collaboration, and how the four case studies in this book – the PSFS Building, Johnson Wax, Lever House, and the Röhm and Haas Building – were precursors of what we understand as architectural branding today. The four buildings studied in the following chapters show how modern architectural characteristics not only served as advertising but also gave companies brand identities. *Building Brands* examines the evolution of corporate modernism through a new lens – that of the development of architectural branding. This scholarship shows that architectural branding existed at a far earlier moment than previously thought and tells the stories of how these buildings, architects, and clients realised and developed it.

These case studies constitute formative models for an architecture and an urbanism that are still with us today. The evolutionary arc of these case studies is still in many ways unfolding. If they provide a history of how corporate clients were involved in modern architecture, they also suggest how corporations still communicate and ultimately expand their brands with specific architectural devices: sign, architect, form, and material.

2 SIGN

The PSFS Building

In October 1929 when the stock market crashed sending the nation into a depression, Philadelphia, like other American cities, had been experiencing a building boom. The Philadelphia Saving Fund Society (PSFS) Building, like other skyscrapers, was in the design phase. The ambitious building project would continue despite the grim economic climate. Designed by the architectural partnership of George Howe and William Lescaze, the PSFS Building was conceived as a symbol of the great, modern company – the new face of the oldest savings fund in America – as the venerable institution reinvented itself to cope with the complex circumstances of the 20th century.[1] Out of these complexities, the PSFS Building alloyed architecture and business in one of the 20th century's most compelling examples of modern architecture.

The building emerged out of many struggles: the struggle between the client and architects, the struggle to define modernism in a context of both historicism and commercialism, and the struggle to create a progressive building in a city where maintaining tradition was the status quo. The architects, George Howe and William Lescaze, ushered in a radical new architectural direction to the city with their clients – the PSFS Building Committee, led by Society president John M. Willcox. But the success of a building cannot simply be attributed to its architects. At the core is listening to what the clients have to say about their corporate headquarters design. Primary materials reveal the extent to which client guidance and leadership as well as the interchange between architect and client influenced the design. Examining the project and emphasising the client's point of view shifts the appreciation of this building from the aesthetics to the intersection of business and architecture, establishing the building as a model for many other buildings.

Modernity and the City

With the late 19th- and early 20th-century development of the tall commercial buildings in Chicago and New York, the skyscraper typology dominated this era in the evolution of corporate headquarters. During this time, the image projected by architecture had become more and more important in communicating ideas about the company it sheltered, with the architecture serving as a powerful means of corporate advertising. The mode of communication chosen for most corporate headquarters was historicising, as exemplified by the neo-classical solidity of the Metropolitan Life Insurance Building (1907–1909) and the Gothic flourishes of the Woolworth Building (1910–1913). Boldly opposing this historicism was the PSFS Building, built as the first modern corporate headquarters in America. The design was very unusual anywhere in the United States at the time, let alone in conservative Philadelphia.

By the 1920s, Philadelphia was a city that had long been an industrial metropolis. Business was at its root, and businessmen were its chief actors. Between 1900 and 1919, the city's skyline changed dramatically. Philadelphia had been slower than Chicago and New York to accept the advantages of tall buildings, largely in light of the prevailing opinion that the city had an almost unlimited area in which to expand horizontally. But increasing congestion as well as rising land values in Philadelphia forced a change in this attitude. The construction of high-rise steel and concrete buildings accelerated, resulting in the completion of a number of 10- to 20-storey buildings. South Broad Street, with its hotels and office buildings, took on an almost canyon-like appearance.

From 1920 to 1930, Philadelphia was marked by economic and urban growth. The building boom produced office and bank buildings that were designed in the Beaux-Arts tradition.[2] But by 1926, a retreat from historicism in architectural design had begun. A predominant alternative was 'modern classicism,' a term coined by Paul Philippe Cret, a transitional approach that was characterised by rich forms of expression based on Beaux-Arts planning and composition with a minimum of elements and details. The clean geometric composition of Davis, Dunlap and Barney's American Bank and Trust Building (1926–1929), with its stylised pilaster and column capitals surmounted by an abstract bas-relief frieze, typified this trend.

In 1930, Philadelphia was the third largest metropolis in the nation, one of only ten cities with a population exceeding one million inhabitants.[3] The city's downtown did not physically reflect the troubled financial conditions plaguing directors of insurance companies, banks, brokerage houses, and building and loan associations. A range of architectural styles stood side by side, from Beaux-Arts eclecticism (Penn Mutual Life Insurance Company's building and The Drake apartment building), to Art Deco (Market Street National Bank and the Pennsylvania Railroad's Suburban Station), to 'modern classicism' (30th Street Station). Among the numerous new buildings of the 1930s, the PSFS Building was a radical departure from the normative.

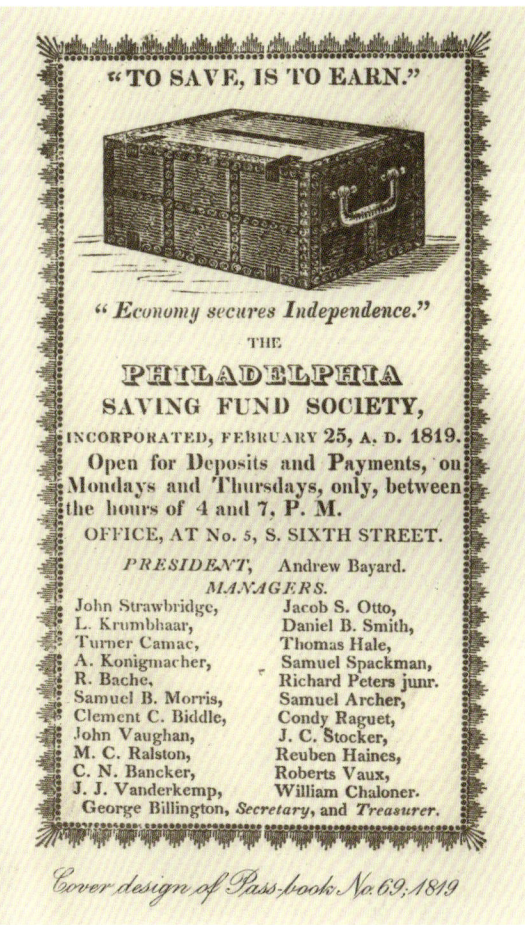

5   Cover design of an 1819 PSFS pass-book, reproduced in James M. Willcox, *A History of the Philadelphia Saving Fund Society, 1816–1916* (J.B Lippincott Co., Philadelphia, PA, 1916).

Client and Architects

Founded in 1816, the Philadelphia Saving Fund Society became the first savings fund to organise and operate business in America.[4] On 13 December of the same year, the institution's philanthropic intentions to encourage thrift and saving among the city's working class were publicly declared in their first advertisement in the *Freeman's Journal & Philadelphia Mercantile Advertiser*:

> To promote economy and the practice of saving amongst the poor and laboring classes of the community – to assist them in the accumulation of property that they may possess the means of support during old age or sickness – and to render them in a great degree independent of the bounty of others . . .[5]

Their founding partners were among the most prominent business leaders of Philadelphia, including Condy Raguet, the founder, and officers Clement Biddle, John Strawbridge, and Roberts Vaux. These individuals were committed to designing a way for working classes 'to afford a secure and profitable mode of investment for small sums to mechanics, tradesmen, laborers, servants and others' (Fig.5).[6] Savings funds had been conceived in the 18th century in Great Britain as philanthropic institutions, and news of their rapid growth disseminated to the United States through journals and pamphlets. Its first depositor was Curtis Roberts, founder Condy Raguet's African American servant. In addition to servants, early depositors of the Philadelphia Saving Fund Society included tradesmen and skilled craftsmen.[7] The benevolent institution first opened in the office of secretary and treasurer George Billington, located on Sixth Street between Chestnut and Market Streets. Strict limits were placed on weekly deposits and the bank periodically reviewed its rolls and returned those with large balances and employed in occupations not representative of 'the thrifty poor'.[8]

The working class, who were the majority of Americans in the mid-19th century, had limited opportunities to securely accumulate savings. It was a fairly safe and convenient method that would yield interest. By the time the Philadelphia Saving Fund Society had received a charter from the state legislature in February 1819, there were savings banks in Boston, Baltimore, and a number of other cities.[9] In its first years, the PSFS grew steadily with resolutions authorising the opening of branch offices outside Philadelphia in Northern Liberties and Southwark.[10] In 1818, PSFS moved its offices to Sixth and Minor Street. In the 1820s, it moved three times due to expansion.

In 1833, PSFS hired architect Thomas U. Walter to design its first commissioned building on Walnut Street. The narrow Greek temple form, completed in 1840, was described in company records with 'a front of white marble from the Chester County quarries and a portico in the style of the Ionic order of architecture'.[11] The hiring of Walter, who was also beginning the design of Girard College for Orphans the same year, demonstrates that as a client, PSFS sought a monumental building that would not only

6　PSFS pamphlet, c.1960, showing PSFS's various banking buildings from 1821 to 1932.

house its savings fund, but would serve as a conduit to their depositors and as an advertising medium for the institution (Fig.6).[12]

By 1850, PSFS had grown considerably and continued to uphold its original ideals with a substantial fraction of all working-class Philadelphians holding accounts there. The company reported 38 per cent of all male account holders were 'mechanics, artisans, or handycraftsmen', and another 13 per cent were 'porters or labourers'. Meanwhile, 43 per cent of female account holders were 'domestic servants, nurses, or housekeepers'.[13] While scholars have questioned whether savings banks in fact enforced their charitable missions, PSFS in particular did. In his book, *A History of the Philadelphia Saving Fund Society, 1816–1916*, James M. Willcox explained that the nature of the depositors – 'laboring classes, the aged, the orphaned and minor' – was consistently upheld and the 'character of depositors' had not been transgressed.[14] He acknowledged that one of the most perplexing problems for savings bank managers had been 'the regulation of the forms in which accounts could be opened, so as to extend liberally the benefits of the system to those entitled to it while at the same time precluding its abuse by those who, on account of the security and the rate of interest offered, seek to evade the rules'.[15]

By 1864, a committee within the board was convened to consider 'more commodious accommodations' for the increasing business of the banking hall and office.[16] It sought to 'purchase a lot and to erect thereon a fireproof and burglar-proof building . . . for the accommodation of the office'.[17] These requirements for the building came out of both the greater security of assets and the aspiration that the new building would inspire the public with a greater degree of confidence. The latter criteria would lead the PSFS to a pedigreed site for its new office.

Two years passed while the committee searched without success for a property within their budget. In 1866, a residential property, known as the Josiah Randall mansion – home of a distinguished Philadelphia lawyer, at the southwest corner of Walnut Street and Seventh Street – came on the market.[18] The property was on Washington Square, which in the mid-19th century was the centre of

a prominent residential area. The location was removed from the busiest city centres but within easy reach from all parts of the city.[19] Standing apart from the banks clustered on Chestnut Street, the site was the beginning of PSFS's pattern of lone-wolf site strategies.

In addition to needing more space, the Saving Fund sought to impart the image of prestige, which this prominent neighbourhood provided. The history of the site as the Randall mansion, with its past guests including 'the most distinguished men of the nation', supported PSFS's desire for stature.[20] The location was considered 'dignified' and was intended to impress the Saving Fund's working-class clientele.[21] After board deliberations, the property was purchased and the PSFS commissioned the new office's design from architect Addison Hutton. Their records describe the historicising design as 'of plain design and solid appearance enhanced by its granite exterior was planned to easily admit of enlargement which the continuous growth of the business in time made necessary'.[22] The stately building on the corner of Washington Square was completed in 1869, the same year that Hutton's design for Parrish Hall at Swarthmore College was built. Future expansion to the office included additions in 1885–86 by Hutton and in 1897–98 by Furness, Evans & Co. (Fig.7).

When the Washington Square office began operation in 1869, most depositors were working class, and the surrounding neighbourhood represented an aspirational goal for their thriftiness and consistent saving. By the 20th century, many PSFS customers who had started out poor became middle class, and in turn the Saving Fund attracted a more middle-class clientele. In effect, the site was self-actualising and the aspiration from working class to middle class was realised through the service of the Saving Fund.

By the late 1910s, PSFS counted the most depositors of any savings fund in the country. It had become one of the city's oldest and most venerated financial institutions, with generations of Philadelphians who first opened accounts as children becoming life-long patrons. Financial institutions began marketing this economic independence just at the time when industrialisation was quickly eliminating the

7   Philadelphia Saving Fund Society main office at 702 Walnut Street, by Sloan & Hutton in 1868 and later in 1900 by Furness & Evans, reproduced in James M. Willcox, *A History of the Philadelphia Saving Fund Society, 1816–1916.*

traditional mechanisms for attaining it: the promise of independence offered by the master/apprentice system receded as machine-based methods of manufacture rose to prominence.

As the nature of work and labour in Philadelphia changed during the 19th century, the 'new morality' revivalists gained influence in American life. The reform movement sought to instil the value of thrift in the working classes. Revivalists welcomed the industrial age, linking strong moral character to industrialisation, and many of the PSFS's founding board members became practising disciples. It was

in this spirit that the PSFS shaped its depositors. It encouraged people to develop habits of frugality and temperance and to avoid needless spending. The institution grew extremely stable and thus crucial to the economic health of the city.

The Society's message of thrift and of saving for the future shifted radically, however, in the early 20th century when by the 1920s, 'thrift' was usurped by consumerism as the Society's advertising slogan. In the 1920s and 1930s, advertising became an economic force, functioning as mass communication in an impersonal marketplace of vast scale.[23] Advertising historian Roland Marchand defined modern advertising as advertisements that transcended or denied their essential economic nature as mass communications and achieved subjective qualities and a 'personal' tone.[24] The PSFS advertising of this time demonstrated Marchand's definition. Taking on a psychological strategy, the modern ads depicted characters experiencing realistic and emotional scenarios. One full-page ad from 1926 features a sentimentalised portrayal of American life, an illustration of an adult son and his elderly mother reading a PSFS brochure. The ad reads, 'Just the thing for me!' and their facial expressions register elation and relief (Fig.8). Most American families could relate to the sense of reassurance offered in this ad, as well as the feelings of economic insecurity motivating it.

PSFS ads elicited many emotions, including fear, in order to reach audiences. 'Scare copy,' as this type of advertising was called, filled brochures advertising Christmas accounts from September 1927.[25] One such ad presents a colourful illustration of holiday shoppers with their arms full of

8   1926 PSFS pamphlet advertising saving fund depositor accounts.

9   PSFS brochure cover advertising Christmas accounts, September 1927.

purchases, walking past a shop. The copy reads, 'Did you have enough?' tapping into the economic insecurities of middle-class Americans (Fig.9).[26]

Beginning in 1923, the Society operated the long running and popular 'School Bank' programme (Fig.10). Organised in cooperation with local schools, the campaign fostered the saving habits of children. Participation was the key ingredient for the School Bank. The School Bank's regularly published newsletter featured company histories and special interest stories, as well as participatory activities, such as poster contests.[27] Children made weekly visits to the banking hall to deposit their savings. They were assigned the roles of receiving teller and entry clerk, collecting and processing their fellow students' savings. As depositors, the students saw interest accrue on their savings, making the School Bank seem worthwhile. The School Bank's two-dimensional advertising and three-dimensional experiences within the PSFS Building joined forces to communicate and deliver a message to children about the benefits PSFS had to offer. PSFS advertising and its commissioned architecture would continue to educate and influence depositors about the institution.

Company president J.M. Willcox was a well-educated and well-travelled man, who possessed much pride in the institution for which he had served as officer on the board of directors since 1902. As the building's client, Willcox proved demanding, constantly testing George Howe on practical as well as aesthetic grounds. Yet he had faith in his architect. The two native Philadelphians shared a similar background of wealth and privilege. Although his preference for historicising architecture would threaten modernist aspects of Howe's design, his involvement in the design process would become a defining factor in achieving the building's final form. The design process that unfolded was not always easy, with the relationship between client and architect becoming contentious at times.

Howe's background prior to his involvement with the PSFS Building commission offers insight into its eventual design. In 1912, George Howe returned to Philadelphia after studying at the École des Beaux-Arts in Paris and began his first job as a draughtsman at Furness, Evans and Company,

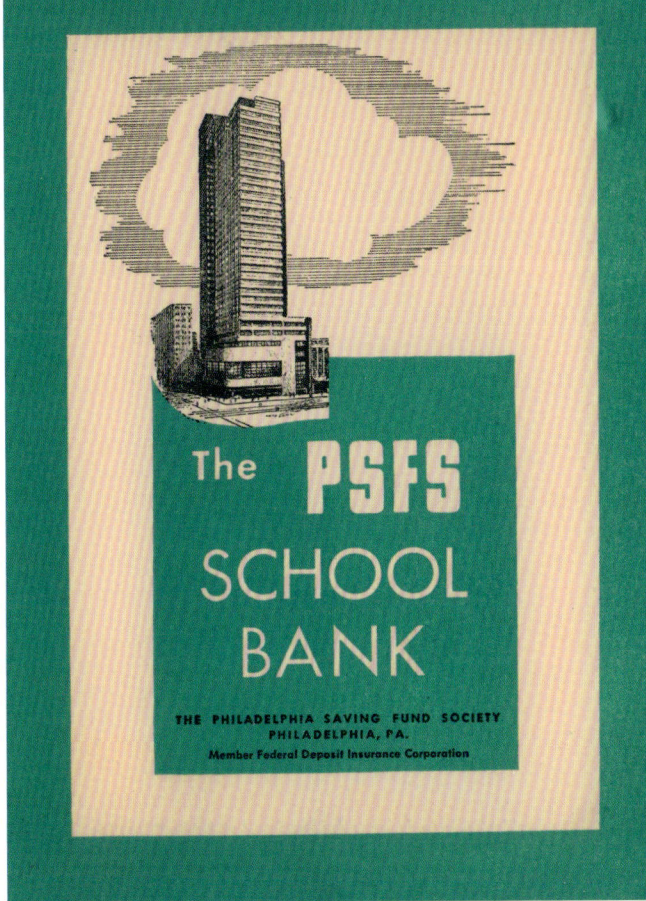

10   The PSFS building was featured on School Bank advertising, c.1955.

the architects of the PSFS's earlier expansion at 702 Walnut Street (see Fig.7). In 1916, Howe joined Walter Mellor and Arthur Ingersoll Meigs in partnership, changing the firm name to Mellor, Meigs & Howe. The 'young firm of established repute' had developed a national reputation for suburban houses designed in the Pennsylvania colonial masonry tradition. Their best-known work looked to post-medieval manors in northern France.[28]

In the early 1920s, before embarking on the skyscraper project, the PSFS commissioned Mellor, Meigs & Howe to design four branch banks. Branch banks were places of access to a financial institution's services, like cash withdrawals and deposits. Prior to 1922, the development of branch banks was limited almost entirely to state banks – PSFS was a state

11   Philadelphia Saving Fund Society branch office (South Branch at Broad and McKean Street),
Philadelphia, 1924, by Mellor, Meigs & Howe.

bank. Their growth was accelerated by the 1927 McFadden Act which permitted national banks to establish branches. Howe, as partner, submitted two designs for the PSFS branch banks, each to be built twice. The design of the first pair was based on Italian Renaissance models and displayed a heavy cornice and rusticated base along with other ornamentation (Fig.11). This represented Howe's initial concept for the branch savings bank as a 'magnified strong box'.[29] This idea informed the way the building communicated to the public. Its 'solidity of aspect' encouraged depositors to feel secure about where they saved their money.

At the same time, Howe also attempted to make the exterior of the buildings less forbidding and 'more inviting to the timid public'.[30] A 'large, hospitable entrance door' gave the appearance of openness and approachability.[31] Architectural form defined the Saving Fund in a tangible way that elicited positive emotion from customers. The design lent the institution personality or gave it a brand.

In 1924, the firm completed construction on two new branches in Philadelphia – one was located in the northern part of the city and one in the southern part of the city. In 1926 the Society added two more branches, known as the West Philadelphia Branch and the Logan Branch. All locations were in prosperous working-class and lower middle-class row house neighbourhoods. This time, Howe designed the buildings in a modern classicist style (Fig.12). The massing of the West Philadelphia and Logan branches consisted of abstract boxes with clean edges, devoid of cornices and rustication, with only minimal moulding applied along the base and around the main entrance. The simplified forms were based in Beaux-Arts traditions but also demonstrated an evolution toward European modern architecture. The design resembled the kind of progressive architectural expression practised by Paul Philippe Cret, Howe's colleague and friend.

In the 1920s and 1930s, Cret exerted an important influence on Philadelphia and beyond. He brought a new approach to classicism that departed from the historicising tradition in Philadelphia.[32] Cret was supportive and encouraging of Howe's experimentation in modern architecture.[33] In an article about the branch buildings published in *Architectural Forum*, Howe noted, 'The austere style of a quarter century ago, with its elaborate classical columns and pediments, has given way to the modern bank – simple, light, inviting, and business-like.'[34] The transition from Beaux-Arts eclecticism to modern classicism had occurred in quick succession in Howe's work, with the simplified, less ornate branch design suggesting the new direction of European modern architecture that Howe's work would subsequently take.

It was in 1926, after the branch banks were completed, that Willcox made an important request of Howe: the bank president asked that electric signs be added to the branch elevations. The client's interest in incorporating modern

12 Philadelphia Saving Fund Society branch office (Logan Branch at Broad and Ruscomb Streets), 5000 North Broad Street, 1926. One of the second pair of designs by Mellor, Meigs & Howe.

signage in this way predicted the brazen display of corporate advertising that turned away from the past for inspiration. At first, Howe refused to design the sign, arguing that the addition of an electric sign would result in an awkward juxtaposition of historicising design and modern technology. But Willcox insisted on including signage as an important advertising feature of modern times.[35] After due consideration, Howe agreed to 'incorporate the most blazing and beautiful specimen in existence' in his 1926 branches for the Society.[36] The resulting sign featured the Society's full name in bronze Roman letters, illuminated by electric lights, mounted on the bottom of a balcony. The technological apparatus of the sign clashed with the historicising characteristics of the facade on which it stood, and Howe's response to Willcox's request was not fully successful in visual terms. Willcox's commercial concerns for advertising his branch banks would soon lead the way, however, to Howe's embrace of modern architecture. In 1928, George Howe left his partners Mellor and Meigs, following a series of professional disputes. But his departure was imminent as it became crystal clear that his bourgeoning interest in modern design was restricted by the firm's historicising approach. This was a major plunge into a new career and unknown future.

It was precisely an interest in modern architecture that brought George Howe and William Lescaze together as partners in the PSFS Building commission. Howe was intrigued by William Lescaze's education in the 'new style' of European modernism, which was in contrast with his own Beaux-Arts training. The younger Swiss architect had been educated at the École Polytechnique Fédérale in Zurich. Under the tutelage of Karl C. Moser, his life-long dedication to the philosophy of a new architecture for a new age began.[37] In the post-World War I era, Lescaze's early work included a brief job with the Committee for the Reconstruction of Devastated France, and a stint with architect, Henri Sauvage in Paris, where he was exposed to Sauvage's pioneering reinforced concrete prefabrication techniques. Frustrated with Europe's stunted economic recovery, Lescaze moved to America in August 1920, making him one of the first European modernists to emigrate

to the United States.[38] While he was eager to realise modern architectural design, the country was reluctant to embrace the 'new style'. Lescaze worked in a series of unfulfilling jobs in Cleveland, finding intellectual sustenance in a small group of creative individuals who shared his interest in modernism, which they explored through poetry, literature, music, and art, as well as architecture.[39]

By 1922 Lescaze's goal to realise European modern architecture seemed to be unattainable. Frustrated, he travelled back to Europe, where he found that, in the two years he had been away (1920 to 1922), many new treatises, exhibitions, and buildings had emerged. Expressionism, having led the discourse since 1918, was coming to a decisive end in a transition to rationalist models. Lescaze was influenced by a number of European avant-garde experiments of the early 1920s, including those of De Stijl, Constructivism, the Weimar Bauhaus and Le Corbusier's Citrohan House project; but it was the architectural expressionism of 1922 to 1923 that most deeply affected the young architect. Lescaze's first-hand observations of German expressionism in Berlin were instrumental in developing his design sensibilities.[40] Expressionism responded to and sought to convey emotional experience rather than physical reality. Originality and sculptural dynamism shaped the outward expression of inner form, and the contradictions of solid and void, light and shadow: these qualities of expressionism commanded the attention of viewers, resulting in spectacles to be admired.

Shortly after his return to America in March 1923, Lescaze launched his own architectural practice, which included mostly interior design projects for showrooms, exhibitions, and lobbies for retail and commercial clients.[41] Recognising Lescaze's showmanship as well as the eclecticism in his design of this period, Henry-Russell Hitchcock described the architect's work as one 'in which he has shown perhaps more virtuosity than integrity'.[42] By this, he meant that Lescaze's modernism was varied. At this point in his career, Lescaze's design approach was influenced by French Art Deco as much as Cubism.[43] Indeed, Lescaze's eclecticism should be seen in the context of gesamtkunstwerk in Europe in the 1910s and 1920s. To be sure, the term incited

13   William Lescaze in his New York apartment and office, c.1927.

much debate in 1914 when Henri van de Velde and Hermann Muthesius famously debated two polarising directions: individualism and rationalism, respectively. The tension between these two concepts can be seen in Lescaze's work of the 1920s. In the years after the influential 1925 Exposition internationale des arts décoratifs et industriels modernes that popularised Art Deco interiors, Lescaze experimented with gesamtkunstwerk in his projects. His 1926 design for his own studio and office at 337 East 42nd Street in New York featured 17th-century Spanish and 18th-century French antique furniture set off against walls covered in expressionist murals (Fig.13). In 1928, Lescaze designed an installation for a penthouse studio apartment for The Macy International Exposition of Art in Industry and a telephone foyer for the S.T. Meyers Company, both in New York (Figs 14, 15). The Macy's design demonstrated an attempt at creating a cohesive interior space that featured highly contrasted finishes in shape, colour, finish, and texture. His telephone foyer design demonstrated a careful composition of rectilinear and curvilinear forms made up of surfaces and materials designed for objects and seating and lighting. These projects and their varied expressions demonstrated his struggle to define modern design and architecture in the years before his partnership with George Howe.

By 1928, Lescaze had moved past eclecticism.[44] He stated that modern design should not be combined with period furniture – that it ought to stand on its own. Modern design, he wrote,

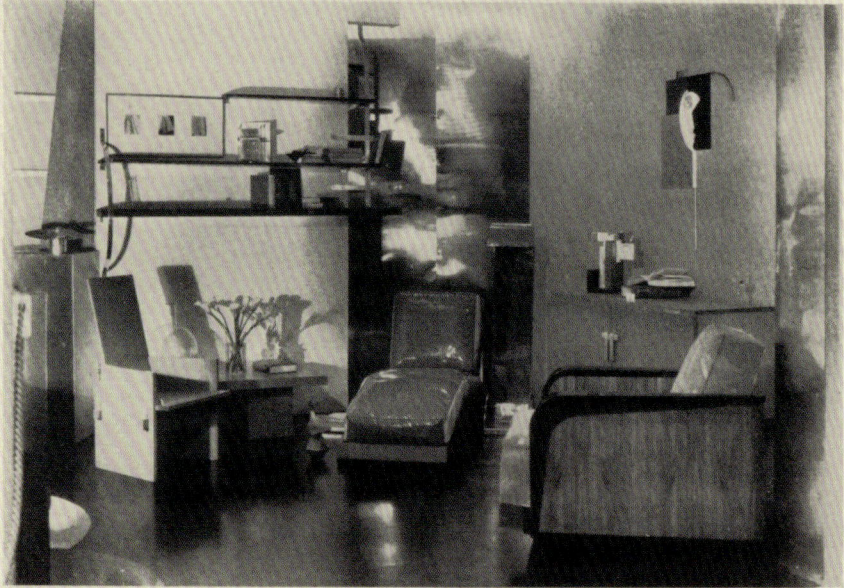

Herbert Photos

PENTHOUSE STUDIO APARTMENT
WILLIAM E. LESCAZE, ARCHITECT
INTERNATIONAL EXPOSITION OF ART IN INDUSTRY, MACY'S, NEW YORK

14   William Lescaze's installation of a penthouse studio apartment for Macy's International Exposition of Art in Industry, reproduced in *Architectural Record*, August 1928, pp 137–43.

15   William Lescaze's design for S.T. Meyers Company telephone foyer, New York, 1928.

needed to be a totality.[45] A modern totality meant a design would have strong visual impact. Lescaze's term for this was 'entity'.[46] His concept of entity provided a new way of understanding architecture as related to the allied disciplines of interior design, furniture design, and graphic design – a precursor to the interdisciplinary design practices of brand consultancies like Wolff Olins that would not materialise until the mid-1960s. As we will see in the PSFS Building's comprehensive design programme, Lescaze's concept of entity provided a strong brand identity for the Saving Fund.

The collaboration of Howe and Lescaze was based on a common pursuit of modern architecture. Their individual struggles to define that style – spanning the Beaux-Arts, Art Deco, and expressionist traditions – informed their collaboration. The architects came together as partners in 1929 with a belief that 'functionalism,' a highly debated term from its inception, formed the basis of their common understanding of modern architecture. What functionalism meant to the two architects can be gleaned from an essay they authored entitled 'Architectural Analysis of the Proposed Building for the Philadelphia Saving Fund Society', dated 26 September 1930, before the design went into construction. In this essay, Howe and Lescaze point to the two tendencies of modern architecture – the 'functional' and 'decorative'. In functional modernism, 'the forms are allowed to grow out of the requirements of our civilization and the modern technique of building.' By contrast, in 'decorative' modern architecture, 'forms are applied without relation over utilitarian and structural functions at the whim of the individual designers [and] without any framework of basic principles.'[47] Both architects clearly placed their faith in the functional tendency of modern architecture, thus fortifying the new partnership.

The PSFS Building

In May of 1925, the PSFS purchased land for a new branch bank at 1200 Market Street – a prime, lone-wolf location in downtown Philadelphia. Five million dollars was a high price to pay at the time, but as a speculative real estate venture, the Society expected a return on their investment. Located at the corner of 12th and Market Streets, the PSFS Building would sit in the heart of the retail district: 'more people passed [by there] . . . than any other spot in Philadelphia.'[48] In fact, the site for the building was specifically chosen 'to attract the frugal middle-class depositor on which savings banks thrive'.[49] The city's largest department stores were concentrated on six nearby blocks, from Lit Brothers at 7th Street to Wanamaker's at 13th Street. The site would generate singularity as the new building would stand as a tall office building amongst a neighbourhood of mid-rise retail establishments. The property's location was fed by a public system of streetcars, subways, and commuter railways including the Reading Railroad Terminal, and two blocks further, the Pennsylvania Railway station. The location of the PSFS site would not only provide convenient access to the vast number of depositors but would attract the attention of new customers. The PSFS's building committee, headed by Willcox, recognised the building site's 'usefulness and prestige'.[50]

The programme for the PSFS Building devised by the client specified not only a bank but also offices and retail space, built on speculation. The combined bank-office building type was not new. In fact, many banks became involved in real estate after the depression of the mid-1890s lifted. *The Journal of the American Bankers Association* advised its readers in 1920: 'If an office building is constructed over a bank economically and with sound judgment, it is a certain revenue producer, often enabling the bank to live practically rent-free.'[51] The PSFS explored this strategy in building a multi-use complex, which expanded its business beyond its original scope. If any time were right to do this, it was during the financial boom of the 1920s. The Society planned to lease the majority of the skyscraper's square footage.[52] Attracted by light and panoramic views of the city, business tenants would rent office space in the tower. Meanwhile, commercial tenants would lease ground floor space, taking advantage of foot traffic generated by the bustling shopping district. The PSFS would occupy the building's prime floors: a banking hall for depositors, and an executive floor with a dining room, a conference room, and a boardroom.

In 1926, as the second pair of branch banks was being completed, planning for a new downtown headquarters began. From the beginning, the project was bold in its intentions. Willcox had high aspirations for the architecture – that the new offices would evoke awe mixed with reassurance in the minds of depositors.[53] He envisioned a skyscraper that would represent the PSFS as a whole, while being inhabited by a variety of business tenants. The goal of the building project from Willcox's point of view was twofold: for the architecture to give a bold new personality for the Saving Fund, and to be a 'sound investment'.[54] In establishing a new personality for the institution through architectural form, the PSFS sought to re-cast itself as a progressive institution, in effect re-branding itself. When Willcox approached Howe (still a design partner at Mellor, Meigs & Howe at that time) to submit a design, the architect was not actively designing modern architecture. Although the modern ethos held his strong interest, he presented a design to Willcox and the building committee that was a Beaux-Arts-inspired skyscraper top with tripartite massing featuring setbacks and ornamental details (Fig.16). Its aesthetic and massing bore a similarity to Raymond Hood and John Mead Howell's Tribune Tower in Chicago, built a few years earlier. Although Howe's design blended well with the contemporary context of Beaux-Arts-inspired and classical modernist skyscrapers already populating downtown Philadelphia, in truth, his aim was modern. He struggled to achieve a modern skyscraper design that would represent the building's structure, in the language of modern architecture. Of this process, he wrote:

> [I] looked about in vain for a precedent that seemed satisfactory from the point of view of architectural expression. Finding none I evolved a design of my own whose chief structural interest lay in an emphasis on the possibilities of steel, in the bold recognition of a great mass of masonry standing on stilts and in the elimination of meaningless mouldings. For its external beauty the design depended on purely decorative elements, such as the great globe at the summit of the tower, and the use of set-backs.[55]

16 PSFS, perspective of the 1926 skyscraper design by Mellor, Meigs & Howe, Philadelphia Historical Commission Files.

By exposing the bolts that held the masonry cladding to the steel structure, Howe's design articulated the building's modern construction system on its facade.[56]

In 1928 Howe terminated his partnership with Mellor and Meigs, having grown increasingly frustrated by the conservative nature of his partners' work and their outright rejection of modern design. The break was not amicable. Howe left, taking with him one of the firm's most substantial clients (the PSFS) as well as two assistants, Louis McAllister and George Daub. The new work of Howe's practice was inspired by changes wrought by the Machine Age.[57] He experimented with forms that symbolised machines, seeking 'simplicity of form and smoothness of finish' and 'to postulate them as necessary consequences and intentions'.[58]

Howe's PSFS Building scheme was placed on hold in 1927, while the Society tested the site by installing a temporary branch. In early 1929 Willcox restarted the skyscraper design process, asking both Mellor and Meigs and George Howe to prepare brand new designs for the bank and office tower. On 29 March 1929, Howe submitted four strikingly modern schemes, which starkly contrasted with Mellor and Meigs's submission.[59] Willcox preferred Scheme #2, dated 20 March 1929, which was most elaborate and contained the seeds for the eventual design.[60] Howe's schematic drawings depicted a thin slab skyscraper with a narrow principal elevation facing Market Street and broad sides facing east and west, features which would eventually be built. Cantilevered canopies defined the upper floors of the slab. The entire composition was rectilinear and devoid of ornament. Its skin was composed of alternating masonry bands and glazed strip windows. The horizontal expression of the slab followed a principle of modern architecture, a second aspect, which would be built in the final design.[61] The slab design maximised the daylight admitted into the skyscraper, with the elevator tower positioned at the back of the site. The modern design won George Howe the commission, over his previous partners.

Despite its modern image, remnants of Howe's Beaux-Arts training and early practice persisted in the design. While the office tower slab was asymmetrically positioned, a strong axial symmetry ran the entire height of the building on the Market Street facade. The design represented both modern and traditional currents, which carried different meaning to the client than the architect. To the client, Howe's modern design was a huge leap away from the kind of architecture that had previously represented the company. According to Isaac Roberts, a member of the original building committee and a PSFS executive, Willcox had decided in all likelihood that Howe would be the architect and perhaps, even, that the building would be 'modern' – that is, 'progressive'.[62] While the client placed great confidence in Howe as a person and as his architect, he accepted Howe's modern design with reservations. Having just abandoned the security of tradition to pursue modern architecture – a new and unfamiliar entity in Philadelphia – Howe knew his design had not yet matured. The struggle to shape the PSFS Building in the modern idiom would continue until five months before the building's ground-breaking.

In May 1929, two months after Howe received the commission, Howe and Lescaze established their partnership, unified by a common goal: to realise modern architecture in the United States. To design a truly modern skyscraper, Howe needed to supplement his skills with the first-hand experience of a collaborator. Lescaze was the perfect candidate as he had established his modernist convictions as a student, was starting to build small projects in his solo practice, and now yearned to realise 'monumental' modern commissions.[63] They established the terms of their partnership. The two architects were often 90 miles apart: Howe would remain in Philadelphia; Lescaze would man a second office in New York City, out of which the Saving Fund commission would be run. Howe assumed the responsibility of establishing a client base, attending meetings, and conducting negotiations connected with the business, while Lescaze, some 90 miles north, was responsible for the architectural designs, the conduct of the offices, and the supervision of construction.

By the summer, the client had warmed, somewhat, to the modern nature of their new skyscraper. At a board meeting on 14 August 1929, Willcox championed the modern office building as a source of additional revenue for a headquarters building – 'a means of paying maintenance charges, taxes, and for gradually amortising the large investment the Society will have there'.[64] The project would include a parking garage, which was located a block away from the bank, north of Market Street. The parking garage was built primarily to help attract office tenants, who were often part of the commuter population. The PSFS acknowledged the new importance of travel by car, suburban life, and the commute to the city for work. Return on investment appealed to the businessmen of the Society's board, who sought to grow the organisation beyond its single purpose of a savings fund. By diversifying, the PSFS evolved in a new, modern business landscape.

Just as the client was growing to accept its new modern headquarters design, the stock market crashed. On 29 October 1929, the booming post-World War I economy in which the Society's building committee had planned its ambitious architectural project ended. This did not delay the project, however. Despite the economic collapse, few major

commercial banks failed during the Depression. In fact, older mutual savings banks, like the PSFS, promised special protections for small depositors. While bank deposits in the city as a whole fell by 21 per cent between 1930 and 1932, deposits in Philadelphia's three mutual savings banks grew by 18 per cent. The PSFS alone gained 53,048 depositors (a 13 per cent rise) during the height of panic in 1931.[65] As a result, their architectural project remained unaffected. In truth, the PSFS found itself in an advantageous position to buy building materials at reduced prices.[66] Despite the grim economic climate, the budget was unshaken, and price seemed to be no object for the client.[67]

In the months following the crash, a major breakthrough occurred in the design of the skyscraper base. Despite the progress Howe had achieved with his design thus far, the street corner condition of the entry and storefront had eluded him. His Swiss partner resolved the base design with his 2 December 1929 sketch, which introduced two new elements: a ground floor store and a raised banking floor (Fig.17). In the months

17   Preliminary sketch of the PSFS building base of the final Building, dated 2 December 1929, by William Lescaze.

since the client had accepted the modern design, the idea of raising the banking hall from the ground floor to the second floor was pursued.[68] By redesigning the base, Lescaze liberated the stagnant symmetry that Howe had carefully established.

In the new design, a dynamic curve swept around the street elevation on Market and 12th Streets. The smooth curve was articulated by a band of horizontal glazing and a receded retail entry area on the ground level. The curved base volume connected with the vertical skyscraper

(*left*) 18   Perspective rendering of the PSFS building base dated 25 December 1929, by William Lescaze.

composition. The design highlighted Lescaze's 'showmanship' and commercial prowess in its spatial complexity and dramatic lighting, and it established his signature design element – the curved volume.[69] The character of his renderings displayed an excitement of the city that was absent in Howe's 1929 drawings. Lescaze's early sketch was further developed in a rendered perspective drawing, dated Christmas Day, 1929 (Fig.18).

Likely sources for the 1929 base design (for which Lescaze was largely responsible) include J.J.P. Oud's Hoek van Holland in Rotterdam of 1924–1927, and Erich Mendelsohn's Tageblatt Headquarters in Berlin of 1921–1923 and the Schocken Department Store in Stuttgart of 1926–1928 (Figs 19, 20, 21). Lescaze admired Oud's Hoek van Holland project, writing to him in 1929

above by a notch at its top, thus creating a transitional composition. The base was high and vertical on the bank entrance facade, with a gradual stepping down to a horizontal 12th Street facade. The introduction of slipped volumes above the curved base reinforced the asymmetry of the

19   Hoek van Holland, Netherlands, J.J.P. Oud, 1924–1927.

20   Schocken Department Store, Stuttgart, Germany, Erich Mendelsohn, 1926–1928.

to ask permission both to include an architectural manifesto and to publish photographs of Café de Unie and the houses of Hoek van Holland.[70] Like the PSFS design, Oud's scheme was designed for multiple uses. Both Oud's and Mendelsohn's designs featured curved plate glass elevations on busy corner streets. Oud's solution was practical: shops needed a big display area and street exposure. But it was also informed by contemporary theoretical notions: the rounded forms represented functionalist principles, an interest he shared with William Lescaze.

While there is no documentation that Lescaze was inspired by Mendelsohn, he was in Berlin in 1922 to visit modern buildings when Mendelsohn's *Berliner Tageblatt* newspaper headquarters of 1921–1923, known as Mossehaus, was newly built, and was likely influenced by it.[71] Like the PSFS project, Mendelsohn's building sat on a prime corner location and was designed for a publicity-

minded patron. Mendelsohn's work on the Berliner Tageblatt Building left the main faces of the existing edifices intact. He inserted a new, rounded corner section and new top storeys above the existing structure. The project was an example of elevation renewal or cleansing, a common practice in Weimar Germany at the time.[72] Instead of renovating an entire building, the elevations were simply stripped of ornamentation. The smooth forms and lines of the resulting building telegraphed architectural modernity. Mendelsohn believed that horizontality was both expressive and emotive – expressing the character of modern machines and construction, and thus alleviating the stress of modern life. The blurring of verticals and the extending of horizontals reflected the way automobile passengers travelling at high speeds perceived buildings as they passed by.[73] The sweeping, horizontal massing of Mendelsohn's Mossehaus appears to have inspired Lescaze as he refined

21   Mendelsohn's Berliner
Tageblatt Building, known
as Mossehaus, was a likely
influence on William Lescaze
in the design of the base of the
PSFS Building.

the base of the PSFS Building. His December 1929 sketches display a similarly dynamic, horizontal curving massing.

At the time, the definition of modern architecture was complex, multi-faceted, and encompassed a number of varied approaches. Both sources of the PSFS base design – Oud's Hoek of Holland and Mendelsohn's Mossehaus – possessed decidedly functionalist characteristics that explored individualism and uniqueness.[74] Oud's work attempted to reconcile 'scientific,' cost-effective techniques in construction with the psychological needs of users. Similarly, Mendelsohn's work featured curving horizontal forms aimed at easing anxiety in the modern world. Like Oud's and Mendelsohn's works, the PSFS Building design exhibited the same kind of singular characteristics. As such, the individuality of the PSFS design in the American business context was just the kind of attention-grabbing

quality that would not only advertise but brand the client.

Lescaze's sketch of the skyscraper base initiated six months of schematic design development. During the spring, the design took shape. It consisted of four major parts: the street-level store; a second-floor banking room approached by staircase, escalator, and elevator; several floors above the banking room dedicated to Saving Fund offices; and an office tower comprising approximately 25 storeys of rentable office space.[75] In April 1930, the contractors, George A. Fuller Company, were able to estimate building costs, and in June 1930, the building committee approved Willcox's recommendation to build a garage nearby for office tenants.

As the design progressed and the architects struggled for modern expression, they met with resistance from the client. Howe and Willcox fiercely debated the horizontal exterior expression, both in person and in a series of letters they exchanged beginning in May of 1929. The two men argued about whether the exterior facade ought to be horizontally or vertically expressed.[76] Willcox profoundly opposed a horizontal emphasis, believing that it would not possess civic presence and appear to some as industrial. News about prospective tenants' criticisms of the horizontally expressed design as 'being ugly and like a loft building' supported his position.[77] The client's concern for an architecture that appealed to the public propelled his heavy involvement in the design of the building elevations. To be sure, the client, with the help of his rental agent, Richard Seltzer, showed concern for the practical rentability of office space. Thus, a number of design decisions were made to increase desirability for future renters. Instead of the ribbon windows that the architects initially designed, projecting columns were used so that partitions could be easily used for division of space.[78] Also, the off-centre position of the tower enabled well-lit offices, and air-conditioning and acoustical ceiling tiles were added to the rental offices.

The architects vehemently disagreed with the criticism. They passionately defended the 'horizontal treatment' as being a 'truthful' expression of structural logic.[79] Horizontality was the 'simple logic of toy blocks' rendered as horizontal brackets. The design's 'aspect' was another reason for horizontality.[80] If the tower were expressed vertically, it would result in the illogical appearance of the whole tower coming down on thin glass. Instead, a steel-frame building, Howe argued, should be expressed horizontally. The use of 'horizontal subdivisions' related to what he called 'the development of the suspended veil'.[81] By 'veil', Howe meant the non-load-bearing curtain wall that hung from a steel structure and no longer carried the burden of structural load. The PSFS Building was one of the first modern skyscrapers to do this.

As Willcox perused the April 1930 issue of *Architectural Record*, he undoubtedly read a relevant article about what Howe had referred to as 'veiling'.[82] In it, Douglas Haskell's essay 'Building or Sculpture? The Architecture of "Mass"' addressed the various expressions that curtain walls took. Structural steel frames allowed the building

facades to serve as 'a mere veil.'[83] In a tongue-in-cheek illustration, Haskell showed a horizontally expressed facade and then turned it sideways to portray a vertically expressed facade. The caption read, 'Horizontal or Vertical? Horizontal or vertical "treatment" is quite at the discretion of the designer, since either is essentially a surface affair, not affecting the inside.'[84] Haskell's commentary put the PSFS elevation debate into perspective: that it was a matter of ornament. Indeed, American architect Louis Sullivan had long since discussed the ornamental nature of skyscraper elevations in his 1896 essay, 'The Tall Office Building Artistically Considered'.[85] In it, he explained that the 'horizontal and vertical' divisions of office units formed the exterior expression. As Haskell would argue 30 years later, Sullivan designed his horizontal and vertical expressions with no connection to the underlying structure. Instead, his tall buildings were articulated into three parts as a plant metaphor of root, stem, and flower. The elevation designs of the PSFS Building would follow Sullivan's lead, with dual expressions as well as a tripartite articulation.

On 3 June 1930, Willcox proposed a compromise. He suggested that the vertical be combined with horizontal lines. 'For my part I don't see why vertical could not be combined with horizontal lines as decoration if they would relieve the monotony and be decorative. That, not structure, would be their justification.'[86] By the end of 1930, the architects had combined vertical and horizontal expression to create a dynamic massing. The north-facing facade was horizontally expressed, while the west-facing facade was vertically expressed. The combined vertical and horizontal, grid-like expression was displayed on the most prominent, east-facing, facade. Thus, the PSFS Building elevations offered a precursor to the modern glass curtain wall.

Curtain wall construction was not new in Philadelphia in the 1920s – for example, the John Wanamaker Building (1902–1910), located a block away from the PSFS Building, was constructed with a skeleton frame and masonry wall.[87] Yet, the execution of a glass curtain wall, which the PSFS Building achieved, was certainly a striking and novel addition to Philadelphia. The client valued the novelty and uniqueness that the curtain wall proposed, as these qualities offered a competitive business advantage. Because modern design was often thought of as industrial rather than commercial, Willcox informed Howe, 'We must recognize the fact that there is something in your design which requires explanation. The first impulse of everyone I have shown it to is [to turn] away from it.' Clarke G. Dailey, the consulting rental agent, was a key person to whom Willcox had shown the modern design. Dailey's response was that 'the architecture, while novel, is striking and modern.'[88] He highlighted the positive attention that the design would surely elicit: 'Opinions will undoubtedly vary regarding its architecture, but the building is sure to be talked about.'[89] Ultimately, Willcox saw potential in modern design for business and told Howe, 'I don't think that there is anything in your design which would decide a prospective tenant against taking space in the building if the matter were properly presented.'[90]

In the end, Willcox recognised the benefit that modern architecture could bring to his business: '[It]s uniqueness – at least in Philadelphia – gives it an advertising value that is worth something', Willcox wrote.[91] Modern architecture would serve not only as advertising but branding, giving a personality to the PSFS. The progressive image would stand out against the traditional context of Philadelphia in the early 1930s. There was no other comparable architecture in terms of height, size, or expression.

That modern design would provide a unique competitive strategy in a commercial context was an idea that Lescaze discussed with Austrian émigré and architect, Frederick Kiesler. As fellow European architects living in New York, Kiesler and Lescaze viewed modern design in American from a similar perspective.[92] Kiesler's design work on store window display gave him keen insight into how modern design was being utilised by American businesses. About this topic, he wrote,

In 1928, a new era began in American retail and manufacturing life. The modern art of the Old World started to take possession of the New World. American business discovered it in an art not only new in itself, but also new in its application as an immense selling force. Characteristically, America used it for one great purpose: increased prosperity through increased sales.[93]

Kiesler built upon the common characteristics of modern industry, life, and design to promote the utilisation of modern architecture by the business client. Howe and Lescaze's design for the PSFS Building, in an analogous way, turned modern architecture into a selling force. As modern manufacturing filled the marketplace with standardised products and displays, individuality in design was increasingly recognised as an attribute. Kiesler described the situation in his 1930 book: 'Too often ready-made, manufactured plans [and] standardized plans are accepted that have been repeated hundreds of times. A different architectural "prescription" is needed for each case . . . [A] store front must each time be individually created for a special store on a special site, playing for a special type of client.'[94] As with Mendelssohn, Howe and Lescaze found a kindred spirit in Kiesler. Kiesler's argument for individuality in a commercial context is precisely the kind of branding that the PSFS Building achieves within the context of 1930s Philadelphia.

Howe had sought out a partnership with Lescaze because of his knowledge of modern architecture. The individualistic architecture that Lescaze had seen on his formative travels in the late 1920s would find its way into the design of the PSFS Building. His first-hand observations of Mendelsohn's and Oud's buildings and their particular brand of modernist expression, the influence of his colleague Frederick Kiesler, and his own commercial commissions in America forged Lescaze's distinctive approach to modern design.

Willcox was careful, however, that the benefits of the building's striking aesthetics would come back to the company – not to the architects. Out of concern that the firm might use the PSFS design to bolster its own reputation, he asked Howe to pledge his word 'as a gentleman' that he was providing the Society with a reputable building and not simply a novelty design for his own publicity. As a gentleman, Howe gave his word. Willcox was a shrewd client, who wanted to ensure that the corporate headquarters would be a monument to PSFS: he did not want a 'signature' by Howe and Lescaze. But despite Willcox's attempt to pre-empt it, the design would evolve in that direction.[95] Of the two partners, Lescaze was more of the showman. His contributions to the PSFS design would give the building its wow-factor. Howe had established most of the main modern design elements before Lescaze became involved in the design as partner, but from May 1929 on, Lescaze's expressionist influences took hold of the project. It was his qualities of showmanship that gave the building its dramatic effects, which would subsequently come to brand and advertise the client. Lescaze's nuanced modern expression – never before seen in Philadelphia – demonstrated what a pioneering architect had to offer a business client in the 1930s.

Even though Willcox found the uniqueness of his architects' modern design appealing, he was not yet satisfied with the 'plan and style of the building'.[96] Much to the dismay of the architects, in the late spring and summer of 1930, the client considered reverting to the 'decorative' scheme that Howe had designed in 1926 (see Fig.16).[97] In an attempt to persuade Willcox of the merits of the modernist design, Howe explained how its 'novelty of forms' naturally evolved from classically based ones. He also promoted the design's 'irregular and organic mass of impressive effect'.[98]

Convinced that Willcox needed more than purely architectural reasoning, Howe also decided to relate to Willcox on financial terms. In the same letter, Howe compared the modern and traditional schemes on the basis of their cost effectiveness. Data was presented in a graph showing the gross area and cost saving that the Society would gain by building the modern 1930 scheme instead of the 1926 scheme. While the 1930 scheme would be realised at a higher cost, the Society would get more for its money. 'In other words, for $930,000 or about 20% more than the cost of the 1926 building, your institution obtains more than 200,000 square feet or over 60% additional floor area. Furthermore, the 1930 building is more completely equipped mechanically than the 1926 building.'[99] Howe used business criteria in his attempt to cast modern architecture as a good business investment.

On 30 July 1930 (upon Willcox's return to work following an illness) the architects presented the design to the building committee. The model showed a transformed building that integrated Lescaze's design with Howe's 1929 scheme (Fig.22). The building had achieved an

(*right*) 22   PSFS presentation model, July 1930.

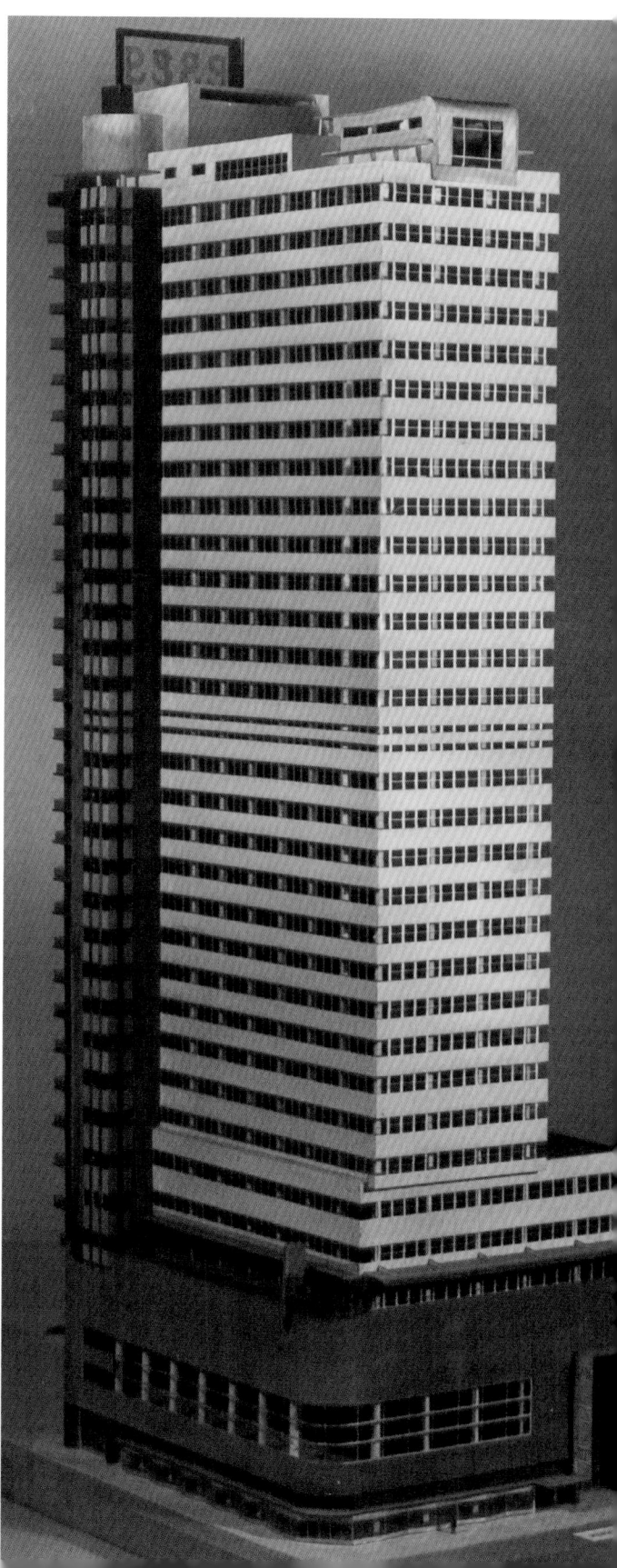

overall asymmetrical, yet balanced, composition. Although each part of the building programme was expressed as a distinct volume, the moments of intersection were no longer awkward. The composition also included several signs, a canopy, and a nascent design for the rooftop 'PSFS' sign. Also new was the shifted rectilinear form that mediated the transition between the banking hall volume and the office tower. Instead of positioning the tower directly atop the banking hall base, a three-floor form was inserted as an intermediary base for the tower. The asymmetry of this base was most evident from the street level. A sweeping curve at the corner of 12th and Market combined the ground floor store and the raised banking hall into a single grand gesture. The curve articulated the equivalent of an eight-storey base. The three-storey-high banking hall space was soaring and impressive. A large swath of plate glass, allowing light in and views out to the surrounding buildings, dominated the banking hall curve.

The asymmetry of the July 1930 presentation model was striking, but more importantly, it was potentially marketable. Asymmetry was a desirable selling device for commercial and retail buildings, according to Kiesler. 'Asymmetry,' he proclaimed, 'is Dynamic. The rhythm, which results from asymmetry, is mobile and kinetic. Therefore, if rightly composed, it directs the eye straight to the point to which you wish it directed. In this case it would be to your merchandise.'[100] It was precisely in this way that the PSFS Building design's asymmetry intended to attract city dwellers and draw them into the Saving Fund's new banking hall, retail spaces, and offices. Although there were other precedents for raised banking halls, the client deemed this a risky move.[101] Yet an unconventional asymmetry of the banking hall would potentially attract welcome attention, a desirable aspect from the client's perspective.

By October 1930, many parameters of the new building project were established. The budget of the building was set at $12,500,000. The building scope would include 'an office, bank and store'.[102] George A. Fuller Company was hired as the contractor. By 12 November, an existing parking garage was purchased. The building committee, however, had not yet approved the building's design.

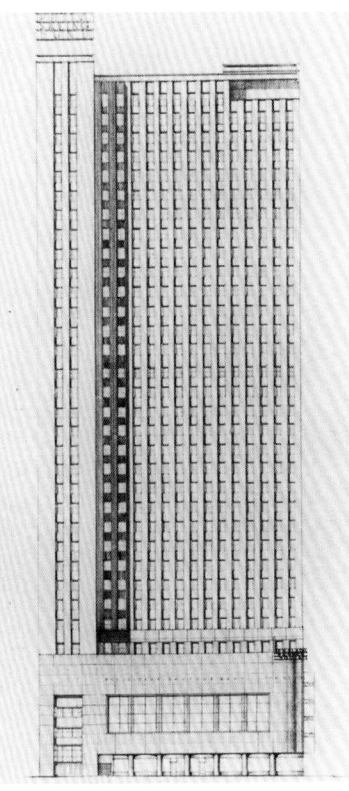

23
PSFS design scheme 2 was symmetrical and expressed verticality. November 1930.

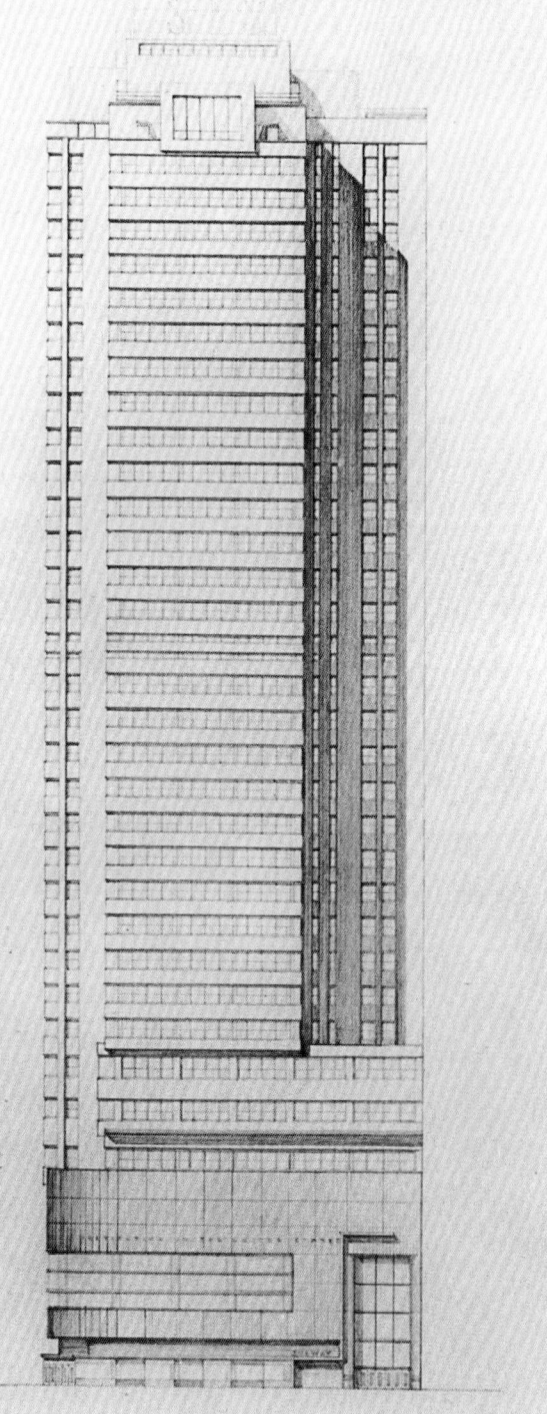

(*left*) 24   PSFS scheme 1, November 1930, showing horizontal expression.

(*right*) 25   Final PSFS building design displayed both vertical and horizontal expression. Rendering, 1927.

In November and December 1930, the architects worked on a series of seven facade studies to examine the various possibilities discussed with Willcox in the summer. From the seven studies, three reflected Willcox's request that the office tower receive a vertical treatment. These schemes, numbered two, four, and six, resembled Howe's 1926 'Beaux-Arts semi-modern' designs (Fig.23).[103] The schemes numbered one, three, five, and seven emphasised horizontality – the architects' preference (Fig.24). Upon reviewing the schemes, the building committee decided against pure verticality and instead chose to go forward with a final scheme based on study number three, which expressed both verticality and horizontality (Fig.25). Verticality was emphasised on the east facade and horizontality on the north facade, facing Market Street, with the banking hall facade serving as a horizontal base.

The chosen scheme accorded with Willcox's request to combine horizontal and vertical expression. The building committee minutes of 12 November 1930 reported the review of 'Two new sketches which the Committee believe point the way to a satisfactory working out of the problem.'[104] With the design approved, the plan was to start construction drawings right away and begin construction in 15 months – as soon as possible after the termination of leases at the Market Street site, 28 February 1931.

Emerging in the immediate aftermath of the stock market crash, the design of the PSFS skyscraper transformed from a Beaux-Arts, semi-modern building to a bold, expressionist, fully modern one. Lescaze's contribution to the design shaped Howe's modern building in a way that predicted the type of architectural showmanship that would dominate later in the century as part of the 'starchitect' phenomenon. Lescaze's expressionistic form, hugging the

corner site, together with its volumetric stone and glass curtain wall, introduced something unique and dazzling to the Philadelphia streetscape. Ultimately, the architects' modern design appealed to their client because of its marketable qualities of uniqueness, and its increased square footage for the price. The PSFS clients understood that modern design equalled good business.

PSFS Sign

Although the overall building design received final approval in December 1930, the design of the sign planned for the rooftop of the PSFS Building was far from resolved at this time. As previously noted, the idea of a modern, electric sign originated with Willcox. In his 26 May 1930 letter, Howe wrote to his client, 'You are aware that ever since you first asked me to design a branch bank around an electric sign [in 1926] I have been looking for a means of architectural expression which would not be in conflict with any form of modern activity outside the field of architecture.'[105] Howe clearly viewed the inclusion of a sign as an opportunity. The awkwardness of his early experiments on the 1926 branch banks made it clear, however, that a more modern solution would be needed.

The sign for the PSFS Building occupied the architects' concern first in 1930 and then again in 1932, as the building neared completion. In between, Howe and Lescaze turned their attention to the design of the building's interiors, furniture, and lighting. The sign and the building were thus conceived not as a whole but rather separately: the building, as we have seen, was a symbolic representation of the company and its values, and the sign, as we shall see, as advertising. At the same time, the architects demonstrated an interest in integrating the letters with the building massing by exploring the space between the letters or adjusting the kerning to correspond with the building. Ultimately, decisions made by the architects and the client around the sign's abbreviation, orientation, and positioning would make the PSFS brand more effective and signal its modernity on multiple levels.

From the beginning of the sign design process, the client's reaction to abbreviating the institution's name was one of strong doubt. The earliest sign design appeared in the July 1930 model as initials, PSFS. The sign was rendered as a framed piece of transparent acrylic, positioned to face north and south, over the south side of the building. The initials were etched into both sides of the acrylic. Upon seeing the initialled sign, Willcox remained unconvinced and asked the architects to consider the full name.[106] At the following 12 November meeting, the architects presented full-name and initialled options for the sign's design atop their seven building schemes. The four even-numbered (vertical emphasis) schemes featured the full name of the organisation, whereas the three odd-numbered (horizontal emphasis) schemes featured only the initials (see Fig.23, Fig.24).[107] An accordance between the client's design preference (vertical emphasis and full name) and the architects' (horizontal emphasis and initials) was clear.

Legibility was an important factor as the client deliberated between the options presented. In the 'full name' schemes, the sign's letters were reduced to a very small size in order to accommodate them all on the rooftop, resulting in a lack of legibility. In the 'initials only' schemes, the letters appeared at a much larger scale. This presented an advertising advantage, as the sign, legible from great distances, could be read by a larger number of viewers. This concern for legibility highlighted the sign's function as a medium for mass advertising: publicity was at the forefront of the client's mind.

The north orientation of the sign was consistent throughout the sign designs. This signalled a consideration to align the sign with the front entrance of the building on Market Street, which housed the entrance to the banking hall. The even-numbered schemes shown with the full name included an additional sign oriented to the east, the building elevation with the 12th Street office lobby entrance. While no resolution of the sign design was achieved at the 12 November meeting, the sign design explorations that took place between July and November provided insight into how orientation and alignment of the building was established within the city's grid.

In the first few months of 1931, and with the exception of the signage design, the final design was set and the architects started drafting the working drawings. The first working drawings were blueprinted on 1 May 1931. Four months later, on 14 September, the final working drawings were submitted. At the construction site, the first signs of building were seen in June, and by the end of July the foundation work was complete. In July and August, the structural steel was shipped to the site, followed by the delivery of the exterior finish materials – grey and black granite. At the same time, Howe and Lescaze's team prepared drawings for the retail and commercial portions of the building, detailing the exuberant, curved storefront on the important corner of Market and 12th Streets. Their instructions from the client were to design the store according to general conditions, without a specific client in mind. Construction of the eighth floor was accelerated, as it was to be used as a showroom for potential tenants.

The next step in the sign design process came as a consequence of adding air-conditioning to the building design. The particularly hot summer of 1931 helped convince the client that the building should be completely air-conditioned. The architects designed the sign atop the building to also hide heating, ventilation, and cooling equipment that would service the entire building. This necessitated the inclusion of a wall-like barrier to hide the gigantic cooling towers of the air-conditioning system, upon which the sign's letters would be mounted.[108] This led to a sign in the form of a billboard (Fig.25). As such, the sign could be understood not simply as a display for a name but also as outdoor advertising. A commuting audience of car and train passengers would figure prominently in the sign design decisions. As such, the sign did not follow the logics of the architectural design but instead was a kind of rooftop billboard calibrated to the surrounding transportation network. In the early evolution of branding corporate modernism, advertising was conceived separately from architecture.

During this time, the north orientation of the sign gave way to one facing east–west, as depicted on a 20 September 1931 drawing.

Eliminating the north-facing sign signalled a shift – from treating the sign like another architectural facade element, to allowing the sign to function on an urban scale and effectively communicate its message. The sign bore the nearly full name: 'Philadelphia Saving Fund'. At this point in the autumn of 1931, the sign studies ceased: the designs would be revisited in 1932.

On 14 January 1932, the building was 65 per cent complete.[109] The architects explored two sign design options: positioning the sign on the building facade or on top of the building. Three rooftop elevations of the top of the tower show the nearly full name, 'Philadelphia Saving Fund', rendered in three ways.[110] In the first, the sign atop the building featured tightly spaced lettering, spanning approximately half the width of the facade (Fig.26, left). In the second, the sign atop the building showed letter-spacing adjusted to span the whole width of the tower (Fig.26, centre). In the third, a sign on the south side of the building spanned the blank space between the window openings (see Fig.26, right).[111]

All three studies took advantage of the relatively blank south facade that covered the elevators and service equipment. Precedents for placing signage on the side of a building can be found in commercial contexts. By the 1920s, billposting, or signage on building elevations, had become a prevalent way of advertising in America. A symbol of the growing commercial culture, the practice of billposting predated the Civil War. The placement of the PSFS sign on the upper south facade was related to this commercial practice. Whether the architects or the client suggested this placement is unknown, but it showed an awareness and acceptance of advertising on the surface of architecture in urban settings. Although ultimately rejected, this option was valuable in examining the pervasive consideration of advertising value within the design process.

Billposting, by the 1920s, had developed a utopian variety, as seen in the Bauhaus Building in Dessau (1925–1926) and the Pavillon de l'Esprit Nouveau at the 1925 Exposition internationale des arts décoratifs et industriels modernes in Paris. The Weimar Bauhaus's radical objective was to reimagine the material world to reflect the unity of all the arts. With the design of their school,

the Bauhaus demonstrated collaborative spirit, which included typography and signage. The Bauhaus sign was vertically hung off the Walter Gropius-designed building as individual, white metal letters in an integral composition with the architectural elements of glass, steel, and reinforced concrete. Austrian artist and designer, Herbert Bayer, who led the Bauhaus typography and printing workshop, was responsible for the sign design.[112] For the letters, Bayer used the 'universal' typeface which he designed in 1925 as an alphabet for print, typewriter, and hand use. The 'universal' sans serif alphabet was boldly rational and efficient, composed of geometrically defined lines of uniform width; its o, b, d, and q were formed with perfect circles and the X created by connecting half circles.[113] To avoid any hint of historical types like calligraphy, Bayer constructed lines with the compass, T-square, and angle. His new typography signalled a larger contextual change. 'The typographic revolution was,' declared Bayer, 'not an isolated event but went hand in hand with a new social and political consciousness and consequently, with the building of new cultural foundations.'[114] While Bayer's universal alphabet was not manufactured as a metal font for letter press printing, it became a symbol of 'Bauhaus typography' and was a great influence throughout the promotional activities of the Bauhaus and beyond.[115]

In his controversial Pavillon de l'Esprit Nouveau, Le Corbusier rejected the decorative arts and affirmed instead the methods of standardisation and industry at various scales of dwelling. Both Howe and Lescaze are known to have visited the exposition and Le Corbusier's principle was certainly one that they explored in their design for the PSFS Building.[116] Of particular relevance is Le Corbusier's sign design: the oversized initials 'EN' – an abbreviation for *L'Esprit Nouveau*, the avant-garde journal Le Corbusier published with Amédée Ozenfant – positioned on the entry facade. The letters 'EN' were painted in illusionistic perspective and appeared three-dimensional (Fig.27). Spanning the entire surface of the exterior wall, the large initials painted white, black, grey, ochre, and burnt sienna not only served to identify the installation and its entry point but also to advertise and promote it.[117] Le Corbusier's use of initials, their

26   PSFS sign sketch showing sign on building (*left*), and on top of building (*centre* and *right*), with name spelled out, 12 January 1932.

PHILADELPHIA
SAVING FUND

HOWE AND LESCAZE ARCH
ELEC SIGNS FOR PSFS
JANUARY 12TH/32. 4B
SCALE 1/16" = 1'-0"

27   The exterior sign of Le Corbusier's Pavillon de l'Esprit Nouveau at the Decorative Arts Exposition, 1925, can be considered a source for the PSFS Building's roof top sign.

placement on the side of the building, and their use of colour influenced many aspects of Howe and Lescaze's PSFS sign.

The placement of signage on the very top of a tall building – Howe and Lescaze's first inclination for the PSFS sign – was called 'skyline lettering'. The skyline was considered to be the most visible position for a building sign.[118] Neon advertising signs on buildings began in 1912 with the Palais Coiffeur barber shop on the Boulevard Montmartre in Paris. In 1913, neon signage was used for the first time on a building rooftop with the all-capitalised lettered sign for the Italian vermouth company Cinzano, in Paris.[119] In the US, the new technology began in Los Angeles with the 1923 Packard car dealership sign. In New York, neon rooftop signs appeared on tall commercial buildings around the same time.[120] These included the Hotel Empire (1922–1923) and the New Yorker Hotel (1928–1930). The McGraw-Hill Building (1930–1931) by Raymond Hood distinguishes itself as a sign integrated with the architectural form of the skyscraper. All were of very different configurations than the PSFS's. By contrast, a sign for the Van Nelle Factory, which pre-dated the PSFS sign, seemed to have influenced the PSFS sign.

28 The skyline lettering of the Van Nelle Factory, Rotterdam, the Netherlands, 1925–1931, was a source for the PSFS Building rooftop sign. Perspective of the main factory building, n.d.

The rooftop lettering of the Van Nelle Factory (1925–1931) in Rotterdam was commissioned and built at roughly the same time as the PSFS Building. The project shares many characteristics with the PSFS Building and is worthy of closer examination (Fig.28).[121] Both projects involved collaboration between a business client and architects; in the case of Van Nelle, the industrialist Cees van der Leeuw and the architects Jan Brinkman, Leendert van der Vlugt, and Mart Stam. Both had multi-purposes: Van Nelle's programme consisted of three factories (for coffee, tea, and tobacco) as well as an office and a glass-roofed pavilion. Both were examples of functionalist modern design. An early proposal showed signs atop each factory identifying the products made in that particular building.

The signs had much in common with the PSFS design. Both consisted of sans serif lettering on the skyline top of the buildings, and both were illuminated at night by neon electric lighting. Both signs obeyed the functionalist design principles of legibility. Most significantly, each sign was angled toward a key infrastructural point. Located on the outskirts of Rotterdam, Brinkman, Van der Vlugt, and Stam's Van Nelle sign squarely faced

29   Direct view of the PSFS sign from the Delaware River Bridge, 1932.

the Amsterdam–Rotterdam railway line, clearly identifying its building to the train's passengers; the signs were thus key to the proper functioning of the factories. While the PSFS Building was commercial rather than industrial, its sign shared with Van Nelle's the essential role of locating its client within the urban space and communicating its brand identity to its inhabitants.

Even after the PSFS sign drawings had gone out for bidding in March of 1932, the design remained unresolved. After abandoning the sign on the south facade, the architects focused on the dual-faced sign directed toward the east and west. It was at this point that the last major change to the design occurred: the east sign was angled a few degrees due north to squarely face the Delaware River Bridge.[122] The PSFS sign faced the bridge upon which many potential customers would be travelling by rail transit into Philadelphia. The sign would now greet commuters, mostly travelling by train, but also some automobile drivers.

Earle Bolton, a staff architect for Howe and Lescaze who attended the design meetings, reported the client's desire for advertising as the reason he eventually approved the use of initials in the building's sign. One of the vice-presidents of the Fuller construction company asked Willcox if he had ever seen a large electric sign reading 'PON' that was visible from the Pennsylvania Railroad as it neared Newark, New Jersey. Willcox had indeed noticed the sign and had wondered about its cryptic meaning. The Society president's own curiosity over the sign demonstrated the advertising value of employing only initials. The Fuller Vice-President voiced his enthusiasm: 'Let's make everyone curious about PSFS.'[123] The new, angled position of the PSFS sign would work similarly to the PON sign through exposure to commuters.

This angling provided further evidence of the Society's awareness of Philadelphia's demographic growth to outlying commercial nodes, which was also reflected in the four branch banks and their decision to provide a car garage for the tenants of the Center City office building. The angling of the sign demonstrated that the client sought integration in the urban infrastructure and transportation network as well as advertising on a mass scale (Fig.29). While the positioning of the sign was resolved, its legibility – whether the full name of the

Saving Fund or its initials would be used – was still unresolved.

On 20 April 1932, members of the building committee held a 'special roof sign meeting' in which full-scale letter samples were viewed.[124] The samples were of two sizes: one at the larger size of the PSFS initial design and another at the smaller size of the full-name version. The client rented a hotel room on a high floor several miles away from which to judge the visibility of sample letters atop the nearly finished skyscraper. The larger, single letter S of the initials option was hoisted into place first. The simple sans serif typeface with an 18-inch stroke proved extremely legible. Next, the smaller sized letter of the full-name option was positioned. It proved illegible. The letter experiment clinched the use of initials on the building. Shop drawings prepared by the Buffalo-based Flexlume Sign Corporation, were produced on 23 May 1932. The final sign design bearing the PSFS initials would confirm what experts in the signage trade already knew – that 'great size . . . takes less concentration to assimilate' and reflected the quick pace of modern urban life.[125]

The rooftop sign's legibility from the Delaware River Bridge determined its final form. Four large letters greeted commuters as they approached the city. According to a 1931 study by the Delaware River Joint Commission, 62,126 people crossed the bridge daily.[126] This represented an impressive 70 per cent of the total number of commuters, who employed various means of travel (including ferries) between Camden, New Jersey and Philadelphia, travelling at 45 to 55 miles per hour. Only a few seconds could be allotted to reading, making the abbreviated, four-letter presentation ideal.

Instead of complicated signs that would be impossible to read in a short amount of time, billboard designs were deliberately abstract and simplified. Their design spoke concisely yet loudly to meet the modern tempo of life created by highway travel. As part of this new aesthetic, 20th-century advertisers refined their use of trademarks, logos, and slogans to create massed images that gave a quick impression. An aesthetics of speed was required, which could deliver messages in a state of unblinking recognition. Initials and logos were the ideal form of communication for

mobile audiences. The sign would serve as mass advertising for a company that was new to a mass scale of business. By using initials, the company would rejuvenate its identity, thus re-branding the institution. The rooftop letters 'PSFS,' while not officially registered until the 1970s, functioned ostensibly as a trademark.

In addition to legibility, architects and clients also tested night illumination at the special sign meeting on 20 April 1932. By the 1920s and 1930s, electrical sign lighting had become an accepted aspect of commercial buildings, especially in the most concentrated district for night-time illumination, New York's Times Square.[127] So while PSFS was not the first building to feature an illuminated sign, it was certainly one of the first modern buildings to do so in the United States. Illumination would significantly add public exposure to the PSFS sign, extending its visibility well beyond the Delaware River Bridge. The 1933 working drawings for the sign showed two alternative treatments for the sign, one with neon tubes and another with four rows of parallel white incandescent bulbs.[128] In the 1920s and 1930s, incandescent bulbs were the standard technology in commercial electric signage.[129] With neon sign technology just emerging, the architects and clients arranged a special sign meeting to test their effectiveness. Neon light mock-ups were designed as one single, two, and three parallel rows, and at different light intensities. The results were studied by photoelectric cells with recording instruments at one-, two-, and five-mile distances. The resulting data was used by the architects to determine the lighting specifications of the final letters. The superiority of neon tubes in terms of colour, cost, and visibility was clear.[130] The sign fabricators, Flexlume Sign Corporation, convinced the architects that neon lights would serve their purpose better and as a result, the specification was changed to high-voltage neon tubing (Fig.30).

Each letter stroke was lit by two twelve-millimetre diameter neon tubes of 10,000 volts, which resulted in a lighting intensity of 140 lumens per foot. While its visibility depended on atmospheric conditions, on a clear day the sign was legible for three miles; at night-time, legibility extended to three-and-a-half miles.[131] The illuminated sign reportedly could be seen (if not

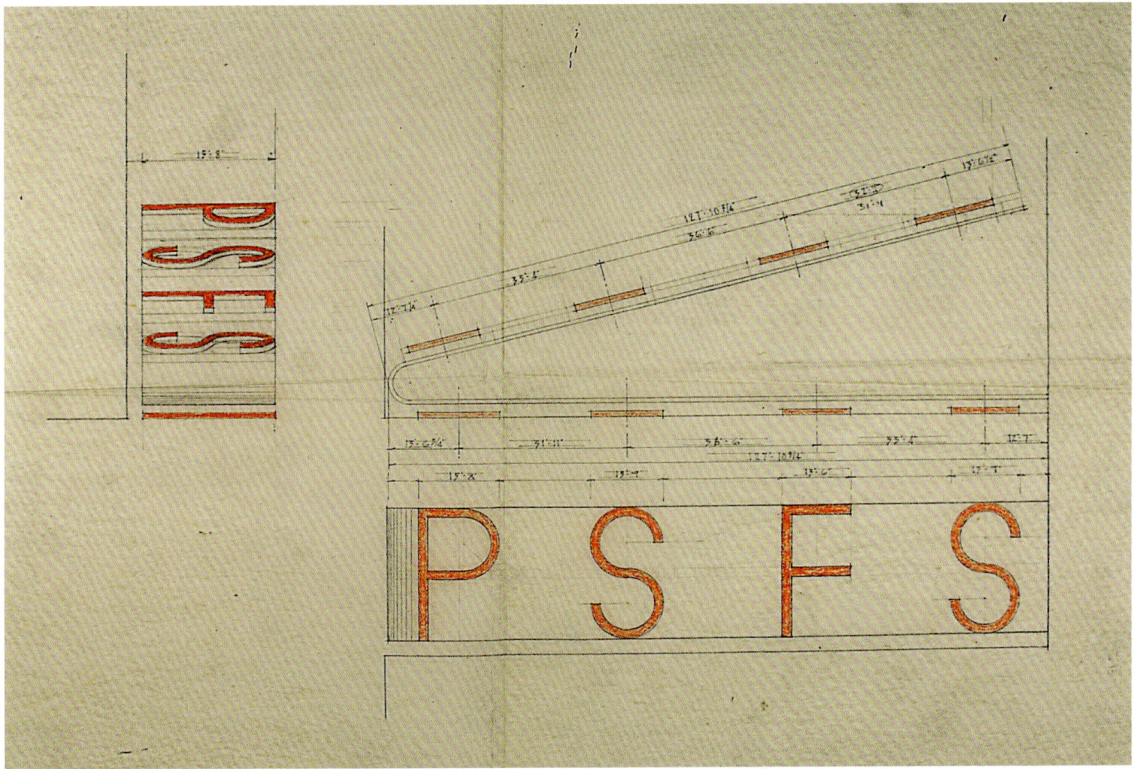

30   PSFS sign drawing depicting red neon letters, n.d.

read) from a distance of 15 miles on the ground and recognised from a distance of more than 20 miles from the air. The sign was automatically switched on at night by a photoelectric cell facing the north sky. Thus, it remained continuously visible, 24 hours a day, seven days a week, 52 weeks a year. The neon PSFS sign atop the 33-floor skyscraper enabled the PSFS to not only speak to its audiences all day and night, but speak in a modern language through the typography of the sign (Fig.31).

Lescaze was responsible not only for the sign's design, but also for its typography. The modern preference for sans serif type was established by Dutch typographer Jan Tschichold, in the 1928 handbook of a movement, *Die neue Typographie* [The New Typography]. The handbook explains how undressing letter forms and stripping them of all ornamental accretions ostensibly reduced type to its Urform skeleton and created the completely functional letter.[132]

Architects designed sans serif typefaces as integrated signage elements on modern buildings. Architecture and lettering were composed as a whole. A good example is the commission for Café de Unie which offered J.J.P. Oud the opportunity to design a modern facade that related to contemporary urban life, complete with illuminated signs, form, and colour (Fig.32). Oud wrote that the contrast 'is evident from the shape and position of the illuminated signs, all of which are directed inwards, that is to say, mounted in such a way to maximise their effectiveness for passers-by on all sides'.[133] Oud had the cafe photographed diagonally rather than frontally – capturing the casual gaze of passers-by on the street.

Oud's approach of integrating signage and architecture in Café de Unie compares well with the signage of the PSFS Building. In his 25 December 1929 sketch of the PSFS Building, Lescaze located a number of signs in similar orientations, scales, and positions as those on the Café de Unie: these included a horizontally oriented, large-scale sign at the top, a vertically oriented sign over the entrance, and a second vertically oriented sign (see Fig.18). The influence of the Café de Unie is clear: the PSFS signage was inspired by the 'Dadaist-like provocation' of Oud five years earlier, even if all of the PSFS signs did not come to fruition.[134]

While the New Typography movement was an important influence on the design of the PSFS letters, the American context of modern typography, which was less utopian and more commercial, was also relevant. Douglas C. McMurtrie, American type designer and typography historian, described sans serif type in 1929 as 'type devoid of superadded or inessential features, which are not part of the primary letter form. This, I think would logically exclude serifs. Scrolls, flourishes and the like are entirely taboo.'[135] Sans serif type in the American context was 'monotone and uniform,' absolutely simple and suitable for fast-paced modern life.[136] In the late 1920s and early 1930s, the American approach to modern typography was based, like the European New Typography, on the easy comprehension of a message. Legibility was the primary consideration, and one of the primary considerations of the PSFS sign.

Unlike the European New Typography, modern typography in America, according to McMurtrie, did not emerge out of an ideology but instead out of, and with, the times. He proposed modern typography as a healthy way out of a stultified historicism, and while critical of European modernism's machine-worship and its more extreme practices, he advocated on behalf of an American variation of the New Typography.[137] In Europe, modern typography was based on engineered type that was evolving toward a standardised and universal alphabet, an example of which was the typeface developed at the Bauhaus in 1925. But in McMurtrie's view, there was too much standardisation in typography. While he felt that modern American typography should not use serifs, scrolls, or flourishes, he still felt differentiation was

(*left*) **31** PSFS sign, designed as a neon billboard.

32　J.J.P. Oud's Café de Unie, Rotterdam, 1926.

necessary. The Ludlow typeface that McMurtrie designed in the late 1920s demonstrated what he meant. The letters were clean and minimal but also possessed a calligraphic quality in the thin and thick variation of line weight throughout the letter. McMurtrie's theories were strikingly similar to those of Kiesler's, who also saw the need for individualisation in modern commercial design for the American market.

Both the European New Typography and American modern typography exerted a strong influence on the PSFS sign's typography. The tenets of the New Typography – ideal, engineered, and standardised type – were aligned with Howe and Lescaze's design approach for both the sign and the building. At the same time, the client, like other American businessmen, saw modern typography as a welcome disruption to the status quo. In a business context, modern typography was thought to be less unified and more differentiated than its European counterpart. These were characteristics that were thought to help stimulate the depressed 1930s economy. Understood by American typographers not as a philosophy but as a 'style,' sans serif typefaces produced in variations entered the marketplace, where they were met with commercial success.[138]

The PSFS sign design also accomplished an International Style principle – an American interpretation of European modern architecture.[139] Lettering was the sole permissible applied decoration on a building because it possessed 'functional purpose in advertising and in indicating the use of different parts of a building,' therefore 'lettering . . . is the nearest approach to arbitrary ornament used by the architects of the international style.'[140]

Since standardised sans serif typefaces, like standardised modern furniture, were not readily available at the time, Lescaze custom-designed the PSFS sign letters and approached it with an architect's sensibility of pure geometries: this meant the letters were largely monoline, with each stroke of a consistent weight. Round letter forms were mechanically circular.[141] By contrast, a typographer's approach to designing type would not be a geometrical exercise but would feature refinements like shortening and lengthening of letter strokes to create readable, coherent, and visually satisfying

text.[142] As a result, Lescaze's typeface resides outside the typographical tradition. The purely geometric underpinnings reveal an architect's approach rather a typographer's. His custom-designed typeface served as an extension of the building's modern architecture and contributed to the coherent identity, or brand, that it created through its design: sans serif typography in effect advertised the modernity of the architecture and the institution.[143]

Lescaze's sign drawing was submitted to sign manufacturer Flexlume for fabrication. Once with Flexlume, a fabrication drawing was made through projecting the sign at full-scale onto a wall. At this point, the sign manufacturer, who was typically a trained typographer, made any necessary adjustments to the design.[144] Flexlume introduced typographic refinements to Lescaze's lettering before the sign was executed. These included the shortening of the lower horizontal stroke of the 'F' and the angled transition between the top and bottom curves of the 'S'.[145] Thus, in the end, New Typography and the American modern typography influenced the lettering of Lescaze's PSFS sign. In an interesting twist, the purity of its letter forms set itself apart from the variants of American modern typography. The architects extended the use of the new font to all of the signage placed throughout the building, from wayfinding signs to teller windows, further defining a unified brand image. The singular sans serif type of the PSFS sign was proud testimony that American business had adopted a design ethic.[146]

After the long debate over its design, in 1932 the PSFS sign was constructed on top of the 33rd floor of the skyscraper. Each of the four letters measured 27 feet tall, 18 feet wide, and 9 inches deep. Their steel structure, which houses the red neon tubes, was painted white. They were supported by steel brackets in front of a solid steel billboard of deep cobalt blue measuring 28 feet tall by 120 feet long. The framework was riveted and cross-braced to the building's steel structure to withstand 200-mile-an-hour winds.[147] One of the two steel billboards was angled toward the north to squarely face the Delaware River Bridge. The other billboard faced directly west. Between the two sign surfaces was a residual space that housed the air-conditioning compressors.

The bold rooftop sign was the result of contextual considerations such as visibility from key transportation routes, and also of expanding modern architectural principles to include typographic expression. By looking beyond strictly architectural considerations, such as aligning the sign with the main entry facade, the architects and clients were able to increase the effectiveness of the PSFS sign as branding – astutely calibrated to the emerging conditions of a modern, mass audience – and make it an icon of the city. After the building was completed, it would be aptly named 'PSFS,' after its rooftop sign. Though 'PSFS' would not be regularly used in the Saving Fund's advertising until almost two decades later, the acronym's association with the institution began with the audacious sign.

The PSFS Brand

The rooftop PSFS sign was part of the architectural branding of the building. Its bold, modern letters announced the Saving Fund as the building owner. Another important component of PSFS architectural branding was defined by the comprehensively designed interiors, furniture, and accessories. Howe and Lescaze designed a large array of items for the PSFS Building, from two-dimensional typography and signage to three-dimensional objects. Many were created during the summer of 1931, in advance of a September deadline for working drawings.[148] That same year, Neil McElroy of Procter & Gamble distributed his now-famous 'brand man' memo, paving the way for branding as the creation of a consistent personality of a company expressed and cultivated through a variety of design media. The architects' seating designs included benches, armchairs, side chairs, upholstered armchairs, and an upholstered sofa. Their table designs included desks, settees, coffee tables, side tables, a table with a drawer for the keypunch room, and an oval boardroom table. Their designed desk accessories included waste cans in two sizes, an ashtray and ashtray stand, a calendar with inkwells, penholders, a letter holder, wall shelves, a desk lamp, a pendant lamp, and a shaving mug holder. The architects also designed products for other areas of the building: writing shelves,

clocks, lamps, telephone booths, grilles, umbrella stands, and coat hooks. The extensive collection of custom-designed items for PSFS did not feature logos, which at the time, was premature. But the cohesive nature of the modern design gave an undeniable identity that was consistent with the company's progressive stance. With its extensive design programme, the seed of branding would be firmly planted in the PSFS Building.

At this time, the term 'brand' referred to the packaging of manufactured products and the identification of product brands as distinct from others. The systemic branding of a corporation did not yet exist. However, gesamtkunstwerk, or 'total work of art'– executing many scales of design to create an architectural whole – had existed for some time, as discussed previously. By the 1920s, gesamtkunstwerk's potential as a selling tool was unlocked by store designers. Heavily influenced by the 1925 Exposition internationale des arts décoratifs et industriels modernes, American department stores including John Wanamaker and Macy's in New York incorporated complete modern room sets in their stores. As spatial realities with strong visual impacts and experience, these interiors as gesamtkunstwerk suggested a modern lifestyle to consumers. Analogously, Howe and Lescaze also extended the principles of gesamtkunstwerk to create brand identity in their architecture and public interiors. If branding creates an identity for a company, then the comprehensive design of a company's spaces constitutes a three-dimensional brand identity.

As architectural historian Carol Willis has pointed out, most skyscrapers in urban centres were in fact speculative, with a very limited number being solely owner-inhabited. In fact, about three-quarters of skyscrapers were built as speculative, income-generating ventures, even if they were intended to brand their corporate owners, including the Woolworth and Metropolitan Life buildings.[149] This was also true for much of post-World War II corporate modernism including the Equitable Building in Portland, the Alcoa Building in Pittsburgh, the Seagram Building, and the Pan Am Building in New York. This was certainly the case for the PSFS owner, which occupied only seven floors of the 33-storey building, as well. Despite the architects' desire to comprehensively design all portions of the building, the 26 floors of speculative office spaces were not to be extensively detailed, as per the client's wishes, and instead, were to be customised by tenants. The Saving Fund offered 26 floors of rentable modern office spaces that were air-conditioned, sound-insulated, and multi-windowed. Howe and Lescaze designed the basic architectural shell of the rental offices including open spaces and large windows which emitted natural light, an aspect that added value and desirability. This was a time before fluorescent lighting was widely used in offices. The architects also designed a few basic interior details, including metal partitions, venetian blinds, and some furniture.

The system of interior metal partitions was an early modern office system, with 'suede gray' metal dividers that provided visual and acoustical privacy. Aluminium venetian blinds were also custom-designed and manufactured for the office windows. Their adjustable louvres allowed occupants to adjust daylight through the large expanses of glass in each office. Nonetheless, Howe and Lescaze persisted in their aim to comprehensively design the portions of the building within their scope. In June 1929, in the early stages of the project, Lescaze wrote to the Bauhaus in Dessau, Germany, requesting 'catalogs showing such articles you have standardised, such as door knobs, hinges, and furniture'.[150] Josef Albers, German-born artist and professor at the Bauhaus, responded in July, informing Lescaze that while a catalogue of furniture was not available, he would send standardised designs in the form of a report.[151] Due to the lack of availability of modern standardised furniture and hardware, Lescaze never received this report, thwarting his original idea to specify furniture for the project. Instead, the architects custom-designed the furniture, fixtures, and details across many scales in the PSFS Building. This was the result of aspiring to furnish interiors with mass-produced furniture in the spirit of Le Corbusier's approach of using off-the-shelf items. But at the time, the mass-produced furniture of the Bauhaus was not available, so the architects proceeded to create a similar modern effect by custom-designing each piece. The comprehensive design approach can also be understood within the context of American industrial designers like

Norman Bel Geddes and Walter Dorwin Teague who designed commercial interiors as extensions and dramatisations of their designed objects.[152]

With his experience designing exhibitions and store interiors, Lescaze took on most of the responsibility for designing the project furniture and accessories. This was unusual for a large-scale commercial office building at the time. Howe and Lescaze did not design the interiors and furniture for the speculative office spaces because their client wished to leave that task to the rental tenants. However, they did design the lobby space and office spaces for PSFS with the same attention to detail that the exterior architecture was treated with. Additionally, significant public spaces including the banking hall, additional lobbies, and boardroom were also designed by Howe and Lescaze. As detailed earlier, the variety of Lescaze's furniture items was exhaustive. The furniture included a myriad of different seating designs, from benches for the banking hall, and upholstered armchairs for executive meetings, to accessories like inkwells for depositors and coat hooks for the board members. The architect's choice of materials varied as well. His use of bent chromed tubing was among the earliest in the United States (Fig.33).[153] Boardroom furniture combined wood-framed chairs with coloured leather upholstery. The furniture was manufactured in limited quantities with little production outside the PSFS commission. The interior design and detailing of the PSFS Building were exceptional in their design.[154] The custom design throughout the building was tailored to its client's needs and as a result, went beyond defining the PSFS brand to expanding it spatially and materially. This led to a deeper connection between PSFS and its depositors and tenants who entered the banking hall and building.

If the PSFS Building's comprehensively designed interior evolved from the notion of a gesamtkunstwerk, it also reflected Lescaze's theory of 'entities'. Upon entering the building, it was clear – even to a distracted pedestrian – that one had reached a distinctive and engaging place. Since beginning his own practice in 1923, Lescaze had designed interior spaces as 'entities'.[155] For him, this meant excluding historical styles and designing all architecture and small-scaled features with a modern ethos and language. Lescaze identified

SD-43-E

C-43-E

Color harmony with any decorative scheme is assured by the complete selection of colors available in the beautiful washable Lloyd Leatherette coverings—Loyd-tex and Redo. In addition to the color selection, there is also a wide choice of "grains" and textures of a "leather-like" quality. There is a color and fabric to suit every taste and every situation. For a complete list of the colors available, see pages 72 and 73.

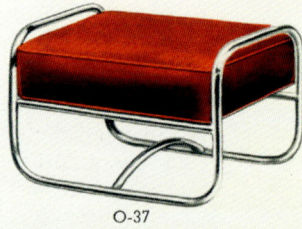

O-37

C-43-E CHAIR

Shaped "No-sag" spring seat has 6½" boxing at front. Padded back. Enameled wood arm rests. 1" tubing.

Seat width, 20"; depth, 21"; height from floor, 16". Back height, 20".

SD-43-E SETTEE DAVENPORT

Shaped "No-sag" spring seat has 6½" boxing at front. Padded back. Enameled wood arm rests. 1" tubing.

Seat width, 60"; depth, 21"; height from floor, 17". Back height, 20".

S-43-E SETTEE
(Not illustrated)
Same as SD-43-E except has 42" seat width.

O-37 OTTOMAN

This ottoman may be used with any of the Lloyd tubular steel upholstered chairs. Has removable spring-filled cushion.

Size of cushion, 15" x 20"; height from floor, 14¾". ¾" tubing.

33   Howe and Lescaze-designed seating for PSFS building, 'Chromium Furniture for 1940', Lloyd Chromium Furniture trade catalogue.

a nested relationship of scales in design, saying, 'the essence of modernism is architecture, first – the architecture of the building itself, then of the different rooms within that building, and then of the design of the furniture in those rooms'. His term for this relationship of scales was 'interdependency'.[156] The interior elements were 'all . . . parts of the whole'.[157] From architecture to rooms to furniture, Lescaze considered 'relation in feeling and form.'[158] Clearly, Lescaze had emotional connection in mind when he conceived his designs. 'The four walls, the ceiling, and floor,' Lescaze wrote, 'should not any longer be passive features, but they should become live parts of the entire design.'[159] As a result, entities were dynamic assemblages of effects, with surfaces that overlapped, interlocked, and slid by one another, bolstered by the contrasting effects of lighting and material finishes. The illusionary space surged with colours, textures, materials, and objects. The black and white photos of Lescaze's 1928 installation for an apartment in Macy's International Exposition of Art in Industry, published in *Architectural Record,* illustrate the emotional potency of Lescaze's 'entity' theory, with its visual effects of shade and shadow, reflection and absorption, and curved and rectilinear forms (see Fig.14).

Another example of entity from the years preceding the PSFS design came in the form of Lescaze's telephone foyer design for the S.T. Meyers Company in New York (1928) (see Fig.15). Tucked into a corner, his functionalist design featured a bench, table, storage space, and light to accommodate the specific activities of looking up numbers and talking on the telephone. The disparate elements were unified through a composition of rectilinear and curved surfaces of contrasting materials and colour. Dramatic shadows cast by an external source of photographic lighting used to capture the design reinforced the effect of contrast. The relationship between the architecture and furniture demonstrated Lescaze's idea of an 'entity' composed of 'live parts of the entire design and not just a shell for furniture'.[160] Again, Lescaze's theory of 'entities' evoked connection with the occupant.

Lescaze applied his concept of entity at a much larger scale in the PSFS commission. In three public spaces – the banking hall, escalator lobby, and elevator lobby – walls, floor, and ceiling came together in compositional balance, with the effects of light and shade and of material reflectivity unifying the space. A perspective rendering of the banking hall design shows dramatic contrasts of light and dark in the marbles of the monumental square columns, of the light finish of ceiling tiles and the dark marble floor (Fig.34). The perspective of the escalator lobby, where materials reflect and

34 William Lescaze's sketch of the banking hall displayed dramatic contrasts of light and dark in the marble surfaces.

35 Perspective drawing
of the escalator lobby
which depicts materials
reflecting and deflecting
light, 1932.

deflect light, shows a similar effect (Figs 35, 36). There, a large sheet of marble is suspended from the ceiling as a light reflector. The ceiling above is washed in light, whereas the area below is cast in shadow. The elevator lobby is also designed with high, light/dark contrasts in both materials' finishes, taking into account the play of daylight and shadow in order to unify the whole. Modernist critic Sheldon Cheney heralded the PSFS Building's coordinated nature, saying, 'Each article or object . . . sheer, gleaming, colorful in its own way falls into harmonious relationship with all else becom[ing] integral to the intangible, pervasive 20th-century atmosphere.'[161] The skillful use of contrasts and reflective materials enhanced the 'entity', enabling the design, according to Lescaze, to 'become live'.[162]

The artificial lighting of interior spaces heightened this effect. Conceived as an integrated element of the architecture, Lescaze's lighting designs were inconspicuous but effective in creating the 'entity'. Cheney described Lescaze's particular talent:

> Lescaze['s] lighting fixtures do not push into the room. They have all but disappeared . . . Lights in hidden recesses or behind glass ceiling areas, or in border troughs, are the original sources. Every wall or curtain or major furnishing unit is considered for reflection or diffusion values, with regard to color, texture, and placement.[163]

Lescaze also used shadows cast by objects in light to his advantage: 'a new method of lighting will create structural shadows, and become an integral part of the whole.'[164] In fact, in photographing his designs, Lescaze often used additional light to accentuate his signature 'shadowy' quality. The shadows cast by the outside light source created lighting effects and thus reinforced the concept of 'entity'.

Two installation systems were used for the interior lighting in the PSFS Building: suspended slabs and coves. This can be seen in the architects' perspective renderings of the three primary public spaces: the banking hall, the bank escalator lobby, and the office elevator lobby (see Figs 34, 35). In all three, suspended marble slabs or cove systems were employed to cast muted light into the space.

36 In the escalator lobby viewed from above, reflective materials play off each other.

Darkness played against lightness, as light from behind the black marble slab bounced light off the light-coloured surfaces of the adjacent ceiling and upper sidewalls. Noting the subtlety of this lighting effect, Leslie Tarleton, consulting engineer on the project, wrote, 'the illumination is so inconspicuous and free from shadow.'[165]

Meanwhile, in the office elevator lobby, the cove lighting system was used to brilliant effect. Tarleton described, 'broad bands of diffused light extend the entire length of the lobby. These strips of light are picked up and the reflections multiplied in the light marble of the walls in such a manner that there is no glare.'[166] The 'strips of light' were cylindrical chromium reflectors located immediately above the elevator doors. They extended the entire length of the lobby and dispersed light on the sidewalls.

An endless effect of repetition resulted from the multiple reflections between two surfaces. The polished marble cladding of the stairwell that connected the banking mezzanine spaces gave a similarly intense reflective effect.

By applying his theory of 'entity' to the PSFS Building design Lescaze created not only a unified and coherent identity for the client, but one that maximised emotional connection with the occupant. Lighting was a fundamental aspect of 'entities,' as the shadowy and contrasting effects, inside and out, became part of the building's striking identity – and in turn, bolstered the PSFS brand. The comprehensive architectural design of 'entities' engaged the building's inhabitants in ways analogous to how modern advertising grabbed the attention of viewers.

The architects masterfully employed lighting on the exterior of the building as well. This enhanced the brand identity of both the retail tenants and of the Saving Fund itself. Tarleton explained that lighting for the PSFS Building was designed 'to augment the appeal of the building, as well as to fulfil the advertising needs of the respective tenants'.[167] The lighting of street-level 'show windows' was designed as a series of grouped reflectors, mounted in the windows' ceilings. Adjustable louvres provided wide flexibility in directing the light. At the same time, a continuous light box ran above the show windows to provide a degree of uniformity to display signs.

Other exterior lights identified the Society-inhabited floors. Floodlights illuminated the facade from the second-floor level up to a height of approximately 17 feet, emphasising the banking hall volume. The architects designed a lighting system for the banking hall windows whereby the lower surface of the horizontal mullions was illuminated at night, giving the windows a soft glow. Floodlights illuminated the 32nd, 33rd, and 34th floors, where the executive spaces were located. At these levels, indirect lighting illuminated the roof parapets from behind, giving the effect of horizontally tiered strips of light. From the roof blazed the gigantic PSFS sign, 'attract[ing] attention to the building from many vantage points for miles around'.[168] Modern lighting design principles – like these and others found in cities like Berlin in the 1920s – aimed at

'effect rather than mere lumen efficiency'.[169] Howe and Lescaze subscribed to these expressionist principles, as they utilised architectural lighting to accentuate the striking and memorable form of the PSFS Building.

The building's overall design amounted to architectural branding for the PSFS. The 'entity' spaces of the banking hall and public lobbies displayed a distinct expressionist style, which served to create a bold and unique identity for the PSFS institution. Its exterior form, interior spaces, and discrete, palpable architectural elements aggregated to form an overall experience that would become a basis for long-standing relationships between customer and institution. These memorable and engaging elements, in addition to the rooftop neon sign identifying the institution through its initials, created an emotional connection to the public, thus achieving the definition of architectural branding.

Advertising PSFS

In the winter and spring of 1932, PSFS launched a new advertising campaign to promote the office spaces of their soon-to-be-completed building. Philadelphia advertising firm Gray & Rogers designed the campaign, titled 'Nothing More Modern'. Like the architecture, the graphics of 'Nothing More Modern' were clean and abstract (Fig. 37). In the trade journal *Printed Salesmanship*, Jerome Gray (founder of Gray & Rogers) described PSFS's ad campaign in an article entitled 'An Ultra Modern Campaign to Let an Ultra Modern Building'.[170] He explained how the graphic design concept took its inspiration directly from the architecture of the building. Gray explained that the ad design was inspired – but not too literally – by the building design. He wrote, 'the advertising must reflect more subtly the originality of Howe and Lescaze.'[171] The ads aimed to capture the 'character,' 'efficiency,' 'unconventionality' of the building. They combined graphic imagery with modern typography to create flat and two-dimensional designs, giving an abstract, sharp impression. Modernist graphic design at the time was characterised by asymmetrical composition, sans serif letterforms, and photographic images,

37 'Nothing More Modern' advertising campaign to rent office space in the PSFS Building, designed by advertising firm Gray & Rogers, 1932.

38   Direct mail advertising – part of the advertising campaign to rent PSFS office space in 1932.

which replaced central-axis page layout, archaic type design, and realistic illustration. 'Nothing More Modern' was a perfect example of modernist graphic design.[172]

The modern design of the 'Nothing More Modern' campaign was supported by traditional sales strategies, as well as an emerging one: newspaper advertising, publicity, and time-honoured face-to-face sales were bolstered by newer, direct-mail advertising. Gray & Rogers created a complete ad portfolio, which included a colourful folder holding numerous brochures as well as simplified floor plans of the building. The folder would not be posted out in its entirety (Fig.38). Instead, to spark interest, separate brochures would be sent, each highlighting a different modern amenity of the building: Garage Facilities, Day Lighted, and Manufactured Weather (Figs 39, 40, 41). Mailings would be followed up with a sales call or the personal delivery of the full 'Nothing More Modern' folder package.

The copy describing the building's amenities, Jerome Gray explained, was written simply and convincingly without exaggeration or unwarranted superlatives, which reflected the spartan graphic design. For example, 'Garage Facilities' were simply described: 'In addition to subway access, a garage was provided for the convenience of tenants within a half block of the building.' Another brochure touted the natural lighting of the offices as 'Daylighted,' offering 'ideal working light,' and depicting 'natural daylight streaming into the interior through continuous glass from column to column, controlled by venetian blinds to any desired intensity.'[173] The building's air-conditioned offices were an amenity that no other Philadelphia office building could advertise: 'Manufactured Weather: The building was air conditioned throughout: de-humidified and cooled in the summer – responding to an especially stifling summer.'[174] The modern graphic design, together with the elaborate sales strategy, resulted in an outstanding response to the campaign. In response to the firm's 10,000 mailings it received 1,500 replies. The 15 per cent return rate far exceeded the projected rate of 4 per cent.[175]

PSFS advertisements in the local *Public Ledger* newspaper featured abbreviated versions of the 'Nothing More Modern' campaign. One ad from 1932 entitled 'Four Reasons Why You Should Investigate Twelve South Twelfth' included practical business concerns with one of Gray & Rogers's graphic three-dimensional images of the building. The ad copy stressed the functional features of the office space:

> You will pay less per square foot – because of 1932 construction costs, strictly functional design, and owner occupation. . . . You will rent fewer square feet, because of Day Lighting . . . Your office will be more efficient – because of Manufactured Weather. . . . You will save business time – because of central location.[176]

The newspaper ad highlights the language in which modern design needed to be pitched and sold to conservative bankers and the larger business world – through a narrative of practicality, efficiency, and cost savings. Thus, the ad reinforces Howe and Lescaze's hard-won success in achieving modern design for a conservative banker client.

39   A brochure advertising the garage facilities for PSFS office space. Part of the 'Nothing More Modern' campaign, designed by Gray & Rogers, 1932.

40   A brochure advertising the plentiful daylight that illuminated the PSFS office space. Part of the 'Nothing More Modern' campaign, designed by Gray & Rogers, 1932.

On 1 August 1932, the PSFS banking hall opened to favourable public opinion. Men hired by the Society were stationed in the room to listen to visitor conversations. Most were inspired by the new building's modern design.[177] The building's appearance instilled confidence that this was a safe place to keep one's money. Visitors saw the modern design as representing a forward-looking institution.[178] On 13 April 1933, the Savings Fund held its first board meeting on the top floor of the PSFS Building. The members convened in the

newly opened boardroom, a superb example of a PSFS branded environment (Fig.42). The various custom-designed elements worked together as a composition: the oval conference table and armchairs veneered in Macassar ebony, indirect cove lighting on the ceiling, and a defining area rug over a wood floor. The varied use of exotic woods both enriched and unified the boardroom. In addition to Macassar ebony on the south wall, the woods included rotary-cut walnut on the east and west walls, and rosewood on the floor.[179] Board members hailed company president Willcox (who was absent due to ill health) as the person responsible for the new building's completion.

The sequence of public spaces to approach the banking hall was dramatic and memorable. In fact, a grand hall served by escalators was without precedent at the time. From the street, the exterior expression of the banking hall's modern aesthetic imparted an uplifting message to the public (Fig.43). The banking hall's bold, curved polished granite and plate glass massing immediately drew attention to itself. The entrance to the banking hall was at the end of the dark grey granite elevation on Market Street. The three, double-glass door entrance continued upwards as a glazed elevation at 52 feet high. Stainless steel letters spelling, 'Philadelphia Saving Fund Society' were installed above the doors, faced with white opal glass, which were lit from behind with frosted sign bulbs. Stainless steel structural elements held the sign and the doors, while the large windows were framed by aluminium.

This entrance led into an escalator lobby, which provided a way to move vertically, by escalator or stairs, to the raised banking hall. The lobby itself 'has been treated to expand visually the narrow, shaft like space and to admit as much light as possible into the area' (see Figs 35, 36).[180] The tall space of the escalator lobby was sheathed in polished black marble, with a large expanse of aluminium-framed glazing that opened into the banking hall. The great reflectivity of the marble wall expanded and multiplied the stair and escalator, whose handrails and mechanical housing were also of stainless steel. In addition to the stair and escalator, the eye was led upwards towards a linear ceiling baffle 'surfaced with acoustical tiles painted a dark brownish-red' that further accentuated the dynamic space.[181] The ceiling baffle

41　An advertising brochure highlighting the largely unprecedented aspect of air-conditioning in the PSFS building. Included in the 'Nothing More Modern' campaign, designed by Gray & Rogers, 1932.

42   PSFS boardroom on the 33rd floor, 1932.

was designed as an indirect lighting cove, along with another vertical cove lighting in the corner of black marble, adjacent to the banking hall doors. The gentle spread of light along surfaces became yet another enriching dimension of spatial effect.

Arriving at the second level, the depositors entered the monumental banking hall through glass doors (Fig.44). As an interior space, the banking hall was spectacular – and, as William Jordy put it, displayed 'sumptuous elegance'.[182] Further, he claimed that photographs of the banking hall did not do the actual experience justice. Once inside, visitors experienced a large soaring space, intensified by contrasting materials, colours, and forms (Fig.45). The chief lighting source was daylighting from the high, oversized windows, through which bank depositors and

employees could look out onto neighbouring buildings. To optimise the natural light, the architects made clever choices in material and in their positioning. Lighter coloured materials were positioned farthest from the windows, while darker coloured materials were installed closest to the windows, thereby visually balancing the light intensity throughout the space (Fig.46). In addition to the natural lighting, the architects designed indirect cove lighting throughout the banking hall.

Like the exterior, the banking hall interior displays the 'play of softness against hardness in both form and color'.[183] The soft, serpentine forms of the mezzanine balconies and teller counter humanised the scale of the large monumental space of the banking hall. Meanwhile, the tall, square window columns provided contrast. Their

(*right*) 43   PSFS Building.

44   PSFS banking hall, 1932.

heaviness was mitigated by the reflecting quality of polished black marble, upon which the images of outside buildings appeared. A two-level curving mezzanine faced with yellow Siena marble in the southwest corner of the room echoed the curving teller counter forms. In front of the mezzanine stood another line of rectilinear columns, alternately faced with black-Belgian and oyster-white marble. The colour scheme utilised the strong contrasts of black and white, which was relieved not only by the Siena marble of the curving mezzanine, but by blue leather upholstered furniture.

The PSFS Building's structural innovation is well documented.[184] In the banking hall, the primary structure was comprised of 14 principal columns that were more than six feet square, spaced 63 feet on centre. These carried the main trusses that measured a full storey in height and supported the skyscraper above. Sixteen-foot trusses had allowed the space to be essentially column-free, giving it the monumental proportions found in the great banks of the classical revival period. The voluminous space provided not only calmness – to counter the bustle of the downtown retail neighbourhood – but also openness that conveyed movement, visibility, and a sense of participation. Massive piers at the edges of the banking hall offered a sense of stability. Its architecture fostered much-needed public faith in financial institutions, which had faltered since the 1929 stock market crash.

At the close of summer 1932, the completed PSFS Building could be seen as an 'entity' (Figs 47, 48). Its clients had described the 33-storey skyscraper throughout the process as a collection of three distinct building programmes, an office, a bank, and a store. These programmes were directly expressed on the building's exterior, in form and in materials. The two tall, rectilinear volumes contained the rental offices and mechanical services, while the curved volume held the banking hall and the store. The contrast between straight and curved forms, in addition to a contrast of materials, gave the building a varied and complex expression. The service core was clad in black brick; the bank and store, both commercial spaces, in polished granite; and the office tower in an envelope of brick spandrels and piers clad in limestone and marble. The material claddings not only expressed interior function but together offered a dynamic contrast in colour and surface effect. The play of reflective and matte surfaces on the exterior massing echoed that of the banking hall interior.

The PSFS Building was conspicuously modern, an anomaly in Philadelphia, if not in America as a whole during this time. The modern architecture that characterised the city was more typically the modern classicism of the Philadelphia Art Museum and the Benjamin Franklin Parkway which emerged from the City Beautiful movement. By contrast, the PSFS Building design was an unabashedly bold and new design. It has famously been dubbed an International Style skyscraper. Yet the truth of this label is limited to its horizontal expression on the north entry elevation – a result of Howe and Lescaze's struggle to design a modern skyscraper. In 1932, upon seeing the completed building, Douglas Haskell wrote that the architect's path to simplicity was cluttered by their 'intellectual baggage from Europe: an "international style"'.[185] Indeed, the PSFS Building was far from a simple design. The architects' internal design struggle was compounded by struggles with their client who fought the horizontal expression for aesthetic and practical reasons. Yet, these client interactions were

45   PSFS banking hall, 1932.

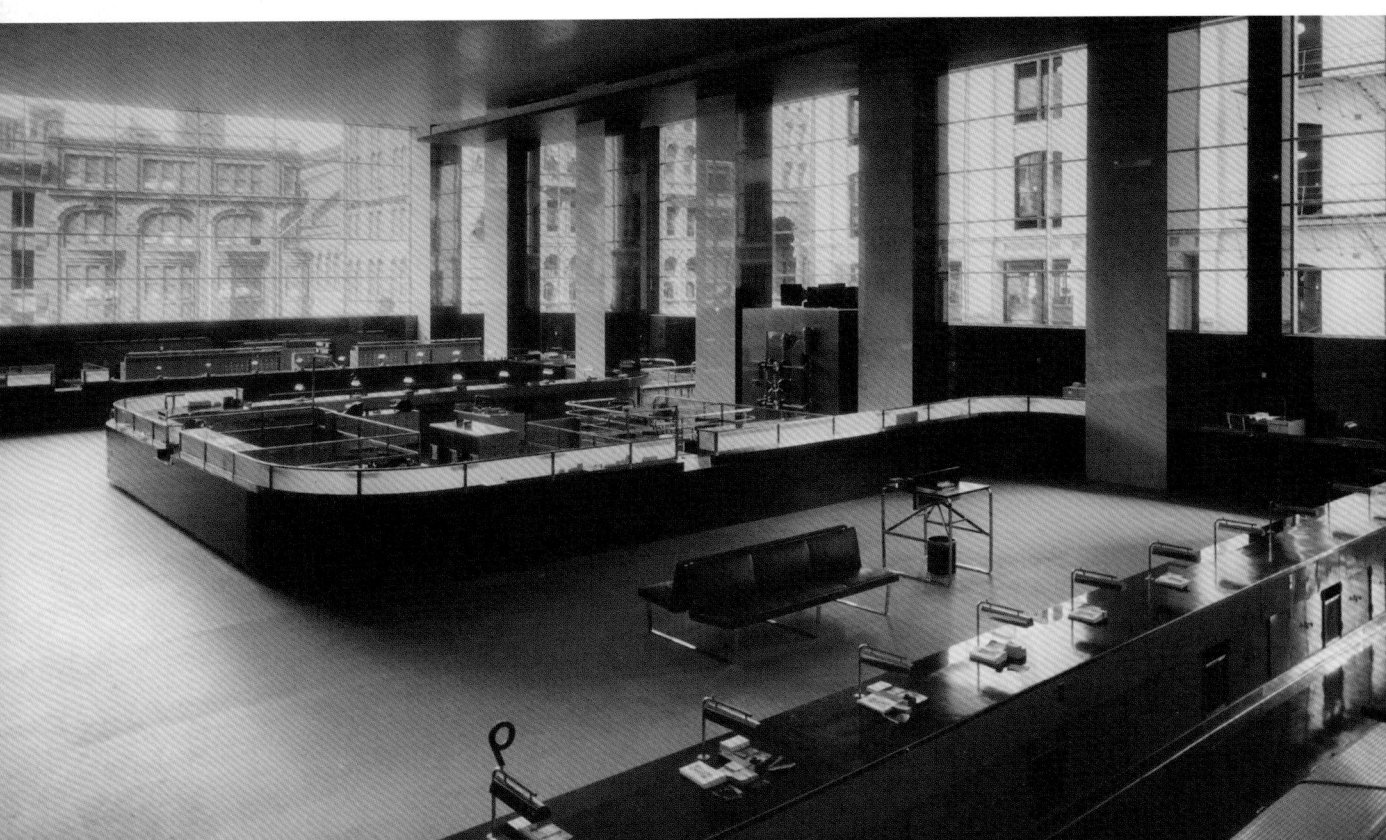

46   PSFS banking hall, 1932.

key to the PSFS Building design's rich complexity. As a result, the design evolved to be a multi-faceted and nuanced example of modern architecture that truly defines the phenomenon, instead of an idealistic representation of the so-called International Style.

The PSFS Building's exuberant massing and varied materials served as architectural branding and, as such, offered the kinds of forms conducive to create emotional connections with the audience. What the clients understood as 'uniqueness' was, in fact, the architects' search for modern design. Further, the architects' sparring with the client over horizontal and vertical exterior expressions was just the kind of client–architect collaboration that can and did have meaningful results.

In September 1943, *Architectural Forum* promoted business patronage of modern architecture in an article entitled, 'Does Modern Architecture Pay?' The journal had sent a questionnaire to business clients of modern architecture and printed a selection of the responses, together with 25 important modern buildings and their clients' comments. *Architectural Forum* editors declared that not only would modern architecture pay off for business clients but it would be embraced: 'In commercial buildings, design is as much a competitive element as merchandising itself. There is no better indication of the soundness of the modern approach than its rapid acceptance by the people who have to examine it most critically.'[186]

47   PSFS Building, view from street level, 1932.

48　PSFS Building, view from across the street corner at 12th and Market Streets, 1932.

Architectural Forum argued that design was a form of merchandising, and modern architecture would promote the sale of a business's goods. In the PSFS's case, its architecture proved outstanding in promoting its services. 'The type of architecture adopted has proved most successful,' Willcox stated, 'and has resulted in a building better adapted for the purpose than would have been possible had the style been conventional.'[187] On his first and only patronage of modern architecture, Willcox wrote, 'I am tempted to hazard a forecast and say that there will be but few large office buildings erected in the future designed along conventional lines.'[188] By commissioning modern architecture, business clients increased their advertising value and identified their brands in powerful ways, the editors argued: 'It should at the very least bring into question the notion that investment return and resale value are answered only when a building turns its face to the past.'[189]

Willcox supported modern architecture by making reference to the building's excellent office renting record, as well as the quick occupation of the ground floor store and restaurant space. In the decades after its opening, the PSFS Building enjoyed steady occupancy, persevering through the Great Depression. This is in contrast to New York skyscrapers like the Empire State Building, which was only 25 per cent occupied throughout the 1930s, and the RCA Building, which only gained full occupancy in 1940. In 1943, the PSFS office space was 92.8 per cent occupied. Willcox attributed these positive results to 'the orderliness and clean-cut arrangement of space, typical of this type of architecture'.[190] When the Society examined the balance sheet of their revenue-generating building, they estimated the total cost to have been $12,360,942.37.[191] When the project began, the estimated cost had been approved at $12,500,000, of which $5,000,000 represented land cost. The construction cost had actually come in under its initial estimation, an important – if not the *most* important – factor for any client.

The PSFS Building rebranded the Saving Fund in architectural terms. The building's exterior, interior, and sign designs created a new, specifically modern image that evinced new and forward thinking by the client. Throughout the building, all scales of design – 'everything from a skyscraper to the hook for the businessman's hat' – cultivated an experiential brand that was memorable and potent.[192] The high level of synthesis, or a kind of gesamtkunstwerk, in the PSFS interior further increased its effectiveness as architectural branding. The architectural branding of the PSFS Building – its dynamic, expressionist skyscraper, its synthesised interior design, and iconic rooftop sign – not only enhanced the client's reputation but created a connection with the public. The four case studies in this book all demonstrate modern architecture as branding. Yet each building offers a particular contribution to architectural branding, and for the PSFS, it is an audacious rooftop sign. If the PSFS Building's particular contribution to architectural branding was a sign announcing the abbreviated name of the client, we now turn to the next chapter, which asserts how a legendary architect's fame played a role in architectural branding for a business client.

3 FAME

Frank Lloyd Wright and the Johnson Wax Building

In 1939, just as the United States was coming out of the economic depression and arming for World War II, 'The Office of the Future, designed by Frank Lloyd Wright' was built.[1] Together, Samuel Curtis Johnson and its renowned architect Frank Lloyd Wright realised the S.C. Johnson & Son Administration Building. *Life* magazine touted the building's progressive design, which opened the same year as the New York World's Fair, asserting, 'Future historians may well decide that a truer glimpse of the shape of things to come than is represented by the New York World's Fair was given in a single structure built strictly for business – the Administration Building of S.C. Johnson & Son, Inc., Racine, Wisconsin.'[2]

From the late 1920s to the late 1930s, Wright's work was subject to negative criticism and his fame had faded significantly, with then-Museum of Modern Art curator Philip Johnson derisively calling Wright the finest 19th-century architect the 20th century ever produced. But by the time the S.C. Johnson & Son Building was completed, Wright was once again acclaimed, which benefited both the architect and his client. In January 1938, Wright was the cover story of *Time* magazine, the subject of an entire issue of *Architectural Forum*, and the subject of a solo exhibition at the Museum of Modern Art. If the PSFS Building, with its glowing neon sign, synthesised interiors, and bold expressionist architectural massing, presented an early model of the urban corporate headquarters as an agent of architectural branding, the S.C. Johnson & Son Building offered similar aspects of the interior and exterior form. Yet Frank Lloyd Wright and his renown offered an entirely different architectural branding strategy – that of the architect's fame.

Racine, *c.*1930

From its inception in 1834, Racine, Wisconsin was an industrial manufacturing centre. Located on the shores of Lake Michigan between Chicago and Milwaukee, the harbour city was also central to the transcontinental shipping industry which emerged later in that century. Racine's growth coincided with the invention and development of agriculture machinery and other labour-saving devices. Known as the 'invention city', it was the birthplace of many modern inventions that would become ubiquitous in 20th-century households. Whirl-a-gigs like the fractional horsepower universal motor (later adapted as Osterizer, Hamilton Beach, and Waring blenders) and the In-Sink-Erator (the first garbage disposal machine) were invented in Racine, as were malted milk, tricycles, and automobiles.

Local industries were vital to the growth of Racine, which served as the headquarters location of a number of companies, including Dremel Corporation, Reliance Controls Corporation, J.I. Case Plow Threshing Machine Works, and Twin Disc. Gold Metal Camp Furniture was started in 1892, the Racine Rubber Company in 1910, Mitchell Motor Car Company in 1903, and Western Publishing in 1908. It was in this context that in 1886, Samuel Curtis Johnson began a parquet floor manufacturing operation that would expand its product line to include floor polishing wax.

S.C. Johnson & Son

In 1886, Samuel Curtis 'S.C.' Johnson bought the parquet flooring division from the Racine

Hardware Manufacturing Company, where he had been working, and named the new business S.C. Johnson & Son. When he and his son Herbert Fisk Johnson learned of a new house being constructed in Racine, they would quickly negotiate a deal with the owner for the home's flooring. The parquet pieces were cut in the company's small factory and loaded onto a horse-drawn wagon for transport to the building site where carpenters installed the parquet flooring.[3] This was the company's business. Clients often asked Samuel Johnson how to care for their floors. Johnson began supplying his customers with finishes used on wood floors: the sealers, varnishes, and shellacs that made the floors look good, but were difficult to apply, maintain, and remove. He developed a better product – Johnson's Prepared Wax™ – a combination of naphtha, beeswax, paraffin, and some harder waxes.[4] Borrowing from the European tradition of caring for old wooden floors by rubbing them with wax, Johnson's Prepared Wax was a success. Even people who had not bought his flooring purchased and used his wax. Johnson recognised an opportunity to diversify his product offerings and thereby safeguard his company's longevity. Parquet floors might go in and out of fashion, and home construction was tied to the ups and downs of the market, but floor cleaners would always be a necessity. Wax cleaner proved to be a versatile product that could be re-formulated for many applications, but most importantly, Samuel Johnson began diversifying his business. Beginning with this early shift from installing parquet flooring to developing floor wax, diversification would be a fundamental element of the now-five generation family business.

The company experimented with additional products, such as wood dye, crack filler, and car wax. As the vogue for intricate parquet floors gave way in the late 1800s to a preference for simpler maple and oak flooring, the company's diversified approach paid off. In 1898, sales of floor wax products exceeded those of flooring: floor wax quickly became the company's main product. By 1906, the company became the S.C. Johnson & Son partnership.

Because of his past experience in the hardware business, Samuel Johnson understood that store owners would prefer selling cans of 29-cent wax rather than waiting for a homebuilder to buy a living room floor. The idea that the wax market might be bigger than the market for floors led Johnson to concentrate on selling Johnson's Prepared Paste Wax. He also understood the value of advertising and promoted the product in *The Saturday Evening Post* and other general circulation magazines, so that Johnson's Prepared Paste Wax soon became a national brand.

Diversifying from parquet floors to floor wax set the tone for the company's future. It stimulated a new way of thinking within the firm. If the wax worked well on floors, why not other surfaces? This shift in thinking came to fruition in 1898 when S.C. Johnson & Son introduced Dance Wax™, a powder product to be sprinkled on a floor to allow dancers to glide easier. Again, in 1914, the company diversified to the auto industry by piggybacking on the success of Henry Ford's Model-T, with Johnson's Autowax and Cleaner™. This opened a new market for wax previously limited to home flooring. Diversifying to auto products was timely. By 1917, parquet flooring fell out of fashion in home décor. The new era for S.C. Johnson & Son was defined by the success of new 'Car Savers' auto products: Stop Squeak Oil, Self-Vulcanizer, Radiator Cement, and Hastee Patch.[5]

With new products for different applications, chemistry would become central to the company's success. Herbert F. Johnson Jr, son of Samuel Johnson, was sent to Cornell University to study chemistry. He returned to the company in 1922. The following years were marked by building upon existing products and branching into new areas. For example, an electric floor polisher, wax for aeroplanes, and a carbon remover for automobile engines were all introduced in the 1920s. While diversification was the consistent strategy of the business, at the core of S.C. Johnson & Son was family.

Family

In 19th-century America, the typical commercial enterprise was small, family-owned and managed, and marketed locally. Transformations in American business encouraged the creation, by the early 20th century, of large, corporately structured firms. Johnson's own competitors, Colgate & Company (now Colgate-Palmolive) and the Procter & Gamble Company, both began with or developed through the efforts of family members during the 19th century, before growing into large corporate entities in the 20th. S.C. Johnson & Son is unique in that it would eventually become a multinational company, but it would remain privately held by the Johnson family. This familial quality – one that resonates universally with people – would become S.C. Johnson's brand identity.

'The one constant', claimed Sam Johnson, 'is the family focus on the long-term success of the company.' S.C. Johnson & Son company operated, and still operates, as a family-owned, private company. As such, they saw distinct advantages of private ownership, especially when competing against public firms. The business edge, in their opinion, is secrecy from the competition. Johnson compared it to a game of poker. Private firms such as S.C. Johnson & Son, he pointed out, can hold their cards tight to their vest, right through the betting and until it's time to lay them down. However, the public firm must expose the majority of its cards almost from the start, keeping only a proprietary ace or two until its hand is called. The private company sees the strengths and weaknesses of its competitor and acts accordingly. Meanwhile, Johnson concluded, the private company is not obliged to show its hand. If it wins, it takes the money off the table, with the public company never really knowing the amount.[6]

In addition to maintaining company secrecy from the competition, S.C. Johnson & Son embraced the longevity of what would be five generations of family leadership. As the company's brand identity, workings of a family business are plentiful in their literature. Johnson recounted an often-repeated scenario: the first generation starts the company, the second builds it up, and the third generation screws it up. Yet the company not only survived, but thrives today, operating in its fifth generation. First, Samuel Curtis Johnson started the company. His son, Herbert F. Johnson Sr, diversified the fledgling product line of waxes and polishes. Johnson Sr's son, Herbert F. Johnson Jr, took a regional manufacturer of waxes and polishes and turned it into an international company. Johnson Jr's son,

Samuel Johnson, further diversified the product line into insecticides, personal care, and industrial products, and expanded foreign operations. The nature of S.C. Johnson & Son as a family company involves both growth and continuity. Also fundamental to the company are its employees, who have always been considered part of the family.

Labour and Profit Sharing

Like most of its American peers, S.C. Johnson & Son did not condone unionised labour organisation; but as an alternative, it actively pursued a counterstrategy by creating a tight-knit, family-like relationship with its employees, forming the basis of a policy of 'welfare capitalism'.[7] With the onset of industrial capitalism, the private sector, not the government or labour unions, in America took the lead in offering benefits like insurance, retirement plans, health benefits, and pensions to their employees. This was in part a reaction to the bitter strikes of the robber baron age. As an example of American exceptionalism, welfare capitalism was a practice that peaked in the early to mid-20th century. In 1914, the Ford Motor Company pioneered the practice when it instituted the five-dollar day. Rather than relying on government programmes or allowing trade unions to organise, private companies offered employees various benefits in place of wage raises. In 1923 Corning Glass Works began providing health insurance. U.S. Steel reduced its workday from 12 hours to eight. In 1927, International Harvester began offering two-week paid vacations. Similarly, S.C. Johnson & Son created its own source of security and stability, and thereby avoided the social turmoil caused by unions in other industries at the time.[8]

In the first decades of the 20th century, S.C. Johnson & Son was one of the first US companies to offer many employee benefits including paid vacations, life insurance, and 40-hour workweeks. With 200 employees in 1917, S.C. Johnson & Son began one of the first profit-sharing programmes.[9] The practice of profit sharing is a system in which the people who work for a company receive a direct share of the profits. In effect, the company extended its family-based structure to its employees. The company understood profit sharing as based in a 'mutual confidence and trust between hourly people, salaried people, and management'.[10]

While S.C. Johnson & Son prospered during the 1910s and 1920s, expanding internationally into a global corporation, financial profits came to an abrupt end when the stock market crashed in 1929. In the aftermath of the crash, many US workers lost their jobs. Millions of unemployed workers were ready to work for any wage in any condition; those who were offered employment were often subjected to appalling conditions and low wages. The U.S. Labor Organization strove to protect workers' rights, and in 1935, the National Labor Relations Act (or Wagner Act) made union membership a government-guaranteed, sanctioned right.

S.C. Johnson & Son was an early pioneer of a myriad of employee benefits that served both the employees and the company itself.[11] From the company's perspective, if the employee's health and well-being are supported by their job, the employer is successful in attracting and retaining good employees and is repaid with loyalty and less staff turnover. The company's welfare capitalism philosophies to increase worker morale would find affinity with its architect Frank Lloyd Wright's democratic ideals.

Advertising

The growth of S.C. Johnson & Son in the late 19th and early 20th centuries coincided with the growth of mass consumption, modern advertising, and expanded media. Since the company's beginnings, advertising had been an important factor in its success. One of its initial promotional efforts was to enclose samples of Prepared Wax with each shipment of flooring. As early as 1888, ads for Johnson's Wax were appearing nationally in *The Saturday Evening Post*, *Ladies' Home Journal*, and other prestigious general circulation magazines.[12] The earliest prepared wax ads in *The Saturday Evening Post* featured mop-wielding housewives who had made their floors shine. A 1918 Prepared Wax ad in *National Geographic* advised, 'Any housewife can easily keep her home bright by devoting a little attention to her furniture, woodwork, floors, and linoleum. All they need is an occasional application of Johnson's Prepared Wax.'[13] Like other cleaning ads of the time, women, specifically housewives, were the target audience. As modern advertising established itself and specialised home cleaning products proliferated in the first decades of the 1900s, S.C. Johnson & Son's message was clear: it would beautify and improve the appearance of a home without increased effort by housewives.

During the Great Depression, advertising suffered like other sectors of the economy. American industry continued to turn out vast numbers of products, but few Americans could afford expensive items, such as cars, houses, and other consumer goods. People who had money to spend reduced their purchases, while factories cut production, reduced salaries, and made workers redundant. Advertisers faced the difficult task of promoting products that Americans could not afford or were hesitant to purchase. Advertisers increasingly turned to the 'hard-sell' and even to sensationalist campaigns. Traditional slice-of-life stories tapped emotions such as guilt, fear, and shame to reinforce advertising appeals. These ads conveyed a common message: if you don't buy this product, you will be sorry.

S.C. Johnson & Son ads of the 1930s relied on just this kind of scare copy. A dramatic colour print ad for S.C. Johnson & Son titled, 'Tragedy of the Young Scrubwoman' depicts a photo-realistic image of a dishevelled young woman wearing an apron over a yellow polka dot dress (Fig.49).[14] Exhausted and despondent, she sprawls in a chair, barely able to hold up her head. A sad-looking mop and pail are at her side. The ad copy begins, 'Young in years – but old in looks', tapping into fears that years of housework depletes the beauty and youth of the housewife. The remedy appears in a small inset: Johnson's Wax Paste products and the technologically advanced electric broom. In this and other S.C. Johnson & Son advertisements, the message was that no housewife should be without labour-saving wax. Throughout the 1930s, cleaning products pitched to housewives continued to promise an immaculate home with a minimum of drudgery.

In addition to dramatic print campaigns, radio ads proved to be a particularly valuable medium for

(*right*) 49   S.C. Johnson & Son ads of the 1930s and 1940s relied on scare copy, which offered narrative stories that tapped emotions such as guilt, fear, and shame to reinforce advertising appeals. 'Tragedy of the Young Scrubwoman', Johnson's Wax Ad, c.1940s.

TRAGEDY OF THE YOUNG SCRUBWOMAN

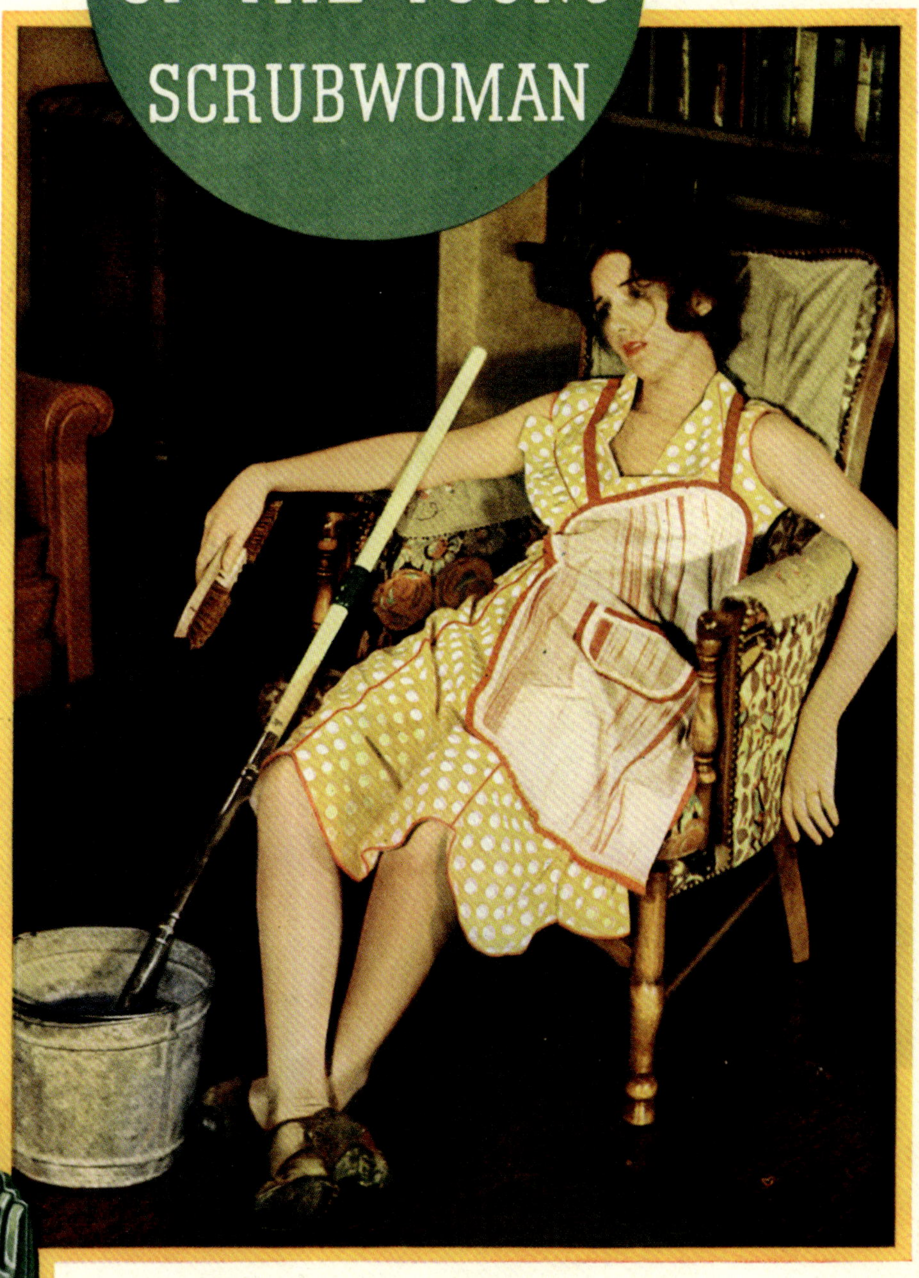

Young in years—but *old* in feelings and in looks. That's what floor-scrubbing has done to this woman—what it will do to anyone. Such ugly work takes the sparkle out of young eyes, tires young bodies, roughens soft hands. In short, floor-scrubbing makes an old scrubwoman out of you, no matter what your age.

• Be glad, then, that you can escape such a tragedy. Modern science has done away with floor-scrubbing. Johnson's Wax and the improved Johnson Electric Floor Polisher give you far more beautiful floors, protected from scuffing and scratching—that stay radiantly polished and *never need scrubbing*.

• It is easy to apply the wax with the long-handled lamb's wool applier. Then it's no trick at all to skim over the floor with the Johnson Electric Polisher. The result is a satin-like glow that resists both wear and dirt. The wax forms an invisible, tough film which dirt cannot penetrate. A little wax on a clean cloth renews any worn spots. Surface dust is removed in a moment with the Johnson Dry Floor Duster. And you *never* have to scrub the floor again.

• Furniture, woodwork, leather and automobiles are protected and beautified by this famous labor-saver—Johnson's Wax. It gives a hard, dry surface which resists scratches, finger-marks, water-spots and stains.

• Johnson's Wax—paste or liquid—can be bought at hardware, paint, grocery, drug and department stores. You can **RENT** the Johnson Electric Floor Polisher from a nearby dealer and transform every floor in your house. This applies to varnished, shellacked, lacquered or painted floors, as well as linoleum.

• Have you any floor, furniture or woodwork problems? Then write to S. C. Johnson & Son at Racine, for 45 years authorities on the care and maintenance of these surfaces.

• Complete floor maintenance outfit includes new Johnson Electric Floor Polisher, Johnson's Wax (paste and liquid), lamb's wool applier, Johnson's gold-striped Floor Duster.

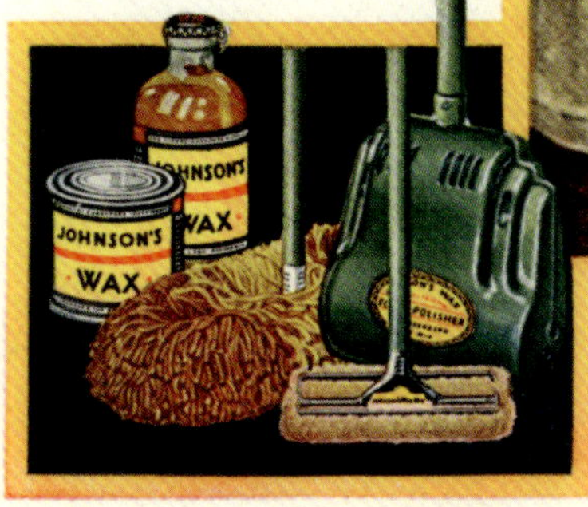

Shi-nup FOR SILVER
Now—at your own store—this remarkable polish for silver, glassware, enamel—nickel. Now made by S. C. Johnson & Son

S. C. JOHNSON & SON, Dept. SP1, **RACINE, WIS.**

Please send me a 25c bottle of Johnson's Wax Polish to try. I am enclosing 10c to cover postage.

NAME ____________________

ADDRESS ____________ CITY ____________ STATE ________

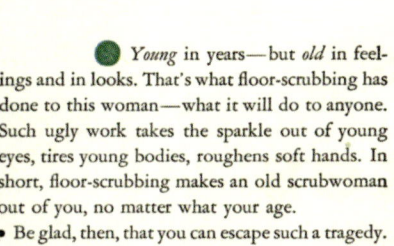

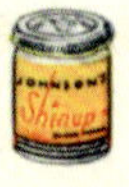

S.C. Johnson & Son. In the 1920s, radio captured the attention of Americans of all classes, but especially of the middle class. Though briefly slowed by the Depression, radio dominated the mass media of the 1920s through the 1950s. Spurred by advertising revenue, radio matured in this era to reach an audience of critical mass, becoming part of the fabric of American life.[15] By 1928, radio had grown into an advertising-based medium with programme sponsorship by companies. Ad agencies developed programmes that fit the needs and interests of their clients.

S.C. Johnson & Son experimented with the new medium of radio beginning in 1931. In 1933 and 1934, the company sponsored the daytime broadcasts of *Tony Won's Scrap Book* and *The House by the Side of the Road*, both favourites of housewives.[16] Won's persona as a benevolent patriarch with a deep, resonant voice appealed to the American public. Advertising that utilised the medium of sound to portray human qualities elicited emotion and reached audiences effectively. The success of sponsorships during the Depression convinced S.C. Johnson & Son to invest more heavily in radio, their most productive advertising medium.

Also in the midst of the economic downturn, the company's leadership changed hands. Known as 'Hib', Herbert F. Johnson Jr, grandson of the founder of Johnson's Wax and heir to the industrial organisation, was an amateur artist and art collector. He possessed a respect for the profession of architecture as well as an experimental spirit, and sought intellectual camaraderie outside of his business life. In 1928, Herbert Johnson Sr suddenly died and Hib took over as president of S.C. Johnson & Son. Herbert Fisk Johnson Jr began his career at the family company as a schoolboy, working summers at the Racine factory making wax, packaging products, and loading freight cars. After graduating from Cornell University in 1922, he joined the company full-time, working first in the laboratory and later as a salesman and purchasing agent. Six years later, after the death of his father, he took over the company at the age of 28. He was a 'shy, retiring man who loved fishing and abhorred personal publicity', but was, nevertheless, a bold businessman.[17] Young Hib's first few years as president of the company coincided with the Great Depression, 1928 to 1931.[18] During this time,

the company's annual sales dropped from $5 million to $3 million, workers' hours were cut, and the company skipped its annual profit sharing in 1931 and 1932. However, retaining employees during the economic downturn was paramount, and no Johnson employee was laid off.

In the spring of 1932, with the company's business at a low point, Herbert Fisk Johnson Jr introduced a major product, a new type of floor wax called 'Glo-Coat'. The move helped the company survive the Depression. In 1932, S.C. Johnson & Son put Glo-Coat, a self-polishing floor cleaner, on the market. Glo-Coat was the commercial success that pulled the company out of the economic depression and transformed it into a profitable model.

At the same time, Hib was concerned that the supply of the carnauba palm would become depleted. The palm frond yields a wax possessing excellent properties for use in the formulation of waxes and polishes, and carnauba wax gave S.C. Johnson & Son products an edge over their competitors. During the 1930s, the young president embarked on an expedition to the carnauba palm-growing areas in northeastern Brazil. A twin-engine Sikorsky S-38 amphibian flying boat was used, giving the party more mobility and allowed them to explore far greater areas and eliminate long overland trips through jungle-like terrain.[19] The trip took one year to complete, and Johnson returned with a wealth of information on the growth, cultivation, and refining of carnauba wax for company products. This contributed to returning S.C. Johnson & Son to a prosperous phase, and the company put its employees back on a 40-hour week and began to hire new personnel.

Radio advertising continued into the 1930s and 1940s, and in 1935, S.C. Johnson &Son sponsored a new comedy programme, *Fibber McGee and Molly* (Fig.50). 'This show gradually picked up an audience which in 1942 included so many millions of listeners that it was rated the No. 1 programme on the air.'[20] At the time, situational comedies like *Fibber McGee and Molly* were popular. Other radio sponsorships included *Amos 'n' Andy* by Pepsodent, and *The Jack Benny Show* by Campbell Soup, as well as other companies at different times including Canada Dry Ginger Ale, Lucky Strike, Jell-O, and Chevrolet.

The S.C. Johnson & Son-sponsored programme was officially titled *The Johnson Wax Program with Fibber McGee and Molly*. *Fibber McGee and Molly* episodes began with a direct advertisement of one of S.C. Johnson & Son's products at the time, which included Johnson's Wax, Glo-Coat, and Car Nu. Each episode featured an appearance by Harlow Wilcox, announcer and pitchman, whose job it was to weave the S.C. Johnson & Son advertisement into the plot without having to break the show for a commercial. Fibber McGee, the comical foil to Wilcox, usually met his pitch lines with groans or humorously sarcastic retorts. 'Waxy' was Fibber's nickname for Wilcox due to Wilcox's constant praises of the company's familiar founding product, Johnson's Wax.

The Johnson Wax Programme with Fibber McGee and Molly was folksy and depicted everyday situations to which most Americans (especially of the middle class) could relate. It focused on the entertaining dialogue between a married couple as well as with their neighbours. *Fibber McGee & Molly* appealed to middle-class Americans as it reflected everyday life and offered comedic relief in domestic predicaments. Beginning in April 1935, the company's long-standing sponsorship of the radio show lasted until May 1950, ending only at the time when radio gave way to the new medium of television.

S.C. Johnson & Son fully embraced the value of advertising and appreciated its role in 'moving people to buy Johnson goods'. At the same time, the company did not want its advertising to be 'blatant, misleading or in questionable taste'.[21] Advertising through mass media not only made the company and its products more visible, it also made itself more relatable and connected it emotionally to consumers. The company felt, 'we have reason to believe that the American housewife has a special feeling for the Johnson Wax Products.'[22]

The national success of Johnson's Glo-Coat floor wax, launched in 1932, drove the company through the Depression without layoffs. By spring 1936, S.C. Johnson & Son had outgrown its makeshift offices in Racine. Within the company compound, the firm's executives worked in a wooden-framed house next to the company's warehouses and factory buildings, while other officers and clerical employees worked in two additions to the house and an adjacent larger office building. 'At first', Hib Johnson said, 'we had no thought of building an office nor of commissioning [Frank Lloyd] Wright to do the work.'[23] He had initially planned to simply have the office remodelled and expanded later. After he and his employees calculated the necessary space to accommodate their growing company, however, Hib decided to build a single structure to unify the scattered clerical workers and executives. He wanted a building in which the employees 'could be happy', as well as one that would 'set us apart'.[24]

In preparing to commission such a building, Hib visited other companies that had recently built similar office buildings. One such project that especially attracted Hib was the Hershey Chocolate Corporation's office building and company town in Hershey, Pennsylvania. The Hershey business, like Johnson's, was privately owned, and the founder, Milton S. Hershey, also took an interest in his workers' welfare. In the first decades of the 20th century, Hershey had a company town built around his new factory, providing employee homes and other community buildings. In 1935, Hershey commissioned a windowless, air-conditioned office. Uncommon in the early 1930s, air-conditioning especially intrigued Hib, as having it would change his company's practice of closing down when the outside temperature reached 90 degrees.[25] The lack of windows, Hershey believed, would dramatically increase cooling and heating efficiency. Unfortunately, daylight was eliminated from the workspace. Hib Johnson visited Hershey's building in 1936 and, inspired, returned to Racine with the intention of commissioning a building that would be similarly windowless and air-conditioned.

That same year, Johnson hired a reputable local architect, J. Mandor Matson, to design the company's new administration building. Matson had worked for the Johnson family before; he was first hired in 1924 by Hib's father to remodel the family's Victorian house in Racine and then again in 1934 for some additional remodelling.[26] Matson's own architecture was eclectic, including a 1928 Gothic Revival church and a 1931 neo-classically designed City Hall, both in Racine. Since there was no vacant land within the existing two-block complex of Johnson's compound, the company bought up half a block of houses to the east and cleared the site. Matson designed a three-storey brick Beaux-Arts building that filled the site. The windowless design would be air-conditioned, following his client's request.

Another request of Hib Johnson's was to design artwork for the proposed building, with the company as its subject matter. Owing much of the company's success to key products and processes, Johnson asked Matson to incorporate icons relating to their products, into the design. Matson's classical design scheme dealt with Johnson's request in a literal and representational way. The architect proposed three niches on either side of the entrance that were to hold bas-reliefs representing the history of wax and wax products, including a boy waxing a table and a woman waxing a floor.[27] Circular stone medallions would portray, in relief, S.C. Johnson & Son products, including furniture polish, paint, varnish, and lacquer. Matson also incorporated as icons the carnauba palm tree, a beehive, and an oil derrick, as well as figures such as a chemist with a test tube, a man with a paint mill, a man waxing an automobile, and a couple dancing on a shiny, waxed floor. Such literal depictions of materials and processes related to the company's products, uses, and identity were part of an earlier stripped-down art moderne aesthetic; yet when compared to the non-representational architectural expression of modern architects such as Frank Lloyd Wright, a strong schism among modernisms comes into focus.

Frank Lloyd Wright

Born in 1867, Frank Lloyd Wright, one of the most prolific and renowned architects of the late 19th and 20th centuries, was a native Wisconsinite, from Richland Center, 166 miles west of Racine. Wright's epoch-defining career made other Wisconsinites proud to declare him a native son. His local roots boosted the state's credibility, its image, and even its businesses. His designs for a handful of commissions in Racine highlighted his particular approach to modern architecture, which contrasted sharply with the building fabric of the city.[28] This polarising relationship would prove to be an apt metaphor for Wright's exuberant persona,

which would later serve to empower him within the context of a media-driven world. More than other 20th-century architects, Wright was shrewd, understood publicity, and employed it to attract prospective clients. He expanded on his renown by casting a narrative of his work and his persona into the world. As a result, clients who commissioned his buildings would benefit through association. Wright's fame served as architectural branding for his clients and their institutions.

Frank Lloyd Wright's fame waxed and waned over his long career and the years preceding the S.C. Johnson & Son commission were turbulent, both personally and professionally.[29] He had left Los Angeles in 1924 and built only three buildings the rest of the decade. Between the late 1920s and the 1930s, important architecture circles considered his career all but over. In 1926, Wright began writing his *Autobiography* at a time when his life was at a low point.[30] Six years later, Wright began the Taliesin Fellowship which helped to keep his family financially solvent. During this time, Wright accepted as many speaking engagements and lectures as he was offered in order to make ends meet. In 1932, Wright would design a house for Malcolm E. Willey in Minneapolis that was completed in 1934, but by then, Wright had fallen into debt. One lecture led Wright to Dallas, Texas in 1934, where he met Stanley Marcus, owner of the high-end department store Neiman-Marcus. Wright ended up designing a house for Marcus, which was never built. That same year, Edgar J. Kaufmann Jr arrived at Taliesin as an apprentice. His father came to visit his son, and immediately hit it off with Wright. This led to Wright designing Fallingwater, the elder Kaufmann's weekend and seasonal residence in Bear Run, Pennsylvania, from 1934 to 1937. By 1936, Wright was prepared and hungry for a larger project and the S.C. Johnson & Son commission fell within reach.

Even though J. Mandor Matson's 1936 design for the S.C. Johnson & Son Administration Building was drawn up, it did not measure up to the client's expectations. Upon viewing the scheme, Hib and his general manager, Jack Ramsey, were underwhelmed. Ramsey told Johnson, 'It just isn't good enough, and it's just another building.'[31] They consulted S.C. Johnson & Son's head of advertising,

William Connolly, on the matter. An important liaison was Jack Louis, Hib's brother-in-law, who was a partner at Needham, Louis & Brorby, a thriving Chicago advertising and public relations firm. Louis and his firm had guided the publicity side of S.C. Johnson & Son to radio sponsorship. In an attempt to solicit suggestions, William Connolly showed Matson's design to the public relations firm's art director, E. Willis Jones. Jones would later recall that Connolly had initially asked him to recommend a sculptor for the frieze at the top of the building. The advertising man's response was similar to those of the clients: the design was 'just "common" and uninspired'.[32] Jones urged Connolly to reject the entire design and hire Frank Lloyd Wright, showing him publications featuring Wright's work. He noted that Connolly, who had been unfamiliar with Wright, was very impressed. Jones called in the firm's Vice-President, Melvin Brorby, and Howard Raferty, a colleague who was an architect, and the three men convinced Connolly to pursue Wright.[33] Raferty, despite admitting interest in proposing a design himself, believed Wright should be hired, saying that he was 'right here under our noses, . . . a native Wisconsonian who was the absolute father of all modern architecture, and it would be a crime not to talk to him.'[34] In current terms, Wright was a 'starchitect'. This was due to his fame, in its different levels, coupled with his charisma and personal salesmanship.

While the internationally renowned architect certainly lived up to Raferty's description, sentiment about Wright in Racine was far from positive. His outstanding debts, as well as the abandonment of his wife and children for a married woman, Mamah Borthwick, had created a scandal and damaged his personal reputation. This was especially damning in the small, family-centric city of Racine. Wright's 1905 design for the Hardy House in Racine had not impressed the Johnson family, his future client, who lived close by. Johnson's sister, Henrietta Louis, recalled that the house was 'kooky – every room is on a different floor. That was crazy in those days . . . Frank never went over in Racine very much.'[35] She even recalled that her father laughed at the house. However, it may be true that any publicity is good publicity, because despite mixed reactions to Wright's architecture and personal life, S.C. Johnson & Son pursued the possibility of hiring him.

Wright had got wind of the Johnson project. Two weeks prior to speaking with Connolly, Jones had spent a weekend at Taliesin as part of a Chicago Art Directors' Club outing. During this gathering, Jones informed his host that S.C. Johnson & Son was planning to build a new office building, and Wright showed great interest in the project.[36] Although aware that an architect had already been chosen to design the building, Wright became determined to quash the company's confidence in that choice and present himself as the better architect for the job.

In 1936, Wright's practice was just starting to pick up. In addition to designing Fallingwater, he was working on a Usonian home in Huron, South Dakota and the Hanna house in Palo Alto, California. At the prospect of the S.C. Johnson & Son commission, Wright recalled years later:

When the sky at Taliesin was dark, the days there gloomy . . . Hib [Johnson] and Jack [Ramsey] were the ones who came out to Taliesin . . . to see about the new building. They came, you might say, like messengers riding on white steeds trumpeting glad tidings.[37]

In preparing for the prospective client's visit, Taliesin apprentices cleaned and beautified the grounds. Jones drove from Chicago and William Connolly and Jack Ramsey of S.C. Johnson & Son drove from Racine, arriving at Taliesin to meet Frank Lloyd Wright.[38] Wright received the three men, giving them a tour of Taliesin, and then served them lunch and tea, over which he delivered his audacious proposal. Jones recalled, 'The pitch that he gave them was masterful and a shocker. In brief, it was not to build on the site adjacent to the ugly old factory, but to raze everything and get out of town four or five miles west . . . plan a Johnson Village around a new factory and office building, homes for employees, their own shopping center . . . the works.'[39] Wright was determined to sell his clients on this idea and it would be the first of a series of conversations he would initiate about moving the site. Edgar Tafel, a Taliesin apprentice, remembered, 'Mr. Wright was trying to get them to move out in the country where there is room to breathe . . . and have an open building.'[40]

Wright's pastoral scheme came out of the previous six years of research and design for

Broadacre City, published in his 1932 book, *The Disappearing City*. As a planning vision, Broadacre City was at once the antithesis of a city and a suburban utopia.[41] Headquartered in a small mid-western city, Johnson's company was nearly the perfect client for the project. Similar to Broadacre City's concept of allotting one acre to each family, S.C. Johnson & Son's business model was also decentralised, based on top executives delegating responsibilities to middle and lower-level managers. Offering more responsibility than less was in line with the company's tradition of treating their employees well. S.C. Johnson & Son was a model of the human economy that Wright advocated.

Wright made a glowing impression on his future clients, building upon his celebrity status and casting himself as 'a kind of artist'.[42] Though Ramsey was not a man easily deceived, Wright captivated him. Ramsey returned from the trip invigorated, anxious to relay his excitement to his employer. He wrote,

> Honest Hib I haven't had such an inspiration from a person in years . . . He's an artist and a little bit 'different' of course but aside from his wearing a Windsor tie, he was perfectly human and very easy to talk to and most interested in our problem and understood that we were not committing ourselves, but gosh he could tell us what we were after when we couldn't explain it ourselves.[43]

At the urging of Ramsey and Connolly, Hib Johnson himself made a trip to Taliesin the next day to vet Wright. Wright liked to meet one-on-one with prospective clients (Fig.51).[44] At the meeting, Olgivanna Wright recalled Frank describing Matson's plan as a 'fancy crematorium', telling Johnson he had designed a far better office building for the Larkin Company in Buffalo, New York, 30 years earlier.[45] Johnson pleaded with Wright, saying, 'Please don't make the building too unconventional!' Laughing, Wright responded, '[Then] you came to the wrong man. You'd better find yourself another architect. The Johnson administration building is not going to be what you expect. But I can assure you of one thing – you'll like it when it is put up.'[46] Olgivanna recalled noticing a bond forming between the two men. Johnson replied, 'It's okay with me then, if you think so. We'll have your kind of building, not the kind of building I had in mind.'[47]

51   Frank Lloyd Wright and Herbert F. Johnson photographed together in front of the completed Johnson Wax Administration Building.

They talked all the time about the building. It was wonderful to hear it because of the harmonious relationship. The younger man was completely absorbing the ideas which are so beyond . . . ordinary business status. [Johnson said] 'I would like to have a beautiful building, I don't want just a business building.' 'Hibbert, you will get it, it is exactly what I had in mind – to give you a beautiful building so that whoever will work there will feel as though he were among the pine trees breathing fresh air and sunlight.' 'Oh! That is exactly what I want. I don't like the feeling of people cooped in without sun, without light. I am happy. You'll go [the] full length [with] your wish in your project.'[48]

Wright's fame as well as his fortitude led to him winning the commission and would define him, in today's terms, as a 'starchitect'. Johnson and his executives believed that they would benefit from Wright's fame and bold architectural vision. From Wright's perspective, this large commission was critical to giving his practice a solid footing again. His promise of a lean budget was an additional factor in ensuring the commission; he agreed to design the building for $200,000, which was $100,000 less than Matson had estimated.

On 23 July 1936, Herbert F. Johnson officially offered Frank Lloyd Wright the commission for his company's new office building in Racine, Wisconsin. The same day, Johnson wrote to Matson to inform him that the company had decided not to build his scheme and to discontinue work. Edgar Tafel remembered the day that Wright opened Johnson's letter, with a $1,000 retainer check enclosed. Tafel recalled, 'What elation we felt . . . our first big, solid commercial project.'[49] After he had hired Wright, Johnson picked up his daughter Karen from her boarding school in Kenosha, Wisconsin. On the way home, he asked her who she considered to be the leading architect in the world, knowing she had been taking Art History courses. She responded, 'Frank Lloyd Wright'. Johnson then proudly informed his daughter that he had hired Wright to build an office building for the company.[50]

Wright and his client agreed that he would provide a design that would give dignity to the company's employees. With this fundamental agreement, Johnson gave Wright the freedom to design the administration building. Indeed, Wright seemed to refer to Johnson in a 1939 lecture, 'No man can build for another who does not believe in him, who does not believe in what he believes in, and who has not chosen him because of this faith . . . That is the nature of architect and client as I see it. When a man wants to build a building he seeks an interpreter, does he not?'[51]

As with the clients of the PSFS Building, Hib tended toward the conservative side in issues of design. With PSFS, Howe and Lescaze compromised with their client in designing the facade with the vertical expression he wanted, as well as the horizontal expression they desired. In the case of S.C. Johnson & Son, Wright did not compromise. Instead, once committed to using Wright, the client gave the architect full artistic freedom. S.C. Johnson & Son's relationship with

Wright resembled a sponsorship agreement. This demonstrated an early example of what we would call today 'co-branding', which is a fluid partnership between celebrity people and celebrity brands.[52] By hiring Wright and allowing him to design his vision, the company would benefit from his fame and recognition – in short, the company benefited from allowing his celebrity status to provide identity and architectural branding.

S.C. Johnson & Son Building: A Vision of Modern Work

With Wright leading the S.C. Johnson & Son Administration Building, the design was an extreme contrast to the company's initial neo-classical design by J. Mandor Matson. Gone were the carnauba palm tree icons and female figures waxing floors. Instead, Wright aimed to address the needs of his client in the medium of architecture, and in turn the design would become a brand identity for his client. Wright's approach in designing a modern office building would shape a new way of life at S.C. Johnson & Son.

The week after being hired, Wright travelled with Tafel to Racine to visit the site for the first time. He found it uninspiring. The half block was surrounded to the south, on Sixteenth Street, by a movie theatre, small shops, and triplexes. To the north and east were two-storey wooden-frame houses, c.1905, built on tiny lots. Johnson was out of town, so Wright and Tafel met with Ramsey and Connolly. Again, Wright tried to convince them that S.C. Johnson & Son should build several miles out in the country. Ramsey, Johnson's right-hand man, was steadfast about staying put in Racine. As manager of operations, Ramsey would oversee construction of the building, but Tafel noted that Wright resolved to deal as much as possible with Johnson, the man who ultimately controlled the decisions and the finances.[53] At this meeting, Ramsey gave Wright a detailed building programme that listed 15 departments for 130 employees and managers. The largest departments were collections, billing, bookkeeping, costs, sales records, files, and accounting. The smaller departments included spaces for mail, branch records, statistical records, general storage, and tabulation. In addition, there was a director's conference room, cafeteria, and loading dock.

The following week, Wright again proposed his Broadacre City scheme for the company to Johnson and Ramsey. Once again, Johnson and Ramsey rejected Wright's proposal, re-iterating that their new office building was to be built near the company's existing plant. As Tafel recalled, this caused a major disagreement between architect and client, bringing Wright to the point of losing the commission. He discussed the situation with his wife when he returned to Taliesin. Olgivanna warned him, 'Give them what they want, Frank, or you will lose the job.'[54] Wright ceded to his wife's point of view and dropped his pitch. His viewpoint, however, remained unchanged, and he would ultimately get his way by designing a building that turned its back on its urban site.

Two previous Wright projects shaped his ideas for the S.C. Johnson & Son Building: the Larkin Administration Building (1903–1906) and the 1931–1932 design for the Capital Journal newspaper plant proposal, which was not built. The Larkin Building in Buffalo, New York was sited with its back to its surroundings, just as the S.C. Johnson & Son Building would be more than 30 years later. Also, the Larkin Building's 'light court' was an early realisation of Wright's idea of an uplifting place for work. One fundamental similarity was the client's intention – both companies committed themselves to the idea of industrial betterment, intended to enhance the workers' morale and commitment to the business.[55] For both client and architect, work was a virtuous pursuit, and the space that housed work ought to be fittingly transcendental.[56] For both companies, Wright created light-filled workrooms, lit by skylights and clerestories. The Larkin design included literal representation in the form of figural sculptures and inspirational inscriptions. In the later S.C. Johnson & Son design, Wright would move beyond the literal and design in a more abstracted, modern language.

Wright stated in *An Autobiography* that the Johnson Wax – as he called it – scheme was based on his unrealised Capital Journal project in Salem, Oregon.[57] He explicitly described the moment at which he began designing the new administration building:

What a release of pent-up creative energy – the making of those plans! Ideas came tumbling up and out onto paper to be thrown back in heaps – for careful scrutiny and selection. But at once, I knew the scheme I wanted to try. I had it in mind when I drew the newspaper plant at Salem, Oregon, for Editor George Putnam, which he had been unable to build. A great simplicity and grace – organic.[58]

For Wright, 'great simplicity' meant a direct relationship between interior space and external form. Wright's approach to the workroom was based on what he had designed for the Capital Journal project five years prior: defining the space with a 20-foot column grid, surrounded with a 17-foot deep mezzanine. Instead, the physiognomic expression of the Capital Journal project was carried out in the S.C. Johnson & Son Building. In both designs, the inner spatial configurations were directly translated to the external form. His design for the S.C. Johnson & Son Administration Building would indeed build upon the 'great simplicity' of the unrealised Capital Journal design, and also provide greater sophistication of the concept in its execution.

Wright immediately began to work on the S.C. Johnson & Son design, basing it on the Capital Journal design and its large workroom filled with columns, supporting a U-shaped upper storey. He developed the design during the next few months, applying two defining principles of his career: the destruction of the box and continuity of space.[59] In a sense, Wright liberated the workroom by separating the ceiling from the wall with clerestory windows, thus destroying the box. The horizontal plane did not meet the vertical, offering not enclosure, but openness. As a result, the design reinforced the 'free plan' of the workroom.[60]

His concept of continuity was also achieved. 'The columns are designed to stand up', declared Wright, 'and take over the ceiling, the column is made a part of the ceiling: continuity.'[61] In the S.C. Johnson & Son design, Wright went beyond his prior projects in advancing the use of curvilinear geometries and 'streamlining' to the next level of his theories. With Frank Lloyd Wright's fame and design serving as architectural branding for arguably all his clients, the different projects may have similar designs. This raises the question of how different clients' identities distinguish themselves. Indeed, Wright addressed each design with specificity and provided ingenuity to each of his designs.

Streamlining

Frank Lloyd Wright's design for the S.C. Johnson & Son Administration Building was 'streamlined'. At the time, the trend of streamlining in commercial design and architecture referred to curved forms based on imagery of mass production and technology. In the 1930s, streamlining was more typical of industrial designers like Raymond Loewy, Norman Bel Geddes, and Donald Deskey. 'Streamline moderne', as it was dubbed, became the preferred style to connote progressiveness for business clients. Wright vehemently renounced the technique, along with the commercial architects who used it, and what he called their 'sloganized dicta'.[62] He opposed the superficial styles and 'effects' that businesses believed would increase their profits. For Wright, 'profit-taking as a motive for a civilization does not seem to be the ennobling basis for one.'[63] This made it all the more baffling when Wright designed the S.C. Johnson & Son Administration Building as a streamlined form.

Wright's highly contradictory statement demonstrated his showmanship. With verve, Wright declared that it was 'high time to give our hungry American public something truly "streamlined"'.[64] This indicated Wright's belief that all previous streamlined designs were somehow incorrect. By adapting the popular commercial technique to his design, Wright would attract attention and prove his design prowess. Taliesin apprentices even suggested that Wright had a habit of taking on contemporary trends as one-time experiments.[65] His co-opting of streamlining came out of a desire to advertise his architecture.

While curved forms were not a fundamental quality of Frank Lloyd Wright's architecture at this point, some of his previous projects did, however, demonstrate interest in circular geometries. Streamlining first appeared in Wright's work in his 1931–1932 proposal for the Salem Capital Journal newspaper plant. Another interpretation of Wright's streamlining tendency comes from architectural historian Neil Levine who points out that Wright made a connection between its geometry and the element of water. Thus streamlining offered a modern sense of business efficiency and provided the employees with a soothing, restful atmosphere in which to work. While Wright dabbled with streamlining, his true interest was elsewhere.

'But I believe', wrote Wright, 'were the "system" aware of it, the capitalists especially would fortify themselves in Architecture that is Organic Architecture.'[66] Here, organic architecture refers to Wright's own theories, as opposed to streamlined design. Despite employing streamlining in the S.C. Johnson & Son design, he still believed his own theories would serve potential business clients better.[67] Reflecting on the early stages of designing the administration building, Taliesin apprentice Wes Peters recalled, 'I remember clearly [Wright's] great struggle to make space flow . . . Part of [his] effort [at] streamlining is understood in the sense of making [the building] a great plastic space enclosure.'[68] Wright emphasised a unifying of discrete spaces, stating, 'the sense of the whole most stimulating to various parts is preserved.'[69] The 'streamlined' skin of uniform brick emphasised the sense of wholeness (Figs 52, 53). This was due to formal articulations of continuity, surface, and volume as well as the consistent use of material: 'Cherokee red' brick.[70] More than 200 custom curved and angled brick shapes were designed to create this overall effect of continuity. The brickwork mortar was raked out horizontally, thus lending the whole massing a horizontal effect. Wright's 'great struggle' culminated in a design that brilliantly redefined streamlining as an 'organic' design in which 'spaces' flowed (Fig.54).

On 9 August 1936, barely ten days after Wright began working, the first design meeting occurred. At the meeting Wright presented his design to Johnson and company executives, highlighting Johnson's, Ramsey's, and Connolly's offices in the 'penthouse', or upper level office area.[71] One of the striking features of the design was the clarity of the company's internal hierarchy. The plans and sections practically doubled as a diagram of the company's personnel relationships. Johnson's office was centred at the fore of the building massing. A pair of pill-shaped forms on either side of the CEO's office housed the executives of the company's two

52   At night, the streamlined aspect of the S.C. Johnson & Son Administration Building is striking.

53   S.C. Johnson & Son Administration Building exterior. Street facade shows the streamlined effect of a solid brick facade with Pyrex clerestory windows.

54   The exterior of the S.C. Johnson & Son Administration Building is a composition of curved building forms.

divisions: advertising and public relations, and operations. At the end, nearest to Johnson's office were the offices of the two heads of these divisions, William Connolly and John Ramsey. Behind Johnson's office and between Connolly's and Ramsey's was a conference room. The executive offices on the penthouse level were isolated from the rest of the employees, yet they had a clear view to the workroom. The mid-level managers' semi-enclosed offices were located a partial level down, on the mezzanine of the workroom as well as in glass enclosed offices under the mezzanine.

Wright's idea for the mezzanine placed managers in an elevated position from which they could oversee employees. It also solved an additional problem related to the noisy office machinery the company required. By placing the

equipment under the low ceiling of the mezzanine and against the back wall, Wright minimised disturbance. Wright included a dining room and theatre as a single, changeable space. There was also discussion of a possible tower, yet its programme was unknown. Johnson was unable to convince the board of its necessity until seven years later, when Wright designed the Research Tower for the company.

Also at the 9 August meeting, Wright presented his concept for 'nostrils', the air-conditioning and ventilation features of the administration building. Derived from the plan for the Capital Journal project, two 'nostrils' on either side of the lobby rose a storey above the penthouse roof, above the surrounding low-rise industrial structures, where they drew in clean air. In addition, these vertical circulation elements served as vertical circulation and air conduits for cooling throughout the building. Wright created the analogy between the building and the body, remarking in a letter to H.F. Johnson Jr that the 'building breathes through "nostrils"'.[72] Wright pointed out that, like the nostrils of an animal, 'the nostrils are for both intake and exhaust.'[73] Fans, compressors, and filters located at the base of the plenums within the mezzanine floor spread conditioned air throughout the Great Workroom.

Johnson's response to Wright's design was positive and enthusiastic. The client's next question regarded the cost of the design, prompting Wright to explain that he worked on a 'cost-plus' basis. Because the construction techniques necessary to realise Wright's work were innovative and at times untested, contractors were unable to accurately estimate the cost; billing therefore occurred as the work progressed.

At the end of August 1936, under Wright's supervision, the apprentices began to prepare working drawings. The set of 20 drawings was relatively small for a 54,000-square-foot building. But Wright had wanted the drawing set to convey the 'underlying simplicity of the building's concept'.[74] The walls were designed as brick on both sides, as Wright intended the structure to read as 'monolithic as possible'.[75] John Howe, a Taliesin apprentice who worked on the project, recalled, that this was 'part of what [Wright] called being a thoroughbred. If a [building] was brick it was entirely brick'.[76] Building construction began in the early fall of 1936.

The press became increasingly interested in the Wright design as the building entered into construction. On 5 October 1936, before ground was broken, Ramsey wrote to Wright, 'We are being pestered by all the newspapers now for some sort of dope and would like to give them a preliminary announcement very shortly.'[77] Wright responded on 11 October with a 1,200-word statement describing the design and publicising it as something new, an 'authentic example of Modern Architecture'. He called attention to its 'organic character throughout.'[78] Wright was famously against the International Style defined by the Museum of Modern Art in New York and its curators. Thus, when Wright used the term 'Modern architecture', he meant his version of it. Wright had agreed

to let Connolly and his advertising department handle all publicity for the building. Connolly investigated *Architectural Record* and its two competitors, *American Architect* and *Architectural Forum,* in an effort to ensure maximum exposure for the S.C. Johnson & Son Building. After learning that the *Forum* had the highest circulation and subscription price and that it was considered the most progressive of the three, Connolly offered the story to *Forum* associate editor Cameron Mackenzie.[79] *Architectural Forum* would dedicate the entire January 1938 issue to the architecture of Frank Lloyd Wright, highlighting his design for S.C. Johnson & Son.

Labour in the Great Workroom: Dignity and Control

While client and architect clashed at times, the two men were of the same mind when it came to employee well-being. Herbert F. Johnson sought to build an office in which the company employees 'could be happy'.[80] Thus, the company was well known for providing life-improving benefits to its employees. Frank Lloyd Wright came to the commission with his own ideas of egalitarian space, which amounted to an architectural equivalent of welfare capitalism. Giving the employees an office where they 'could be happy' dovetailed neatly with Wright's democratic ideal of preserving people's dignity through architectural means.

Throughout his career, Wright consistently pursued the idea of a single, dominant space that effectively brought inhabitants together. In fact, a dominant space was central to a number of Wright designs both before and after the S.C. Johnson & Son Building, including the Larkin Building (1902–1906), the V.C. Morris Gift Shop (1948–1949), and the Guggenheim Museum (1943–1959). While these single, dominant spaces varied in programme, they possessed several common attributes: they were symmetrically organised spaces; their light sources were not from the walls but rather from above, emulating a natural forest environment; they were multi-storied in height and ringed by mezzanine levels. Wright viewed these symbolic spaces as ones 'wherein he [humankind] seeks refuge, recreation and repose for body, but especially mind'.[81]

About the administration building in particular, Wright wrote, 'Organic architecture designed this great building to be as inspiring a place to work in as any cathedral ever was in which to worship. It was meant to be a socio-architectural interpretation of modern business at its top and best.'[82] Among other contemporary theories of modernism, Wright's emphasis on nature was uniquely American. Based on 19th-century Transcendentalist thought derived from Ralph Waldo Emerson among others, Wright's theories did not accept the idea that industrialisation should occur through the domination of nature.[83] Instead, Wright sought to achieve harmony with nature through architecture.[84] He achieved this in the Great Workroom by creating his own interpretation of nature within the building. Tafel recalled that at the first design meeting, 'Wright's presentation was very dramatic and right to the point. He described the site – wax and paint factory building to the west, movie houses, stores, and houses on the other sides. It was all mediocre architecture. There was nothing to look out to, no views. So [the solution was to] turn everything inward.'[85] Once inside the Great Workroom, the grid of interior columns offered the experience of being in a forest, with light penetrating the space from high above. Wright promised his client that the inhabitant would 'feel as though he were among pine trees breathing fresh air and sunlight'.[86] Wright intended the design as an uplifting illusion of nature as a way for the company employees to maintain their dignity in the workplace (Fig.55).

By designing a unifying and uplifting space, Wright aimed to reverse the deleterious effects caused by the modern division of labour. With an interest in utopian social change, he sought to humanise the industrial character of labour, re-casting it as an uplifting activity. Wright's own social ideals were based on empowering the individual through self-sufficiency, as advanced by his Broadacre City design. Just a few years earlier, in contemplating high unemployment during the Depression, Wright proposed a social reordering of the country that aimed to instil pride in the American worker. All families would be allotted an acre of land on which to grow their own food. Urban infrastructure included decentralised schools, modernised transportation, and utilities managed by state and county governments. He also applied his social theories to his own life and to those of his apprentices at Taliesin, who farmed the land and achieved a degree of self-sufficiency in the context of his and Olgivanna's frameworks.

In the architectural form of his Great Workroom, Wright attempted to instil his ideal of self-sufficiency within the framework of a large company. The realisation of this ideal would, however, depend largely on the management and operations of S.C. Johnson & Son. In consolidating their employees in a new company headquarters, both client and architect believed that gathering workers – who had previously been scattered throughout different buildings – under one roof would result in a greater sense of cooperation. By doing so, S.C. Johnson & Son reinforced its 'family' brand. The workroom was organised for clear visibility and good communication among employees. The cantilevered columns supporting the roof kept the space free of structural walls that would have obscured the views. At the same time, in efficiently grouping the company's employees together, the organisation of work became modernised.

The mezzanine provided managers with clear views of their subordinates. The positioning of file storage – the functional and legal core of any office – within the space posed an important functional consideration. In a practical sense, the activity of an office revolves around the placement and organisation of documentation and records (Fig.56). Files produced by Steelcase were centralised as well as customised within Wright's design for modular desks. Compared to the typical office of the time in which small rooms allowed employees to hide and inefficiencies to fester, Wright's large, open space encouraged transparency, accountability, and efficiency. The floor plan granted clerical employees' direct access to one another. Departments were organised within the overall layout to promote the most efficient flow of information through the room. Related departments were positioned adjacent to one another, allowing paperwork to move quickly along a linear route.

55   The Great Workroom in the S.C. Johnson & Son Administration Building.

In the 1930s, conflicts of modernisation continued to persist. For example, in the 1936 film *Modern Times*, a worker, played by Charlie Chaplin, hilariously struggles to keep up while working on a mechanised conveyor belt. This provided a commentary on the domination of industrial control over human nature. Wright began designing the S.C. Johnson & Son Building in the same year that *Modern Times* was released. It was duly sympathetic towards the film's viewpoint. Thus, he worked to reverse the dominance of machine over human. Wright promoted a world in which the human figure stood at the centre: the 'soul' of the machine, just as it had been in medieval times.

Yet the artisan spirit of labour was in conflict with 20th-century models of scientific management and Taylorisation. Instead of structuring an agreement between master and apprentice that involved the apprentice's eventual independence, modern work, segmented labour, and stratified classes denied the apprentice the promise of independence.

While the Great Workroom's spatial characteristics were uplifting for those who worked there, aspects of corporate control could be seen in the design as well. For example, the top-down office hierarchy was literally expressed in the configuration of the offices, with the senior managers above and clerical workers below (Fig.57). Meanwhile,

56   Centralised files in the Great Workroom open office plan allowed for efficiency,
clear visibility, and good communication.

middle managers located on the mezzanine had visual surveillance of every clerical worker on the workroom floor. The immensity of the room, while mitigated by cork-lined undersurfaces, discouraged talking and encouraged silence. The other perspective of the uplifting atmosphere exposed corporate control. Ultimately, Wright and his client, Hib Johnson's, combined vision for an uplifting place to work was achieved. While the Great Workroom design was, understandably, unable to resolve larger issues of industrial labour, it did offer progress towards humanising modern work.

The Impresario

Wright's impresario spirit materialised in his use of technical innovations, which provided plenty of advertising value for his client. One example was his unique design using Pyrex glass tubing to form the building's clerestories and skylights. Another was the dendriform columns that supported the roof of the Great Workroom, thereby allowing the ceiling to hover above the walls. The gap created between wall and ceiling boldly demonstrated Wright's ingenious 'destruction of the box'.[87] As

57　View of the Great Workroom, in which the managers on the mezzanine level could oversee clerical workers on the floor. The office hierarchy was literally expressed in the configuration of the workspace. In this photograph, we can also see the dissolution of corner where the wall meets the ceiling at the clerestory window. Photograph, c.1939.

Wright described it, 'in the Johnson building you catch no sense of enclosure at any angle, top or side. You are looking at the sky and feel the freedom of space.'[88] Wright's ideal vision for the space relied purely on natural illumination from the roof and clerestories and avoided artificial lighting altogether. But Ramsey questioned Wright specifically about how employees would be able to work when the sun was not out. Wright initially suggested desk lamps but he eventually agreed to design an artificial lighting system for the building. Lumiline bulbs were concealed between the double layers of glass tubing in the clerestories and skylights.

Although Wright wanted to flood the Great Workroom with sunlight, he refused to use plate glass in the clerestories. Because of his anti-urban stance, Wright had designed translucent, rather than transparent, glass windows through which the outside surrounding neighbourhood would be obscured. Wright's initial thought had been to use glass block, because of its obscuring properties, to build the clerestories. Wright also required that the material could be angled or curved, to conform to the profile of the streamlined building. In September 1936, he sent inquiry letters to Steuben Glass, Libbey-Owens Ford, American 3-way Luxfer Prism Company, and Corning Glass about the possibility of their company custom-designing glass block. With the exception of one company, correspondence ended in the manufacturer's lack of interest in working with such an experimental and costly application.

Wright found a willing glass manufacturer in Corning Glass of Corning, New York. Represented by product salesman E.J. Winship, Corning Glass was interested in innovation and willing to invest in Wright's endeavour. After many conversations, Winship and Wright decided on using Corning's Pyrex tubing.[89] By March 1937, the glass manufacturer agreed to produce the custom curved glass for the building. Having only been used in chemical and industrial applications, this patented form of glass would resist extremes of temperature and would not discolour. Wright directed Taliesin apprentices to experiment with the architectural application of Pyrex tubes as windows for the Great Workroom. Subsequently installed as a mock-up, the design included aluminium racks to support the Pyrex tubes and couplers to seal and connect the lengths of tubing. By early May of 1937, Wright had taken out seven patents on his Pyrex Glass Construction units. The process was not without delay as innovations in the custom manufactured

aluminium racks and glass tubing were complicated to produce. Ultimately, Corning produced Wright's innovative structural glass design for the clerestories in curved segments, thus enabling his vision of running continuously around the curved corners of the building (Fig.58). S.C. Johnson & Son would later advertise the Pyrex tubing detailed clerestories as '43 Miles of Glass But No Windows'.[90] Corning would also advertise its work for Wright and the S.C. Johnson & Son Building in an advertisement that stated, 'The windows go around and around' (Fig.59).[91]

Another instance of Wright's showmanship was the technical innovation of his 'dendriform', or tree-shaped, cantilever columns. Wright's vision of the Great Workroom was as a forest with natural light filtering down from above. He achieved this by filling the space with dendriform columns, whose gentle tapering from the bottom to the top connected with a circular pad, which supported a circular slab. Between the slabs, natural light would shine into the room through a ceiling of custom-designed Pyrex tubing (Fig.60). Using botanical terms, Wright named the column sections as stem, petal, and calyx. Circular slabs that topped the petals interconnected with short beams at the roof level. The petals and slabs form a continuous rigid frame that enables the columns to come down to the floor at a narrow-hinged connection. Together, the stem and calyx are reinforced with steel mesh.

58 The ingenious custom-detailed Pyrex clerestory windows.

The windows go around and around ...

ORDINARILY the opening of a new office building in Wisconsin doesn't stand the world on its head.
But it was different recently when architect Frank Lloyd Wright finished this ultra-modern building for S. C. Johnson & Son, Inc., famous wax manufacturer. Nothing like it has ever been seen! And one of its most striking features is a complete absence of windows. Instead, broad bands of glass tubing completely encircle the building.
It was no easy job to cut and bend the tubing Mr. Wright required. But it's the kind of job Corning likes to tackle. In 6 months a little group of glass experts furnished 43 miles of tubing, selected for size and straightness, curved to round the corners; cut 9,538 sets of miters to form perfect angles!
Exciting "firsts" are common at Corning. For here glass research gave Thomas A. Edison his first electric lamp bulb; gave women durable, attractive Pyrex brand Ovenware. Recently the papers carried the story of an amazing new glass developed by Corning research that can be heated cherry red, then plunged into ice water without breaking!
Glass research in America got its start at Corning and here it has remained paramount for over 70 years. And after all these years, researchers are continually impressed by the ever widening possibilities of glass. As a material of amazing and unexpected strength, able to resist unusual wear and corrosion, research is finding new uses for glass in many industries where it replaces materials long used but essentially less adapted to certain jobs.
If you have a problem in your business where you think the intelligent application of glass, or the development of new glasses with new characteristics, might save money and increase efficiency, write today. Corning Glass Works, Corning, New York.

CORNING
means
Research in Glass

59   'The windows go around and around . . .', advertisement for Corning Glass, in *Fortune*, November, 1939.

60   The lobby of the S.C. Johnson & Son Administration Building is a double height space with the executive offices facing onto it. The ceiling is constructed of custom-designed Pyrex tubing, which gives daylighting between the circular slabs of the dendriform columns.

Wright was able to design such thin columns because of a new, unusually high-strength concrete manufactured by Marquette Portland Cement.

Wright realised the dendriform columns with the help of talented engineers Wes Peters, who was a Taliesin apprentice, and Mendel Glickman, who taught structural engineering at Taliesin.[92] The unique columns were mocked up on the construction site with theatricality. In 1937, the Wisconsin Industrial Commission had denied permission to build the columns, refusing to accept the structural integrity of Wright's design.[93] A test of a single column was held on 4 June after the concrete had cured for one week. Johnson, Wright, contractor Ben Wiltshek, and a group of Taliesin apprentices were on hand for the test, which was presided over by the Wisconsin Industrial Commission representative, the Racine city building inspector, the city engineer, an engineer from the Marquette Cement Company, and representatives from the steel mesh manufacturer. Also present to document the column loading were photographers from the local, state, and national press.

As the event began, sandbags were loaded onto a platform over the circular pad at the top of the column (Fig.61). When the load reached 12 tons, state inspectors declared they were satisfied. However, Wright demanded that additional sandbags be loaded onto the tops of the columns. At 30 tons, the loading crew was instructed by Wright to keep loading. The crane continued to load loose sand in the centre of the ring of sandbags. As it became clear that heavier material could be endured, pig iron was also loaded atop the column. Periodically, Wright, with great confidence, would kick the column and strike it with his cane.[94] Finally, at 60 tons – five times the load required by the state – the loading ceased. The column was still structurally sound and had only then begun displaying slight cracks at the calyx. As a result of this show of technical bravado, Wright was not only granted permission to build his column design, but his image as an innovative modern architect was renewed in the eyes of the public. A year later, in January 1938, an entire special issue dedicated to Frank Lloyd Wright was published by *Architectural Forum*, with the administration building and S.C. Johnson & Son taking centre stage along with the architect.

61   Frank Lloyd Wright and S.C. Johnson & Son executives observing the fully loaded test columns, 1937.

Life and *Time* magazines also ran cover stories on Wright in January 1938.

Local building commission permitting delays and last-minute changes slowed down construction. Wright's prolonged illness with pneumonia after construction began in winter 1936 was yet another factor, because many details required his personal supervision. In the end, the construction process lapsed for two and a half years, finally concluding in

1938. Completing construction of the administration building was slow and painful for both client and architect. 'I wish the construction would go faster', lamented Wright, 'but I can't demand it because the workmen are doing their best. They have to be taught everything. They have never built anything like this and it is tough. I feel sorry for them and sorry for myself.'[95] Ramsey and Johnson voiced frustration with Wright because of the numerous changes and delays in construction. Manifold complications in the design and installation of the glass tubing pushed back final completion of the building. In February 1939, after much delay, it was opened. To the joy of client and architect, the general reception of the building at its opening was exceedingly positive.

While the administration building was complete, Wright had envisioned a tower and courtyard enclosure as a companion to the administration building. But Johnson was hesitant to hire Wright for the research building based on previous countless delays and cost overruns. Instead, he sought a 'plain factory kind of job'.[96] Johnson even entertained a proposal by his head research scientist, Dr J. Vernon Steinle, who submitted a memorandum describing a potential design that was antithetical to Wright's vision: a U-shaped, two-storey plan, north of the administration building. Eventually, Wright's persistence paid off and he was able to convince Johnson to hire him for the research building.

Eight years later, in 1947, Wright began design on the S.C. Johnson & Son Research Tower. Wright proposed an innovative vertical structure based on the strong centralised taproot structure of a tree. This was a concept he had explored from 1927 to 1929 for the St. Mark's-in-the-Bouwerie apartment building designs. His building design was vertically expressive and was organised around a giant central stack with hollow reinforced concrete floors branching from it. As a result, the labs received abundant daylight. He designed two-storey units for the labs, a square floor level and a circular mezzanine level. The space in the corners was double height. The Research Tower continued a number of aspects from the administration building, including the exterior cladding material of Cherokee red brick, the nostril concept for ventilation, and the Pyrex glass tubing for the exterior enclosure.

While the administration building had used 47 miles of tubing, the Research Tower employed 17.5 miles. Visually, its vertical nature complemented the horizontality of the administration building. In contrast with the relatively low-lying city of Racine, the Research Tower's visibility gave the S.C. Johnson & Son company an architectural brand identity in the minds of Racinians.

Wright's Synthesised Interiors

As discussed with the PSFS Building, the concept of gesamtkunstwerk, or total work of art, can be understood as a key element of architectural branding. To be sure, the term applied here does not refer to its 19th-century formal and handcraft implications, but instead, it should be understood as cohesively designed and engaging interior environments. Thus, they are a powerful strategy for branding design. Frank Lloyd Wright synthesised the interiors and their furnishings with the architecture of the S.C. Johnson & Son Administration Building, bringing together the various scales into a cohesive whole. Gesamtkunstwerk defined most of Wright's projects over his long career. The harmonising of modern architecture, interiors, furniture, and objects was particularly poignant in the early to mid-20th century. For Wright, the 'organic' was a unifying concept that was implemented throughout the S.C. Johnson & Son Building, from its exterior massing, to its structure and interior, down to its desks and chairs. Colour was another cohesive element throughout the building, as the cast aluminium portions of the interior were painted to match the 'Cherokee red' brick. S.C. Johnson & Son not only benefited from Frank Lloyd Wright's fame, but the gesamtkunstwerk interiors created an impactful brand identity for the company that engaged its occupants. Spaces including the lobby, the Great Workroom, and advertising offices were especially powerful. Like the PSFS Building and Peter Behrens's design for AEG, the S.C. Johnson & Son Building design gave its client an architectural and design brand identity. Good branding is achieved through an immersive experience, and Wright's particular design ethos, applied at many scales of design, achieved just that.

The desk served as an important core component of Wright's unified vision for the administration building. Prior to the 1920s, most desks bred individual privacy by compartmentalising office space. From the 18th century on, desks performed multiple functions, and were generally ornate and clunky. The ultimate Victorian desk, an ensemble of writing surface and varied storage compartments, was realised in the Wooton Patent Cabinet Office Secretary. The Wooton was a hulking mass, equipped with plenty of pigeonholes for tucking away papers and supplies. Antithetical to this was Wright's desk design for the Larkin Building. The Larkin desk (1906) formed a simple, integral part of the workroom and its architecture, with built-in metal file cabinets and cantilevered seats that swivelled in to facilitate cleaning of the floor.

By the 20th century, the nature of production was rapidly changing. Desks became modern 'standardized designs that allowed them [designers] to adopt more efficient mass-production techniques'.[97] The spread of modernity brought an obsession with rationalisation in the workplace – with employees as well as with furniture design. For example, Frederick Winslow Taylor's influential theories attempted to reconcile labour and capital through scientific management. The Metal Office Furniture Company was founded in 1912 in Grand Rapids, Michigan and would later change its name to Steelcase and manufacture Wright's furniture for the S.C. Johnson & Son Building. The modern ethos transformed office furniture design in the 1930s with streamlined designs by designers such as Gilbert Rhode, Norman Bel Geddes, and Raymond Loewy. In response to the growing need to equip business concerns throughout the US, Steelcase had, by 1933, become the largest furniture manufacturer in the US and abroad. Like his desk for the Larkin Building, Wright's design for the Great Workroom of the S.C. Johnson & Son headquarters addressed modern life in the workplace with organisation and efficiency. In doing so, it went beyond the definition of the desk to become a true workstation, predating Herman Miller's 1947 George Nelson-designed workstation. Wright's workstation design was not simply a desk; it possessed a writing surface, storage elements, and files.

Like the streamlined building exterior, the geometry and form of the S.C. Johnson & Son desks and their chairs were also circular and elongated (Fig.62). At 84 inches, Wright's desk was two feet longer than the standard desk at that time. Corners of the desk were not orthogonal, but curved. The three layers of work surface – a desktop, with shelves above – were detailed to suggest floating slabs of wood. Wright punctuated the integration of building and furniture with a dramatic detail, the intersection of column and desk. Although this design remained unbuilt, it appeared in a plan and elevation of the desk and chair design.[98] The coming together of two important design elements eloquently demonstrated the design's comprehensive nature and cemented a brand identity for S.C. Johnson & Son.

Wright's Great Workroom desks were meticulously designed for different employee roles. Nine variations on the desk accommodated specific clerical tasks. In addition to the desks, tables were designed for the mailroom and other departments. Custom-designed individual pieces included a desk for the company president, a conference room table, and the receptionist's information table. In all, Wright designed more than 40 different pieces of furniture, each accommodating different business functions. Business machines, such as typewriters, rested on the lower surface at a comfortable working height.

Wright innovated further with interchangeability of furniture in the S.C. Johnson & Son headquarters. Instead of designing two chairs – a desk chair and a visitor's chair – Wright designed one that would serve both functions, with interchangeable feet. Variations in the basic design for the secretary's chair were used for the officer's chair as well. The desk provided an early prototype for use in an open office employing workstations rather than partitions. Its design resulted in an open and light-filled workplace. In this sense, Wright pioneered open office systems with the Great Workroom of S.C. Johnson & Son and in the light court of the Larkin Building. Open office systems would not become truly standardised or mass-produced until 1964 when Herman Miller introduced the Action Office designed by George Nelson and Robert Propst. The Quickborner office landscape, designed by Eberhard and Wolfgang

62   Wright-designed desks and chairs for the administration building, 1939.

Schnelle in Quickborn, Germany, was introduced in the same year.[99] Wright's design initiated a trend toward today's open office and flexible furniture systems.

The S.C. Johnson & Son Brand and the Architect's Bravado

Frank Lloyd Wright vehemently denied accusations against him of self-promotion. In 1957, near the end of his illustrious life, television journalist Mike Wallace asked the famed architect if he was a 'PR artist'.[100] Wright indignantly replied 'No!' feigning a lack of interest in the matter of promotion altogether. Yet Wright's charismatic personality and personal salesmanship made him a de facto PR artist. Architectural historian Neil Levine has called Wright the 'first superstar architect of the 20th century', adding, 'it was a role he relished, but one that also deflected criticism from the work and to the person.'[101] Thus, it was the person, or more precisely, the persona, of Frank Lloyd Wright that people could relate to, and thus make connections with, that served as a brand identity for S.C. Johnson & Son.

Although he contested it, Wright was a tireless promoter of his ideas, as much as he was a creative genius. In addition, his personal life was sensational and as a result its most shocking details were printed in newspapers and circulated in the rumour mill. Not only was his lifestyle the subject of public discussion but his projects made headlines, in part because of Wright's tendency to describe his work in proverbial sound bites. In addition, Wright devoted much of his energy to activities that disseminated his ideas and projects: he was committed to training the next generation of architects at Taliesin, as well as to writing and lecturing a considerable amount. He also granted many interviews, not only to architectural writers within the field but to the mass media. Self-promotion was the by-product of Frank Lloyd Wright's bold confidence. All of his buildings were brought into the spotlight with him.

The rise of a celebrity-based culture in the 20th century can be attributed in part to the shift from a producing society to a consuming one. Along with this shift came the media machinery that provided information to the masses: the flourishing print, broadcasting, recording, and film industries that would create a ravenous market for celebrity culture. Such a quickly changing milieu brought on social fragmentation in Americans. As a response to the malaise, society produced a cult of personality. Image and charisma, rather than character, became a means to distinguish individual selves from the masses. In a culture preoccupied with fame, 'celebrity' became a measure of success.[102] The public looked for personalities and celebrities, and Frank Lloyd Wright fit the role perfectly.

From October 1936 – three months after S.C. Johnson & Son hired Wright – Connolly began 'the publicity programme in connection with the new office building'.[103] Immediately, Wisconsin newspapers and architectural journals began to demand stories on the project. As Connolly saw it, publicity about the building divided into two audiences: one within the field of architecture and another to a general audience (Fig.63). While he understood that the architectural community would have a great interest in the Wright building, Connolly believed a broader audience was more important to reach as it consisted of the company's consumers. 'A second and very valuable kind of

63   William Connolly, Head of Advertising at S.C. Johnson & Son, here with Herbert F. Johnson Jr, in the new administration building. Photograph in *Life*, 8 May 1939.

publicity', wrote Connolly to Wright, 'may be expected in newspapers, particularly in the building and business pages and in lay publications of various kinds.'[104]

Wright fully cooperated with Connolly's lead on advertising and even stated he would 'hide behind' the ad executive. Wright agreed to Connolly's request that S.C. Johnson & Son's advertising department in Racine would act as 'a clearing house for all releases', with the help of their publicity agent in Chicago.[105] Wright responded that he was already 'beset by architectural magazines for "exclusive" presentations on any scale [he] desired'.[106]

On 24 April 1939, the Johnson Wax Building opened, with S.C. Johnson & Son's advertising department orchestrating the events of the day.

MILWAUKEE, MONDAY, APRIL 24, 1939.

'Fair' Atmosphere as Wright Building Opens

Extraordinary design of the new Johnson Wax office building in Racine, a Frank Lloyd Wright architectural gem, Sunday gave a "world's fair" atmosphere to the gathering of throngs of curious to view its many features. The blank wall seen above is built above glass sections, hidden by the line of spectators awaiting admission.

Racine on Civic Holiday As Throngs View Plant

64   '"Fair" Atmosphere as Wright Building Opens', *Milwaukee Sentinel*, 24 April 1939.

'Spectacular as the showiest Hollywood set', reported *Life* magazine, 'it represents simply the result of creative genius applied to the problem of designing the most efficient and comfortable, as well as beautiful, place in which S.C. Johnson & Son executives and clerks could do their work.'[107] *Businessweek* also reported on the intense attention the building received upon its opening:

> Last week-end was open house at the new Johnson office. Factory employees and their families were admitted Friday afternoon, office employees' families Friday evening, the general public Saturday and Sunday. In Racine, with only 70,000 population, more than 26,000 visitors trudged from basement locker rooms to penthouse squash court, while outside block-long queues waited as much as two hours and broke two revolving door glasses in the Sunday Push.[108]

Another local news headline read, 'Racine on Civic Holiday As Throngs View Plant'.[109] The article described the opening of the 'unique' office building

as Racine's 'miniature "world's fair" of its own' (Fig.64).[110] Visitors were escorted by 'two hundred uniformed Boy Scouts' and 'half a dozen police officers were required for special traffic duty.'[111] Journalists, including *Businessweek,* focused attention on the design's 'functional' quality.

> Discarding all conventional standards, he [Frank Lloyd Wright] started with a study of what a wax-maker needs to accomplish in the office. Net result is a building fitted to a business – a structure that's 100% functional.[112]

Wright's design made the S.C. Johnson & Son publicity department's job easy. His innovative architectural elements were easily rendered as superlatives for ad copy. These included 'Golf-tee columns', 'The World's Most Modern Office Building', and 'The Office of the Future' (Figs 65, 66, 67).[113] The publicity department pitched the building as singular and as a pioneering design of the future. *Engineering News-Record* deemed it the 'Office Building Without Precedent'.[114] *Life* magazine declared, 'New Frank Lloyd Wright Office Building

Shows Shape of Things to Come'.[115] A journalist for the *Spring Valley Democrat* thought it surpassed another architectural spectacle, calling it the 'Newest Thing Since the Skyscraper':

> Built entirely without windows or glass brick, it utilizes 43 miles of glass tubing for lighting. More than 200 kinds of specially shaped bricks, molded to order, were used in construction. Heated through the floors, air conditioned, the building is expected to set the pace for office structures of the future. Even the furniture was specially designed by the architect.[116]

News journalists were fascinated by the architectural curiosities designed by Wright, including a 'windowless' office, 'golf-tee columns', and 'nostrils'.[117] Only the term 'nostrils' was uttered by Wright himself: the others were invented by journalists. It was important, not that architects understood and appreciated these terms, but that the general audience of S.C. Johnson &

Son's product users did. That product users linked Wright's progressive design to Glo-Coat or Jubilee would make architecture part of the company's brand identity. Wright's most repeated description of the building was that the administration building was 'to be as inspiring a place to work in as any cathedral ever was to worship in'.[118] The reference to a cathedral was crucial because most people could immediately relate to the kind of awe-inspiring environment a cathedral provides. The term 'cathedral of commerce' had already christened the Gothic-inspired Woolworth Building more than 40 years prior. In his statement, Wright communicated the idea that an office building could be as uplifting as a house of worship.

An article in the May 1939 issue of leading trade journal *Broadcast Merchandising* discussed not only the link between radio and advertising, but also among radio, advertising, and architecture. First, the article established the importance of S.C. Johnson & Son's sponsorship of *Fibber McGee and Molly*. Its headline read: 'Johnson's Wax Program Smoothes Sales Approach to Dealers and Consumers: Fibber McGee Credited with Great Achievement in Winning Dealers Friendly Interest and Appreciation of Extensive Advertising Campaign.'[119] S.C. Johnson & Son's advertising manager, William Connolly, boasted, 'Our sales volume has steadily increased since 1932 . . . we feel that much of the credit for this steady increase in business is due to that medium.'[120] Radio became the quintessential medium for mass culture. Unlike movies, radio was a household presence; by the mid-1930s, 60 per cent of all American households owned at least one set. And unlike records, radio was live, with entertainment and information available at the touch of the dial. Radio stars such as Jack Benny and Burns and Allen became more than celebrities – they were virtual members of the family.[121] The same article in *Broadcast Merchandising* explained how a popular and folksy radio show humanised a business.

> A great many deals [customers] apparently listen to the program regularly and most of those who do seem to like it. As a result our men are often greeted jocularly by dealers and their salespeople

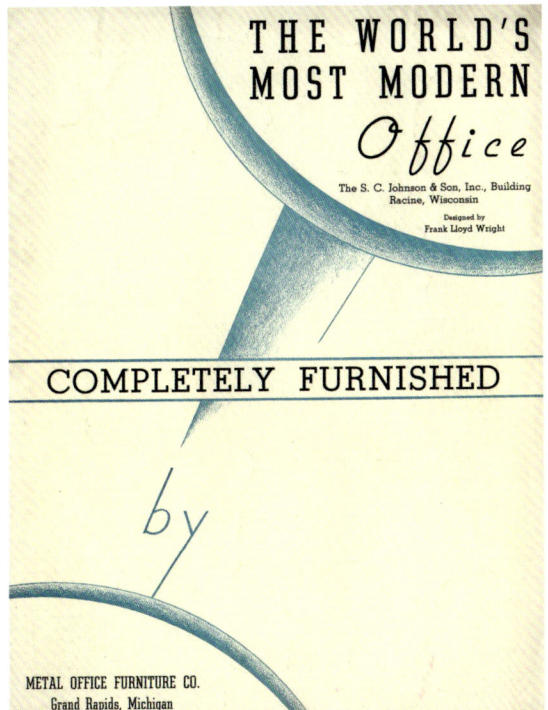

65   Metal Office Furniture Company advertisement, featuring 'The World's Most Modern Office . . . designed by Frank Lloyd Wright', composed with a stylised sketch of the dendriform columns, 1939.

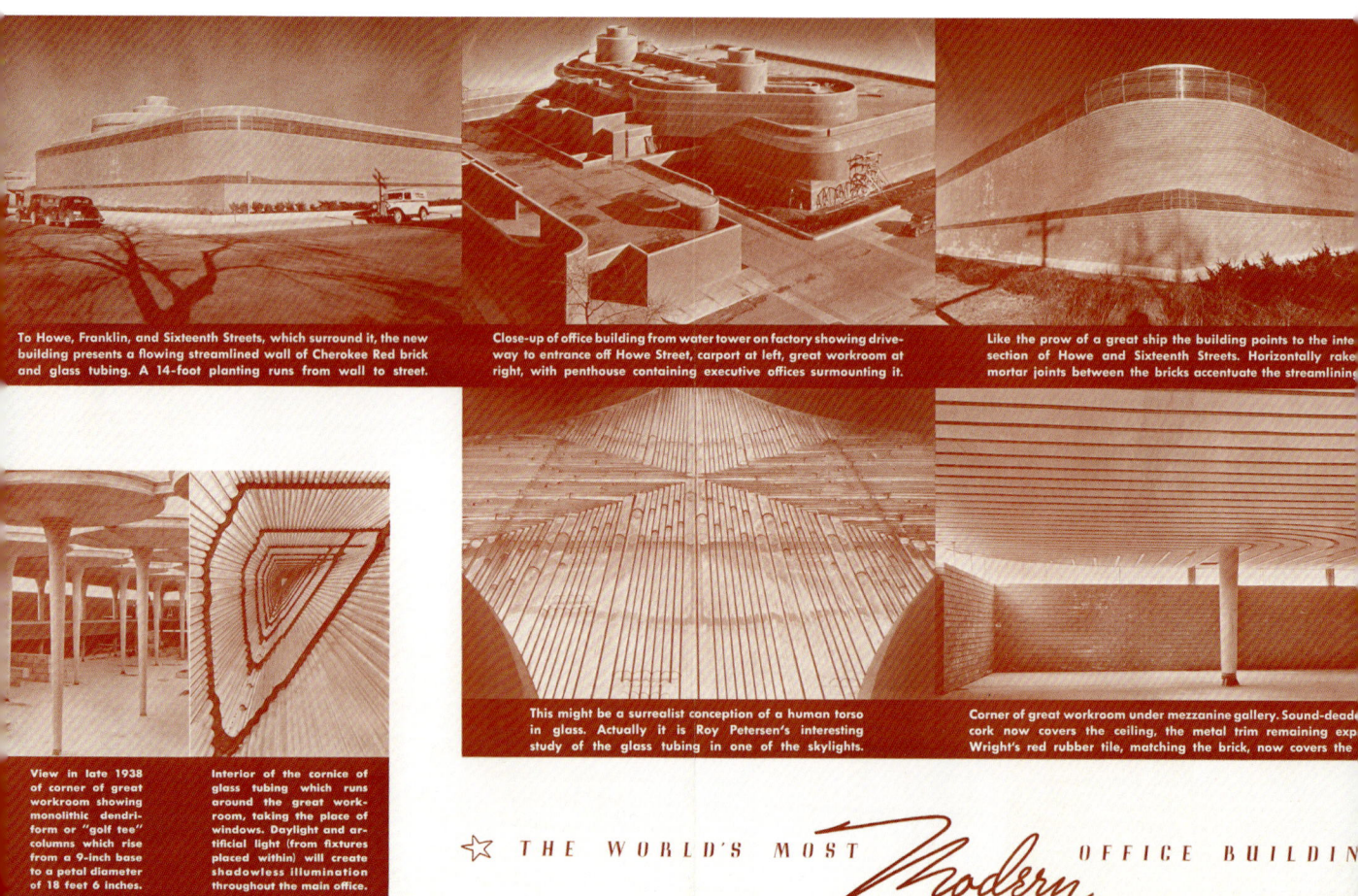

To Howe, Franklin, and Sixteenth Streets, which surround it, the new building presents a flowing streamlined wall of Cherokee Red brick and glass tubing. A 14-foot planting runs from wall to street.

Close-up of office building from water tower on factory showing driveway to entrance off Howe Street, carport at left, great workroom at right, with penthouse containing executive offices surmounting it.

Like the prow of a great ship the building points to the inte[r] section of Howe and Sixteenth Streets. Horizontally rake[d] mortar joints between the bricks accentuate the streamlining

View in late 1938 of corner of great workroom showing monolithic dendri-form or "golf tee" columns which rise from a 9-inch base to a petal diameter of 18 feet 6 inches.

Interior of the cornice of glass tubing which runs around the great work-room, taking the place of windows. Daylight and artificial light (from fixtures placed within) will create shadowless illumination throughout the main office.

This might be a surrealist conception of a human torso in glass. Actually it is Roy Petersen's interesting study of the glass tubing in one of the skylights.

Corner of great workroom under mezzanine gallery. Sound-deade[ning] cork now covers the ceiling, the metal trim remaining exp[osed] Wright's red rubber tile, matching the brick, now covers the

☆ THE WORLD'S MOST *Modern* OFFICE BUILDIN[G]

66 Ad for 'The World's Most Modern Office Building', highlighting the building's innovative features.

Frank Lloyd Wright Designs
THE OFFICE OF THE FUTURE FOR
S. C. Johnson and Son, Incorporated

Many advanced structural, lighting, heating and equipment ideas used for the first time in the new office of S. C. Johnson and Son, Inc., are described and pictured by candid camera

Top: This photograph, made from a tower above the factory shows the striking and unusual features of the new Johnson building, which houses the officers, executives and office employees of the famous Racine company

Below: Made without photographic lighting, this picture shows, in the white areas, the double layers of glass tubing; between these layers is the electric lighting which is needed only on darkest days. Note the graceful columns

BY JOHN GARTH

AS YOU approach the new office building of S. C. Johnson and Son, Inc., you naturally look for the entrance in the conventional place, near the center of the building where entrances usually are. But all you see are solid brick and mortar walls and two bands of glass tubing, with no openings whatever, and not a window in sight. Apparently there are no doors.

Then you reach a covered arcade or court, extending east and west between a garage and the north side of the building. Entering this court you find, midway between the east and west walls, half a block from any street, solid glass revolving doors. You enter, walk across a high ceilinged lobby, with flowers growing and blooming in boxes overhead, to the reception desk, an enclosure built of brick topped with polished maple. A step to the south and you enter the great workroom, which is the general office of the company, where several hundred clerical work-

67 'Frank Lloyd Wright Designs the Office of the Future for S.C. Johnson & Son, Incorporated', headline image in *American Business*, May 1939.

with 'Hello, McGee' . . . Insignificant though these things may seem, they break the ground for our men, who find it easier to lead into a discussion of our products and their promotion as a result. Much has been said about the importance of humanizing a business . . . Radio helps in keeping us human to our customers.[122]

If sponsorship of a radio show humanised a business through the association of a product with a radio personality, then the sponsorship or commission of a building with its association with a famous architect would also create a bond with customers. In the same article, a major portion was an inset highlighting the company's new administration building.

> Not only do S. C. Johnson & Son, Inc. believe in using radio, the modern advertising medium to sell their products. They also believe that modern merchandising methods can be successfully applied to every part of their business. Convincing evidence of this modern point of view is found in the 'World's Most Modern Office Building', which Frank Lloyd Wright designed for them . . . it is expected that many thousands of Fibber McGee fans will come from all parts of the country during the next several years to see this building.[123]

By proposing that Fibber McGee fans would visit a Wright-designed office building, this *Broadcast Merchandising* article brought the two media, radio and architecture, together in a constructed reality of two spokespeople. By pointing out that architecture was just as potent an advertising medium as radio, *Broadcast Merchandising* poised Fibber McGee and Frank Lloyd Wright on equal footing as agents of advertising. This role was not lost on Wright as he boasted that his brilliant design attracted incredible media attention to the company.

> Bill Connolly, competent 'man on the job' for the advertising of the S. C. Johnson Co., calculated that two or more millions of dollars could not have bought the front pages in newspapers and top-notch magazines which the building had attracted to itself. Of the media attention that

the architecture garnered, Connolly declared, 'And the movie "shorts" took it up . . . to this hour.'[124]

Wright wrote about his ideas on advertising and the S.C. Johnson & Son project in *An Autobiography*. In particular, he had noticed the similar role that architecture played with radio in advertising the company. Wright pointed out: 'And observe – although a building is not radio, it was the psychological world-moment for the more serious sort of thing we now did. Hib knew it (his "hunch") and he took the gaff with only a stab or two at his architect now and then just for luck.'[125] The 'hunch' Wright referred to was that architecture served as advertising. What the client knew from the beginning became a reality.

As with the medium of radio, S.C. Johnson & Son became active in television sponsorship. In 1948, the company began television advertising and by November of that year had launched its own television show, 'Starlight Theater', half-hour romantic dramas directed by Yul Brynner. A consistent element of the show was 'a big-name Broadway or Hollywood star . . . supported by well-known Broadway players'.[126] Stars appearing on 'Starlight Theater' included Dorothy Gish, Nancy Kelly, and Julie Harris. Like their choice of architect in the famous Frank Lloyd Wright, S.C. Johnson's interest in celebrity sponsorship was reflected in the medium of television.

S.C. Johnson & Son understood their Wright-designed building as modern merchandising. Architecture advertised and ultimately branded the company as 'dynamic, and forward-looking' to the public. In the company's in-house employee publication, the *Jonwax Journal*, William Connolly explained that, 'one of the important facets of our public relations is based on the world-wide interest shown our Frank Lloyd Wright-designed buildings.' Connolly went as far as to state, 'Modern architecture has done much to enhance the public image of S.C. Johnson as a dynamic, forward-looking company', thus confirming that Wright's architecture branded the identity of the company.[127]

S.C. Johnson & Son's advertising department produced the pamphlet 'Welcome to the Home of Johnson's Wax', in which the narrative described

68   'Welcome to the Home of Johnson's Wax', pamphlet for visitors. The graphics depict the stylised dendriform columns. Pamphlet, c.1939.

the exceptional architecture and made sure to point out its famed architect. Throughout the pamphlet, a graphic device based on Wright's dendriform column is used (Fig.68). The stylised golf-tee shape is rendered in different shades of orange on the front and back covers. Inside the pamphlet, the company highlights the fact that the architecture was 'Frank Lloyd Wright-designed', and that Wright was 'the greatest architectural genius of his time'. Illustrating the narrative is a sketch of Wright drawing at a draughting table (Fig.69).[128] S.C. Johnson clearly invested not only in Wright's architecture for their headquarters, but in his persona and fame for their company identity.

An interoffice memorandum from Jack Ramsey to William Connolly provides evidence

The Administration and Research Center

The buildings you will see on your tour were designed by Frank Lloyd Wright, a native of Wisconsin who has been called the greatest architectural genius of his time. Asked what he considered the most important factor in designing the Johnson's Wax buildings, he replied: "The human values involved. If you make men and women proud of their environment, and happy to be where they are and give them some dignity and pride in their environment, it all comes out to the good where the product is concerned."

Since the Administration building was completed in 1939, this business structure has attracted the attention of people all over the world. Photos of it have appeared in publications of many lands, and 500 architects recently selected the Center as one of the "Seven Wonders of American Architecture."

Although the Research Tower and adjoining buildings around the courtyard were constructed 10 years after the Administration building, the composite units look alike. They have the same warm, reddish-brown brick, called "Cherokee Red." More than 200 special shapes of brick were used in the construction.

The circumferential bands of pyrex tubing not only admit light but add to the interior decoration. If laid end to end they would extend for 63 miles.

Mr. Wright not only designed the building but also the unique round and oval desks, tables, and chairs.

69   'Welcome to the Home of Johnson's Wax', pamphlet for visitors. The narrative points out the fame of the building's architect and features an illustration of Frank Lloyd Wright at a draughting table. Pamphlet, c.1939.

that S.C. Johnson & Son fully understood the value of hiring Wright. Ramsey pitched the company's approach to the new building by making an analogy to the design of a furniture polish container.[129] Just as S.C. Johnson & Son did not choose an ordinary, mass-produced bottle for their remarkable new furniture polish, but instead 'asked the best designers we knew' to 'clothe [the furniture polish] as it should be clothed', so did they not choose to use 'stock office space' for their new administration building.[130] Instead, the publicity-minded company hired the renowned Frank Lloyd Wright.

'Mr. Wright has interpreted our desires', writes Ramsey, 'in a building that will be as beautifully efficient as it is structurally beautiful.'[131] Ramsey notes that the building would be 'modern' and not 'modernistic, in line with today's fads in everything from architecture to cork-screws'. The building's 'modern' design was creative and positive. Ramsey's memo concludes by aligning the architectural

qualities of 'innate honesty of purpose, proper use of materials, real craftsmanship, human consideration' in the building as 'express[ing] the good Johnson Wax, Glo-Coat, paints, and all the other products we make and sell'.[132] For S.C. Johnson & Son executives, the architecture of their headquarters expressed, and effectively branded, the company and its products.

Despite their disagreements, Hib Johnson had great respect for Frank Lloyd Wright. As a businessman, he believed in his role as one that advanced architecture (Fig.70). In a speech given during a panel discussion in 1957, Hib stated, 'businessmen are largely responsible for the advancement of education, the arts of painting, architecture, music, the theater, television. . . . Some of the most dramatic aspects in contemporary culture.' For the S.C. Johnson & Son leader, the arts were part of advertising 'because they have become part of the mechanics of advertising in America'.[133] To reinforce his point, he named a

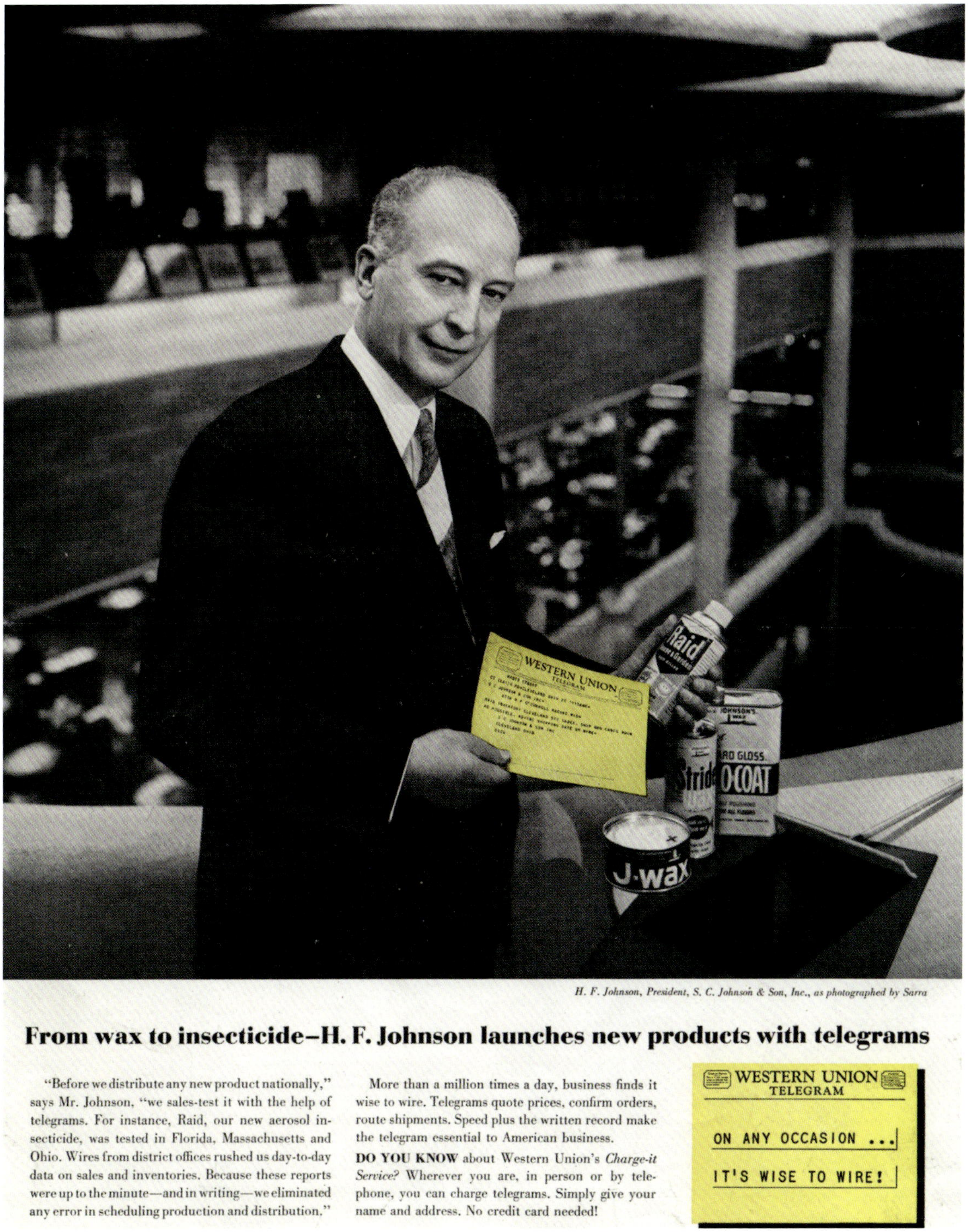

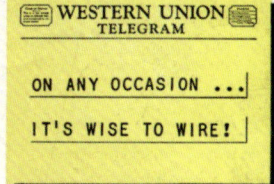

WESTERN UNION
TELEGRAM
Raid
J·wax
H. F. Johnson, President, S. C. Johnson & Son, Inc., as photographed by Sarra
From wax to insecticide–H. F. Johnson launches new products with telegrams
"Before we distribute any new product nationally," says Mr. Johnson, "we sales-test it with the help of telegrams. For instance, Raid, our new aerosol insecticide, was tested in Florida, Massachusetts and Ohio. Wires from district offices rushed us day-to-day data on sales and inventories. Because these reports were up to the minute—and in writing—we eliminated any error in scheduling production and distribution."
More than a million times a day, business finds it wise to wire. Telegrams quote prices, confirm orders, route shipments. Speed plus the written record make the telegram essential to American business.
DO YOU KNOW about Western Union's Charge-it Service? Wherever you are, in person or by telephone, you can charge telegrams. Simply give your name and address. No credit card needed!
WESTERN UNION
TELEGRAM
ON ANY OCCASION ...
IT'S WISE TO WIRE!

70 One of Frank Lloyd Wright's greatest clients, Herbert F. Johnson, photographed in the S.C. Johnson & Son Administration Building. This 1956 ad for Western Union Telegrams depicts the company president with S.C. Johnson & Son's most successful products, including Glo-Coat.

71 Frank Lloyd Wright in the
S.C. Johnson & Son
Administration Building,
c.1950.

few Italian companies who shared the view that architecture and other arts were integral parts of business: Olivetti, Fiat, Necchi, and Cinzano.

Later, when Hib's son, Samuel C. Johnson, became president of the company, he wrote, 'From the day the building opened we achieved international attention because that building represented and symbolised the quality of everything we did.'[134] The company promoted Frank Lloyd Wright as the architect of its headquarters, thus associating him with the company and creating what we understand today as a co-branding arrangement. The S.C. Johnson & Son Buildings are considered architectural branding because Frank Lloyd Wright and his designs both defined and enhanced the company's identity. All who had knowledge of the project and experienced the building and its interiors would associate Wright and his design with S.C. Johnson & Son. The cachet of Wright's high profile and his design expertise expanded the brand (Fig.71). As such, Wright's fame as branding for the S.C. Johnson & Son headquarters makes it a unique example of architectural branding that stands apart from the other case studies of this book. While the architectural design certainly expanded the company's identity through Wright's modern, and gesamtkunstwerk design, the architect himself and his fame were the key branding strategies that connected the company with the public. While Wright's fame cemented S.C. Johnson & Son's identity, the next case study will shift focus to a corporate headquarters' striking architectural form as branding strategy.

4 FORM

Lever House

As the Cold War developed in the years after World War II, the United States experienced phenomenal economic growth. After 1945 the major corporations in America grew even larger, propelled by the expansion of the automobile industry, a housing boom, and the rise in defence spending. The nature of work shifted from an industrial economy to one based on service, and by the mid-1950s Americans increasingly held white-collar jobs. In 1952 the newly constructed Lever House stood as a proud modern monument to its creator, Lever Brothers (Fig.72). The iconic form of the headquarters building provided the company with 'millions of dollars of free advertising', and its modern architecture provided it with a new, bold, brand identity.[1]

Lever House was completed in December 1951. Four months later, the building received universal praise from architects, critics, and laymen who acclaimed the new architectural image it created for New York City business. At that moment, the city had seen little of European modernism and the success of Lever House gave other large corporate clients confidence in commissioning modern architecture.[2] While the 24-storey slab skyscraper was largely praised when it opened, this study of Lever House offers a new interpretation of the building as it expanded the client's branding through specifically architectural terms in the post-World War II era, as the forces of the corporate client converged with Skidmore, Owings & Merrill's bureaucratic architecture, Raymond Loewy's interior styling, and the building's urban stance.

New York, c.1948

After World War II, New York prospered, both economically and culturally. By the late 1940s, the city had become the world's financial capital. Of the nation's 500 largest industrial companies, 135 were located in Manhattan, including Standard Oil, General Electric, U.S. Steel, Union Carbide, IBM, and RCA. Manhattan was dubbed the 'headquarters city'. Skidmore, Owings & Merrill (SOM) founder Nathaniel Owings described the midtown site of Lever House:

> Park Avenue was still lined with beautiful, nearly authentic Renaissance palaces. The luxurious Marquery Apartment House was typical. Designed by John Russell Pope, it faced on tree-lined courts, giving the avenue a quiet elegance which was further enriched by Saint Bartholomew's Church, designed by Bertram Grosvenor Goodhue; and McKim, Mead and White's masterpiece, the Racquet Club.[3]

Modern architecture of the International Style was rarely seen in New York at this time. Notable exceptions included the New School for Social Research, designed by Joseph Urban (1929–1931), and the Museum of Modern Art, by Philip Goodwin and Edward Durell Stone (1937–1939). Instead, Art Deco and Streamline Modern works were more prevalent at this time, with Rockefeller Center (1930–1939), the McGraw-Hill Building (1930–1931), the Chrysler Building (1928–1930), and the Empire State Building (1930–1931) reaching new heights in a streamlined, moderne style. Lever House's modernism would bring a striking new presence to Park Avenue, and to the city of New York.

At the moment when the emerging trend of corporations, institutions, and families was to move to the suburbs, Lever Brothers decided instead to relocate to New York City. At this time journalist and activist, Jane Jacobs voiced strong opposition

72   Lever House, 53rd Street and Park Avenue, New York City.

to de-urbanisation, advocating just the opposite – urban growth. The postwar New York City office boom reflected her cause. In a 1957 *Architectural Forum* article, she reported, 'What is happening in New York is less an expansion than an explosion of office space. The 40 million square feet added or about to be added represents more than a 40% increase of the city's office space at the war's end' (Fig.73).[4] Jacobs argued that invaluable social phenomena would disappear if business moved to the suburbs. She realised that businesses and their employees 'hanker[ed] for big, horizontal, flexible spaces', but this put the face-to-face meeting – 'the shared Martini' and 'the subtle sizing up' – at risk; in short, 'the chance to bring the full weight of personality to bear' – which had been an influential aspect of American business up until that time.[5] By locating its American headquarters in the socially vibrant urban environment of New York City, Lever Brothers' business would benefit in many ways, not least of all through the innovative architectural branding of its headquarters building.

The Client

By the mid-19th century, Bolton, England, one of the most bucolic towns in the region, had been almost obliterated by industry, leaving it transformed into a factory town.[6] In 1850, Bolton was filthy, disease-ridden, and overcrowded. William Hesketh Lever (1851–1925), the founder of Lever Brothers, had grown up in Bolton. Having witnessed the detrimental effects of industrialisation, with its billowing clouds of soot and layers of grime, he would eventually market and sell its antidote: soap. As the standard of living of industrial workers rose from 1860 onward, a viable market for soap grew alongside a vast need for the product.

From the 1860s, soap was the key product of the Lever family's wholesale grocery store in Bolton. Their soap was exclusively packaged as 'Lever's Pure Honey'. By the 1870s many grocers had begun selling a competing soap called 'Pure Honey'.[7] To customers, the two soap products were nearly indistinguishable. In 1875, the Trade Marks Registration Act introduced registered trademarks to Britain. Having learned the hard

way that a distinctive trademark was as important as the quality product itself, William Lever sought the help of the best trademark and patent agent in Liverpool.

Lever considered half a dozen names for his new trademarked soap. 'But really', Lever later revealed, 'none of those names appealed to me. I had big ideas of some sort of name – I did not know what – but it was going to be such a marvel.'[8] He eventually found the name for which he was searching, 'Sunlight', which he would later trademark.

73   View of Park Avenue looking north, with Lever House on the left and Nikita S. Khrushchev's motorcade going up Park Avenue, September 1959.

Port Sunlight

In 1886, William Lever began plans to build not just a factory but an entire company town. It would be called Port Sunlight, named after Lever Brothers' most successful product, Sunlight Soap. Located in Warrington, England, near Liverpool, Port Sunlight would be a 'garden village' – self-consciously rural, an alternative to urban industrial towns. Like the well-known contemporaneous town Bourneville, built by Cadbury's at the rural fringe of Birmingham in the 1890s, Port Sunlight was based on the romantic rural villages of the 18th century, such as John Nash's picturesque cottages at Blaise Hamlet, and on the parks of Frederick Law Olmsted. These works, like Port Sunlight, tapped into the myth of rural life as benign and healthful, as counter-posed to city life, with all its evils.[9] The health and well-being benefits of Port Sunlight's architecture were supplemented by Lever's 'prosperity-sharing', an experiment in sharing profits, intended to further enhance the lives of Lever's workers and their families, and at the same time cultivate loyalty.[10]

Along with his business, Lever's great interest was architecture. He actively involved himself in the development of Port Sunlight village and worked in close collaboration with its architects.[11] The architecture reflected the influence of the Arts & Crafts movement, of William Morris, and of late-Victorian aestheticism. The architecture at Port Sunlight was notable for its attention to materials, texture, and detailing. It was an environment in which the visual richness and design unity were in dramatic contrast to the dull and oppressive cities of England's industrialised north.[12]

The village's architectural lavishness demonstrated what could be done with unlimited money. Yet while character was displayed on building exteriors and their fronts, the interiors and backs of the buildings were plain and utilitarian. And though the individual living units were small, the architects designed them in clusters, giving the false impression of larger middle-class houses.[13] Despite Port Sunlight's sophistication and aura of quaintness, there was a great sense of artificiality and drama. As architectural and urban historian Margaret Crawford has pointed out, the community's retrospective styles and replicas of well-known Tudor and Elizabethan buildings offered a deliberate nostalgic image of the pre-industrial village.[14]

While Lever sought to improve industrial working conditions and give employees a balanced life, the design of Port Sunlight displayed a high degree of paternalism. Lever's pleasant company town came at a price: ethical values were imposed upon its dwellers. William Lever became notorious for creating a stifling atmosphere at Port Sunlight, imposing strict controls over its inhabitants.[15] When realised, Lever's hope that the design of Port Sunlight architecture could shape human behaviour fell short.

Lever Advertising

Lever's soap – while it was a solid product – was nothing new. What made 'Sunlight' truly unique was its trademark and packaging. Lever understood the magical power of advertising. In 1909 he wrote, 'We want to have [a] hypnotic effect with soap. . . . The whole object of advertising is to build a halo round the article.'[16] Having identified its key market as the working class, Lever's advertising aimed to convince working-class housewives that Lever soap was not a luxury but rather an indispensable necessity for the home and a better choice than its competitors. Lever's advertising campaign was thus twofold: to capture the working-class housewife's attention, and to make consumers of Sunlight soap out of people who had purchased little or no soap before.

One of Lever's advertising themes depicted Sunlight soap as an effective and time-saving device for the housewife. A Sunlight soap advertisement of 1887 read, 'Sunlight Gets the Washing Done Leaving Time for Sport and Fun'.[17] Another theme portrayed soap as a cure for women's premature ageing. Melodramatic ads exploited the insecurities of working-class housewives, who had little time to devote to beauty regimes. In 1888 Lever debuted the famous slogan, 'Why Does a Woman Look Old Sooner than a Man?' (Fig.74).[18]

A second phase of advertising, after 1900, established interactive strategies, including 'how-to' pamphlets, such as 'Sunlight Soap and How to Use

74 Early Lever Brothers advertisement for Sunlight soap, n.d.

It', as well as highly competitive 'prize schemes' in which customers who collected a prescribed number of soap wrappers were promised rewards.[19] Devices like this not only created demand but also broke into other products' markets. By studying human psychology and exploiting human emotions around ageing and maintaining a clean, healthy home, Lever thrust his goods into the consciousness of potential users. William Lever was quoted as saying, 'The cost of advertising is not paid for by the consumer; it can only be paid for by increased sales.'[20]

Lever's soap business prospered in the late 19th and early 20th centuries. In 1895, Lever Brothers expanded to US soil, opening a small New York office to handle sales of Sunlight and Lifebuoy soaps. Three years later, Lever Brothers acquired a small soap factory in Cambridge, Massachusetts, and a few years after that, another in Philadelphia. In 1929 Lever Brothers merged with the Dutch company Margarine Union to create Unilever Ltd. Lever had a wide geographical span, instantly making Unilever multinational.[21] Meanwhile, Margarine Union was a stronger, more profitable, company.[22] The two companies used the same sources of supply (oils and fats) for their most visible products (soap and margarine), as well as for their diverse, lesser-known products (meat, cattle food, and ice cream). Another important commonality was that the two companies shared a key customer: the housewife.

The Lever Brothers Company in America, which kept its name, was among Unilever's most successful subsidiaries. This was due in part to advertising, which effectively alerted American consumers to a series of new menaces.[23] In 1930, a Lever Brothers advertisement promised consumers that Lifebuoy soap would 'protect' them from the social disgrace of 'dishpan hands', and 'B.O.', short for body odour (Fig.75).[24] Similarly, Lux detergent

75 Lifebuoy ad, *New York News*, January 1951.

promised to prevent 'undie odor' with an ad admonishing, 'She never omits her Daily Bath, yet wears underthings a second day.' As a result of these anti-odour sales pitches, Lever Brothers' business boomed. They had effectively created demand for their own products by magnifying the insecurities of their target audience.

The man responsible for these ads was Lever Brothers' head of US operations, Francis Countway, whose keen understanding of American culture and marketing led to a long run as president, from 1912 to 1946. By the 1930s three giants made up the American soap industry oligopoly: Proctor & Gamble, Colgate and Palmolive-Peet, and Lever Brothers. Together they controlled 80 per cent of the national soap market. Lever's success peaked in the early 1930s, when they made substantial advancement over Proctor & Gamble. After 1933, Lever encountered tougher competition due to that firm's launch of synthetic detergents like Dreft in 1933 and Drene in 1934, both of which were more effective than solid soap in regions with hard water. In 1944 the three competitors were reduced to two, when Lever acquired Colgate and Palmolive-Peet toothpaste company Pepsodent, where Charles Luckman was president.

In the 1940s, as Francis Countway's tenure was ending, Lever Brothers' American business experienced a downturn, due not only to the competition introduced by synthetic detergents but also as a result of its own managerial problems, which created an ineffective workforce. Although Countway was a brilliant marketer, his management skills proved inadequate. Brothers Laurence and Geoffrey Heyworth, co-chairmen of the Lever Brothers enterprise, sought to improve the situation as well as usher new blood into the company. They summoned the 34-year-old Luckman to London where they vetted him and eventually offered him the job of president of Lever Brothers at the American headquarters in Cambridge, Massachusetts.

Charles Luckman, 'jet-propelled wonder boy of U.S. sales promotion', became president of Lever Brothers America on 1 July 1946.[25] Unilever took a particularly hands-off approach to managing its foreign operations. Luckman had a keen sense for management (as well as a natural talent for sales) and brought a much-needed fresh approach

to the company. Business, however, was not his first passion: his boyhood dream, which had been interrupted by the Great Depression, was of becoming an architect. Luckman studied architecture at the University of Illinois, graduating at the height of the economic downturn. Unable to find work in architecture, Luckman took a job at Colgate and Palmolive-Peet. His drawing skills led to a job as a draughtsman within the advertising department, at $20 a week. Thus began his 'two-decade detour in the marketplace of business'.[26] Luckman told himself, 'In six months when the depression is over, I'll be going back to architecture'.[27] However, the depression lasted rather longer than expected, and the lucrative salary, which supported his growing family, further delayed his return.

At Colgate and Palmolive-Peet, Luckman turned an opportunity into a career. He went beyond selling the product to 'merchandising' it. His first effort with Palmolive soap combined engaging displays with strategic pricing placed in grocery stores. Signs read, 'Palmolive Soap 10 cents each; Special Sale Today; 3 bars for 27 cents while they last.'[28] This created the desired effect – selling more, faster, and for more profit. While advertising moved the customer toward the product, merchandising moved the product toward the customer. He understood that the scope of merchandising was larger than advertising's, and he was soon transferred to the sales department. In 1935 Luckman's success at Colgate and Palmolive-Peet led to a promotion to sales manager of the Pepsodent Company, where his marketing techniques were credited with quadrupling profits.[29] By the age of 30, Luckman had become president of Pepsodent.[30]

In June 1944, Lever Brothers bought out Pepsodent for $66 per share. Luckman owned 15 per cent of the company stock, which he had bought at $6 per share. This deal made Luckman a millionaire, and it put Lever Brothers in a better position to battle its chief American competitor, Proctor & Gamble. When Luckman took over the post of president in 1946, he faced many obstacles to his future success at the company. In addition to inheriting a company that had begun to lag in sales, its middle management was riddled with nepotism: 89 per cent of the employees (an unusually high number) had relatives working within the company. As a result, one of Luckman's first major tasks was to initiate a massive layoff. While this was a necessary action mandated by the Lever Brothers chairmen in Britain, it made him extremely unpopular. Luckman would learn that 'if you fired one, you would have problems with the relative.'[31] This purge would become an indicator of other tumultuous events in Luckman's early tenure as president. Architecture once again entered Luckman's professional life, as his leadership at Lever Brothers required him to take on the role of client representative for a new US headquarters.

Architects

The ups and downs of Luckman's first few years at Lever Brothers caused the head office, Unilever Ltd., much concern. As a result, in 1949 it hired the Chicago-based business and real estate consultant George Fry to conduct a study of the US headquarters. Based on Fry's findings, Unilever would make some significant changes. Through Fry's connection with Nathaniel Owings, a partner of Skidmore, Owings & Merrill, the Chicago-based firm was hired to design a new headquarters for Lever Brothers in New York City.

Nathaniel Owings was a self-professed 'huckster': the type of architect who hatched big ideas but relied on others to execute them.[32] Born in Indianapolis, Owings credited his interest in architecture to witnessing 'the miracle of cathedrals'.[33] In the summer of 1920, he won a trip to the World Boy Scout Jamboree in London. While touring France on this trip, the 17-year-old visited Chartres Cathedral, Mont-Saint Michel, and Notre Dame de Paris. After receiving his architecture degree from Cornell University in 1927 he moved to New York to begin work at York and Sawyer, whom Owings described as the 'classicists of their day'.[34]

Owings's younger sister Eloise was married to Louis Skidmore; the two had met on a 1929 trip to Europe, she with her mother studying fine arts and he on a Rotch Travelling Scholarship. In a quick turn of events, the young Skidmore became head of design at the 1933 Century of Progress International Exposition in Chicago, and

he invited his new brother-in-law to join him.[35] Like Owings, Skidmore was from Indiana. His interest in architecture began as a young man, but he studied electrical engineering instead. After graduation, he served in World War I with the Army Air Corps in Liverpool. While stationed there, he visited Gilbert Scott's Gothic Revival Liverpool Cathedral, then under construction. Like Owings, Skidmore was also deeply inspired by the dramatic architecture of European cathedrals. After the war, Skidmore began studying architecture at the Boston Architectural School. He subsequently transferred to Massachusetts Institute of Technology, graduating in 1924.

Technological innovation was the theme of Century of Progress, offering the public hope as they emerged out of the prolonged Depression. The 1933 exposition portrayed modernity largely in the form of Art Deco architecture. This formed a stark contrast to Chicago's previous vision – the 1893 World's Columbian Exposition – whose Beaux-Arts architecture linked American progress to the classical past. Companies represented in the exposition sought to use design to distinguish the virtues of their products and services.[36] Skidmore and Owings explained to company heads that, 'the building dollar could also be an advertising dollar; that architecture could be an expressive idea as well as weather protective.'[37] From early on, Skidmore and Owings appealed to their clients' business and advertising interests. At the same time, they created room for their own architectural interests.

Skid's Boys

In 1935, one year after the hard work of designing and managing the Century of Progress International Exposition had ended, Skidmore and Owings agreed 'out loud, in words, the final agreement creating the firm of Skidmore and Owings'.[38] 'Skid and I', recalled Owings, 'pledged our lives to share and share alike – to offer a multi-disciplined service competent to design and build the multiplicity of shelters needed for man's habitat. We would build only in the vernacular of our own age.'[39] Although disavowing eclectic architecture, Skidmore and

Owings's aspirations sprang from their common passion for cathedrals. It was more than just the physical attributes of Gothic architecture – monumentality, openness, and light – that inspired them: it was also the process that led to it. Owings wrote, 'We felt we knew how to build a modern "Gothic Builders Guild" practice.'[40]

Owings outlined the means by which the new firm's goals would be achieved: 'Through combining group practice and good design, social change, [and] showmanship, we would marinate our architectural demands in sound economics to meet the criteria of our doubting critics – who didn't believe that one could have both economy and aesthetics – with proof that they were the same.'[41] Indeed, their particular skill of combining economy and aesthetics would propel the firm to become one of the largest in the world.

On 1 January 1936, Skidmore and Owings opened their first office in Chicago. Set against the backdrop of the economic depression, the first few years were a struggle. They cultivated the contacts they had made through the Century of Progress project. In these early days, the firm ran like a typical small office. Architect Ambrose Richardson, who was hired in 1937 in Chicago, recalled his job as varied: doing renderings, answering the phone when the secretary was at lunch, filing drawings, passing out the evening mail, doing some small design jobs, and running errands.[42] Soon, a New York office was opened literally 'on paper', because a client would not guarantee a commission without proof that Skidmore and Owings had a New York office.[43] The partners created a false letterhead with the office address of Joseph Urban and Otto Teegen, their former colleagues from the Chicago World's Fair project. The trick worked, and soon an actual office materialised in New York, with Louis Skidmore as the resident partner.[44]

The New York office, headed by Skidmore, was an assembly of specialists that together formed a strong whole. Skidmore hired the core architects that would run the New York office for the next 30 years. The stable of dynamic and productive young men became known as 'Skid's Boys'. Each contributed a specialised skill: Robert W. Cutler (1905–1993) focused on hospitals; J. Walter Severinghaus (1905–1987) had experience in housing; William S. Brown (1909–1999) was

an expert in prefabricated housing; and Gordon Bunshaft (1909–1990) served as a designer.

'Tomorrow's Office Building'

After months of observing the Lever Brothers' operations, real estate consultant George Fry recommended closing the Cambridge office and opening a new headquarters, due to 'complex circumstances' which had developed. In truth, the office was in turmoil as a result of Charles Luckman's first few tumultuous years as president. On New Year's Eve 1949, Nathaniel Owings and George Fry celebrated together at the Chicago Club. The two drinking buddies played a game of craps that ended with Owings winning all of Fry's cash. Owings returned Fry's money, and in turn, Fry was so moved that he asked him to help in 'a confidential matter of business'.[45] This led to SOM being considered for a major office headquarters commission for Lever Brothers, Fry's client.

In the summer of 1949, a series of preliminary meetings led to the provisional hiring of SOM as designers for Lever Brothers' new headquarters. The meetings were held in private so that Lever employees would not know about the impending move. The client's identity was even withheld, initially, from the architects. At an early meeting with the client, Owings presented a schematic 'toy'-like design model.[46] SOM's schematic design model was based on 'Tomorrow's Office Building', an architectural prototype first conceived in 1946, and one that Nathaniel Owings had previously pitched to building owners and managers at the 1949 National Convention of Office Building Owners and Managers in Hot Springs, Virginia.[47]

As a showman who managed to 'irritate, titillate, disturb and unbalance the status quo', Owings promoted the strikingly simple, modern building design.[48] 'Tomorrow's Office Building' had received serious attention at the 1946 North Central Conference of building owners and managers (Fig.76). Owings's slab tower promised to create a memorable identity; the building would thus provide advertising value to its managers and owners. His speech to building owners and managers pointed out the design's individuality:

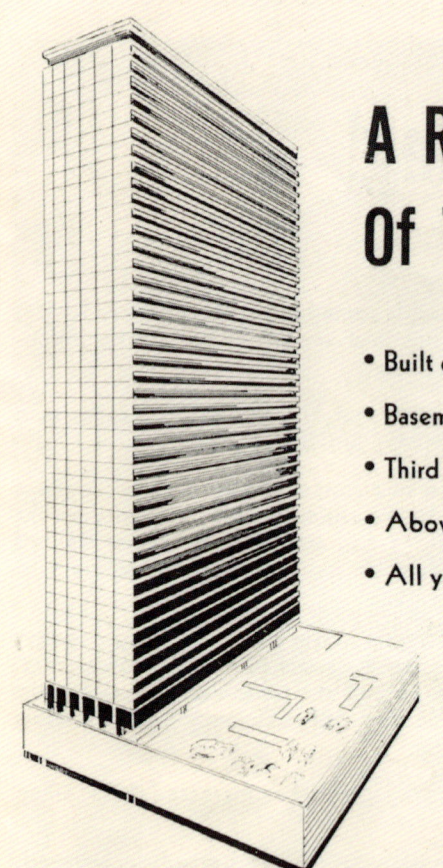

A Radically New Conception Of Tomorrow's Office Building

- Built on a site eight times larger than the floor plan of the building above the third floor
- Basement, second and third floors used for parking
- Third floor level an outdoor park with real grass and trees
- Above third floor a straight shaft, no setbacks
- All year air conditioning, sealed sash, acoustical ceilings, permanent sunshade controls
- Exterior materials requiring no painting or tuckpointing
- Windows washed with vertical type of automatic squeegee run on tracks

By NATHANIEL A. OWINGS
Architect, Skidmore, Owings and Merrill
New York, Chicago and San Francisco

76   Nathaniel A. Owings, 'A Radically New Conception of Tomorrow's Office Building',
National Real Estate and Building Journal, January 1948.

Our environment is established. We are self-contained. Because of our size we are clearly identifiable as a single important unit. We have individuality. We have character! Our office building is a clear simple rectangular shaft rising from a pedestal or base, free of obstructions on all sides permitting perpetuity, lifting, air, and view.[49]

He approached postwar urban density in a new way. 'Satellite and decentralized business centers grow up', Owings argued, 'not necessarily because the central ones are going down, but because the central ones have reached their maximum capacities, traffic-wise, parking-wise and merchandise volume-wise. This means, to us, that the busy centres of cities are here to stay and that our office building must be at that point.'[50] This statement demonstrates Nathaniel Owings doing what he did best – selling his design and its urban site. In doing so, he attempted to counteract the trend at the time which was the construction of research facilities and insurance company headquarters in outlying parts of cities.

Owings's argument was analogous to urbanist Jane Jacobs's sentiments about cities. She pointed out that doing business in the 1940s and 1950s benefited from the kind of 'pedestrian proximity' that only dense cities like New York or Chicago could provide.[51] In fact, Jacobs would later praise Lever House's design in discussions of the New York City office boom.[52] Like Jacobs, Owings recognised that, while there was a trend of businesses moving to sprawling suburban headquarters, it was an important urban and sociological statement to remain in a city.

In an article for the *National Real Estate and Building Journal*, Owings urged business owners to buck the trend of moving their offices to the suburbs. Office buildings, he argued, did not need to be 'dark, grimy, dismal canyons of stone'.[53] Instead, his proposal for a new 'tomorrow's office building' offered what the typical masonry office buildings of the 1930s and 1940s did not. 'Tomorrow's Office Building' offered not only advertising value with its striking modern design, but many desirable amenities for employees including plenty of daylight, air-conditioning with sealed windows, outdoor green roof spaces, and parking.[54]

'Tomorrow's Office Building' was composed of two slabs raised on pilotis – one vertical slab and one horizontal base slab. Owings envisioned the glazed and louvred elevations as composed of prefabricated combination window and spandrel units with air-conditioners. He pointed out that the prefabricated glass panels could be literally 'snapped' onto the building frame, and that a wider scope of permissible materials could be used for the spandrel material including aluminium, stainless steel, or even plastic. These materials would be low maintenance, requiring no painting, and the windows would be 'washed with vertical type of automatic squeegee run on tracks'.[55]

'Tomorrow's Office Building', according to Owings, was the prototype for Lever House. 'Lever House was built in 1952 but goes back to 1946 in Chicago, where I arranged a debate with George Bailey, on "the Office Building of the Future [Tomorrow's Office Building]."' 'The idea', Owings wrote, 'lay flat and moribund until George Fry and

I got drunk together on New Year's Eve two years later.'[56] Indeed, the design's key elements – including the dual slab composition, pilotis, aspirations for prefabricated windows, spandrel units, and proposed window-washing equipment – clearly show that 'Tomorrow's Office Building' was the genesis of the 1949 Lever House design. With 'Tomorrow's Office Building', Owings spoke the language of business.

At the same time, the Lever House design was clearly influenced by architectural sources. Gordon Bunshaft would dismiss the influences, but they are undeniable.[57] The pilotis imply a Corbusian influence. The Le Corbusier-designed United Nations Building was under construction just blocks away. Lever House's glazing of the entire ground floor implies a Miesian influence. At the time, Mies van der Rohe's built work was present and important with the Lakeshore Drive Apartments in Chicago, designed and constructed in 1948–1951. Also, a retrospective of Mies's work opened at the Museum of Modern Art in New York in 1947. Lever House's design countered the status quo of urban office buildings with its speculative nature, and by taking Le Corbusier and Mies's work as precedents.

New York, 'Where the advertising was'

The 'confrontations' and 'linkages' of a dense urban environment were precisely the reason that the president of Lever Brothers' American operation, Charles Luckman, sought to relocate the company.[58] The final decision to move to New York, rather than Chicago, was motivated by a related concern: to have advertising firms in local proximity. Lever Brothers' reorganisation left it with a deficit in its marketing department. Luckman needed to recruit employees with experience in sales, advertising, and merchandising, a task best accomplished in New York, where 'ad men' were in large supply. Company heads were also convinced that they would be able to work more effectively with their advertising agencies in New York if the frequent and immediate meetings between these consultants and Lever management could be conducted in person.[59] Indeed, Lever Brothers would become one of the first and largest television advertisers at this time.

By the late summer of 1947, Lever Brothers decided to move to New York City. Although the potential site in Chicago was desirable, New York had the concentration of advertising firms needed to handle the company's promotional activities. A Lever Brothers executive made the revealing comment: 'The price one pays for soap is 89 per cent advertising . . . and the advertising agencies of America were there [New York].'[60] After Lever Brothers decided on New York for its headquarters, Fry revealed the client's identity to the architects. At his first meeting with Luckman in New York, Owings brought both Louis Skidmore and newly made partner Gordon Bunshaft.[61] SOM was officially offered the job – their first office building commission – which they eagerly accepted, having been turned down previously for three other office building commissions. Luckman considered their lack of experience with the office building typology an advantage. 'Frankly', he explained, 'the main reason I hired your firm was because you've never done an office building. This will help you keep your minds open to some of the ideas and concepts I want for the new Lever House.'[62] Their inexperience also enabled Luckman to pay SOM a mere three per cent fee for the job, which was lower than the standard fee schedule set by the American Institute of Architects. To add insult to injury, the bargain deal had another condition: Raymond Loewy & Associates would design the interiors. This particular collaboration would prove awkward, least of all because of Bunshaft's disdain for his former employer.

During negotiations for the building lease at 390 Park Avenue, Owings presented a fateful design change. He proposed that the slab tower be oriented perpendicular to Park Avenue, rather than parallel. According to Owings, an east–west tower orientation would improve both advertising value and exposure of light. He explained,

> The conventional way to have placed the tower would have been parallel to the Avenue. We placed it perpendicular to it to provide north and south orientation, considered ideal exposure for offices. When placed perpendicular to the street,

the tower's visibility gains greater prominence, the mass is much greater and, in perspective, the building appears more graceful and slender.[63]

Changing the orientation would accentuate the office building's advertising value. Yet Bunshaft did not agree, arguing, 'You expose the adjoining buildings, the side walls, the ugly stuff, and the empty space in between, the back yards.'[64] These aspects bothered the architect so much that he had an additional design study made in which the office tower faced Park Avenue. This exploratory design would have hidden the adjoining buildings; still, its disadvantage was that people working in the building would have had a close view of the adjoining building walls. The planned office tower thus remained perpendicular to Park Avenue.

On 16 September 1949, Lever Brothers (the American subsidiary was named as such, even though the parent company was Unilever) signed a 40-year lease with Goelet Estates. Lever Brothers, with the help of Fry and SOM, searched for companies that would be interested in financing the building construction, eventually finding the Metropolitan Life Insurance Company. While the lot was initially too small to allow efficient floor sizes with 25 per cent site coverage due to the zoning ordinance, an additional 3,300 square feet of land was purchased at the west side, making the total square footage 83,000. A 1916 New York City zoning provision permitted a building to rise without setbacks provided that its footprint covered only one-quarter of the lot. Its purpose was to prevent massive buildings from blocking light and air to the pedestrian street level. The building would take three years to complete.[65] Design development and construction drawings were executed over the next ten months, from the end of September 1949 to 1 July 1950.

Gordon Bunshaft

With the perpendicular slab in place, Gordon Bunshaft took over as design principal and led the Lever House design to fruition. Bunshaft had started working at SOM in 1936, after two short-lived architectural stints at Edward Durell Stone's and Raymond Loewy's New York offices. He had enjoyed working for Stone on a hotel project in Honolulu but was let go when work ceased. Stone then recommended Bunshaft to industrial and interior designer Raymond Loewy, who offered him a job. He took the job but found the experience unsatisfactory. Bunshaft left Loewy's office after just a few months, stating flatly that the office 'didn't do architecture. It did interiors and products'.[66] To Bunshaft, 'Raymond Loewy was a phony. He's put a gold line on a cigarette or on a railroad train, and he'd get a fee for it. It was a very casual place. . . . [T]hey used to have tea dancing around ten in the morning.'[67] Desperate, Bunshaft made a plea to his old boss, Stone, bluntly telling him he couldn't stand it there.[68] Stone made a call to his friend, architect Louis Skidmore, who was looking to hire.

In August 1936, just months after SOM had been established, Bunshaft interviewed with Skidmore and was hired. He became one of 'Skid's Boys', part of the founding core of architects, with his particular expertise being architectural design. Bunshaft would become the design partner in charge of many of SOM's most critically acclaimed buildings in addition to Lever House, including Manufacturers Trust Company Bank in New York, 1951–1954, and Connecticut General Insurance Company in Bloomfield, Connecticut, 1954–1957, among many others. Up until 1960, as architectural historian Nicolas Adams has stated, Bunshaft 'controlled' design at SOM, which meant that while he was not the designer of every SOM project, his strong opinions on most projects were usually accepted.[69] His life-long career with SOM began in 1937 and would end when he retired in 1979. In September 1949, when Bunshaft became involved with the Lever House design, he had recently become a design partner at SOM.

Lever House Design

'I'm sick . . . of these goddamn liars', Bunshaft later declared, referring to Owings, Luckman, and the narratives both crafted about the Lever House design.[70] Of the three accounts, Bunshaft's would be the most comprehensive, informed by his

oversight of the general, day-to-day design and construction of the building. Bunshaft credited Owings with landing the commission. 'At MIT', Bunshaft recalled, 'there was an old French professor, the head man, who said there were three important things about doing a building. There is, one, getting the job, two, getting the job, and three, getting the job. So Owings has that credit.'[71]

Another major player, according to Bunshaft, was Charles Luckman. Luckman, who served as the client, brought to the table an unconventional idea of keeping the ground floor of Lever House free of retail tenants. To all others involved in the project, this seemed like an absurd and unprofitable idea since retail facilities on the ground floors of commercial buildings often were the highest revenue generators on a per-square foot basis. But Lever House boldly broke that trend. 'He [Luckman] wanted a building to identify Lever', Bunshaft said, '[and] they were not interested in making bucks out of stores or renting extra space.'[72] Without Luckman's support behind this idea, the base of Lever House would not have been designed the way it was.

Also instrumental, according to Bunshaft, was SOM project architect Manny Turano. Though there were other SOM employees working on the project, Bunshaft singled out the talented and hardworking design assistant for praise. Turano was one of 'the others' – the architectural staff – who did most of the actual design and production of the buildings.[73] '[T]he others', Bunshaft explained, 'take care of all the headaches', while he remained 'in charge of design'.[74] Yet clearly Bunshaft appreciated Turano's efforts, crediting him with making 'some beautiful drawings of the proportions and the mullion system and all that'.[75]

The fourth key contributor was William Brown, the administrative design partner at SOM. Working jointly with Bunshaft, Brown was the person who managed the project. Brown's most significant contribution was to supervise the curtain wall effort and, in general, to manage the technical achievements of Lever House. The curtain wall, Bunshaft said, 'forced the glass industry to develop a spandrel glass and to find and design an outside window washer. That was the first real one that worked in the world.'[76] While the design looked 'neat' and 'simple', Brown explained that its realisation actually entailed a challenging set of 'technical problems that had to be solved'.[77] Compounding this achievement was the fact that a 'comparatively inexperienced and unqualified staff' would solve those problems.[78]

Bunshaft's account of Lever House's development was just that: his own interpretation. Although he had spent the most time of anyone on the project, he told only one side of the story. Both Owings and Luckman made more substantial contributions than Bunshaft would ever acknowledge. Although Bunshaft had knowledge of Owings's several meetings with George Fry, he never formally acknowledged Owings's early design contribution:

> Owings told me he took along with him a small toy plastic rectangle, a little box. It could have been like the size of a pack of playing cards, but just plastic with some little lines on it for floors.[79]

Bunshaft disparaged Owings's 'Tomorrow's Office Building' model as a toy, thus diminishing the latter's contribution to the Lever House design.

An 'Architecture of Bureaucracy'

The discrepancies among the Lever House narratives were a consequence not only of the individual recollections of its design contributors but also of its corporate organisation. In the Lever House commission, corporate structure defined the client's company as well as the architectural firm designing its headquarters. In comparison to the earlier Johnson Wax case study in which Frank Lloyd Wright was a singular voice over his apprentices for a family-run company, the Lever House case study offers a large corporate architecture firm, designing for an even larger corporate client. This shows change and evolution in both corporations and architectural practices between the two world wars. While SOM was not the first large architectural firm to design large office buildings for large corporate clients – a number of firms, including D.H. Burnham & Co. and Smith, Hinchman & Grylls, had accomplished this far earlier in the mid- to late-19th centuries – its

Lever House design became the built prototype for many future designs of the firm, which were run more efficiently because of the lessons learned.

Incorporated in 1936, SOM cultivated what architectural historian Nicholas Adams has called 'a collective enterprise'.[80] SOM employed recent graduates from architecture school. These young designers modelled and drew building designs, developing them until the point of construction drawings necessary for building. These young men and women were encouraged to specialise according to their natural skills. Some architects focused on project management or programming while others were responsible for structures or materials.[81] An employee would develop an expertise in a specific subject and be assigned to work on that particular aspect of multiple projects, in any one of its three offices.

SOM grew to become decentralised and operated from multiple branches. The firm's services were broad, providing engineering, landscape design, urban planning, and interior design services. SOM opened a third office in San Francisco in 1947. By 1952, SOM had 14 partners and more than 1,000 employees. What made SOM's structure particularly corporate was that it was both departmental and hierarchical. It was run by a partnership, with the primary organisational division existing between the partners and the architects.[82] At least two partners, tasked with distinct responsibilities, supervised each project: a design partner who defined the design approach, and a management partner who oversaw the business interests of the firm. SOM defined a new architectural approach to teamwork, while providing comprehensive design services.

SOM's secret to well-organised, large-scale architecture was to cultivate specialists who together possessed collective strength. Through a structure similar to the corporations who were their clients, SOM trained their employees as specialists, then assigned them to different projects. The firm was able to operate at an economy of scale, reducing the cost per project through increased production, realised through operational efficiencies. According to William Brown, the story of SOM is actually the story of 'a few hardworking and idealistic individuals who found that together they could give a scope to their ambitions that they could not accomplish alone'. Indeed, in 1947 Henry-Russell Hitchcock praised SOM's work as an 'architecture of bureaucracy', asserting that the firm was 'animated by two disciplines . . . the discipline of modern architecture and the discipline of American organizational methods'.

In describing the firm's designs, Hitchcock emphasised 'organizational genius, which can establish a fool-proof system of rapid and complete plan production'.[83] He likened bureaucratic architectural organisation to a precision of parts coming together into a finished product on the assembly line. In contrast to the way Johnson Wax headquarters was designed by a strong-willed individual whose apprentices realised his vision, the relatively unknown architects at SOM designed Lever House as a collective, represented only by the initials of the three founding partners. In a reversal, Lever House's architectural form came into the limelight, while its architects took a backseat.

Despite suggestions to the contrary, SOM did not consider itself a firm of bureaucratic architects. Instead, Nathaniel Owings, the firm's resident impresario, considered himself 'a catalyst'.[84] In this role, Owings utilised his social skills to achieve 'great architecture designed by great architects'.[85] He thought of himself as the key individual who provided the groundwork for genius architects.[86] Owings was an organiser of people; a man who could get things done by pulling together the complex forces of clients, contractors, planning commissioners, and other building and design specialists.

In this role, Owings's outsized personality served him well. He appeared on the cover of the popular magazine, *Time*, in August 1968. *Time* magazine's editors wrote of Owings: 'In bridging the gap between aesthete and politician or businessman, nothing comes in more handy than a touch of boisterous good humour and the forthright logic of the black-dirt belt of Indiana from which Nat Owings sprang.'[87] In his autobiography, *The Spaces In Between: An Architect's Journey*, Owings described himself in the following way:

> My contributions have been – and still are – in the preparation of an environment within which others might create, and operate fully within the structure, framework or armature of SOM.

. . . I as an individual cannot point to any major building for which I am solely responsible. But I can point to individual, brilliant architects like Gordon Bunshaft, Charles Bassett, and Walter Netsch who are products of this entity.

Instead of operating as a singular architect designing signature building forms, Owings's contributions were made at the level of upper management and were ultimately responsible for the designs that the firm produced. In the structure of a large corporate architectural practice, this hierarchy was defining and vitally important. In this bureaucratic framework, SOM realised Lever House.

'Verticals and Horizontals'

When, in September 1949, Bunshaft and his team of young architects began to design Lever House, Luckman charged the architects with developing a building that would serve to identify the Lever Brothers corporation. He asked for a distinguished building devoted entirely to 800 to 1,000 Lever employees and their services. Bunshaft's first step toward creating an architecture of identity was pragmatic. Most real estate developers considered the 1916 New York City zoning provision a hindrance as it prevented them from maximising rentable space: Bunshaft and his team turned it into an opportunity. He desired a pure form; his solution was to respect the ordinance and restrict the size of this prismatic slab on the site. The law also limited a building's height: 108 to 130 feet, or 10 to 12 floors, along the avenues (in this case, Park Avenue), and 85 feet, or seven floors, on streets (here, 53rd and 54th Streets).[88]

Eventually, as designed, Lever House covered even less than its allowable lot size, leading the architects to wonder whether it was 'mad that such a small sized building [would be] sited on [such] valuable real estate'.[89] But the design made the tower slab look far slimmer and ultimately sleeker than other towers built in New York City and elsewhere. Its strikingly minimal use of prime real estate would become one of Lever House's most distinguishing features. Its distinctive massing satisfied the client's desire for creating a strong architectural identity and what we understand today as architectural branding.

To Bunshaft, the Lever House overall design was a composition of 'verticals and horizontals'.[90] The 18-storey slab tower comprised the vertical plane. Each floor contained 8,700 square feet of office space, allocated to the various companies that made up Unilever's American holdings. (Luckman insisted that the building be exclusively occupied by Lever Brothers: 'I did not want tenants in the new building; it was to house Lever and only Lever.'[91]) The slab configuration allowed the architects to reduce the size of the building's central core and created light-filled, open spaces. The architects created highly desirable private offices, which ringed the perimeter of the building.

The most innovative aspect of the vertical slab was its orientation perpendicular to Park Avenue. Its massing was composed of two forms: a horizontal slab floating above the ground level, and a vertical slab, both clad in a novel, blue-green glass curtain wall. Buildings on Park and other avenues generally maintained a consistent street frontage with their front elevations. Lever House's perpendicular vertical slab was detailed to appear as if it were floating above the horizontal mass. This was enabled by the design of a 'notch', which was articulated as a deep shadow recess at the third-floor level, where the cafeteria overlooked a landscaped roof terrace.[92]

The horizontal element of the building comprised a 22,000-square-foot rectangular slab. This element housed office support, including mail and stock rooms, as well as business machines. The slab was raised one storey above the street on columns and was punctured to create a courtyard below. On the recessed third floor was the employee dining room, which opened onto a terrace for leisure activities, with plantings and a shuffleboard court imprinted onto the paving along the southern edge. The terrace allowed a continuous visual link between both slabs of the buildings and also permitted daylight to enter the ground floor plaza. The tower slab was located 40 feet from the northern property line. This positioning achieved the architects' vision of asymmetrical volumes, while adhering to zoning laws restricting the tower allowance on the side street. The 'verticals and horizontals' of Bunshaft's massing made a striking image in the urban landscape. An image of the building became a logo for Lever Brothers and was used as the letterhead on company correspondence.

'Stilts with no shops'

Luckman advocated enthusiastically for keeping the ground floor clear of retail space, and as a result Lever House was built accordingly. The president of American operations believed that the inclusion of shops would 'make Lever unrecognizable'.[93] It was such a distinctive idea that when Louis Skidmore saw the design model in the SOM offices, he rebuked, 'You'll never get away without stores. It's crazy.'[94] Bunshaft replied, 'Well, it's the whole goddamn design.'[95] Skidmore insisted, so Bunshaft inserted retail spaces. When Luckman came into the office for the next meeting, he asked, 'What happened to it? What's that stuff in the bottom, Skidmore?'[96] Skidmore replied, 'Stores. You've got to have them.'[97] To Skidmore's answer, Luckman replied, 'You've ruined the whole design.'[98]

Bunshaft applauded Luckman's audacity in going against the typical businessman's inclination toward profit: 'If [Luckman had] gone along with that, the building would have been nothing.'[99] Gordon Bunshaft was not the kind of architect that involved himself with theory. Instead, he prided himself on the use of practical parameters. In Lever House, 'stilts with no shops' was 'as far as the philosophy went'.[100] In the 1950s, the Park Avenue neighbourhood in which Lever House was sited was residential, not commercial. According to Owings, an atypical block of commercial stores had previously occupied the site of Lever House: 'On that particular vacant lot on Park Avenue between 54th and 55th Streets on the west side of the street there had been some shops, what were called "tax-payers": one story, tacky.'[101] This kind of commercial environment was exactly what Luckman believed would distract the public from recognising the character of the building's owner, Lever Brothers. By building a progressive, owner-occupied office building in an upscale residential section of Park Avenue, Owings argued, Lever House would be a trendsetter for businesses to relocate to midtown.[102]

Lever House's ground floor plaza was unique for New York at the time.[103] Privately owned but open to the public, it established a precedent that would become widely emulated – perhaps most notably by Mies van der Rohe's neighbouring Seagram Building of 1958. Lever House and Seagram's catercornered plazas inspired an appreciation for urban public space that other office buildings' owners were quick to capitalise on. In 1961 New York City enacted a major revision of its 1916 Zoning Resolution that offered incentives for developers to install such spaces. Soon, Luckman would need to convince the Unilever leaders of the value in 'stilts with no shops'.

Unveiling the Model

While the SOM architects developed the Lever House design, Charles Luckman travelled to London to present a model of the schematic design to the 24 English and Dutch directors of Unilever to obtain their approval. Luckman planned to present the 'sparkling and beautiful' presentation model to the council of his bosses 'without any fanfare', intending to 'underplay it'.[104] He would rely on 'the dramatic effect of this remarkable building' to 'speak for itself'.[105] He brought the glass-and-aluminium architectural model into the boardroom of the London headquarters covered by a black satin cloth. When the time came, he slowly unveiled the model, announcing quietly, 'Here it is.'[106] The gleaming model was met with a silence which Luckman attributed to shock. He waited as the minutes went by; no one looked up or said a word. Finally, the Vice-Chairman of Unilever, Arthur Hartog, said with his heavy Dutch accent, 'Shuck, it's dif-f-f-er-unt!'[107] The other board members laughed, and Luckman went to work selling the building design.

Luckman knew that he would have the most difficulty in selling the idea of not including income-generating stores or banks at the street level to Lever Brothers executives.[108] He argued that although the building only used half of the buildable space allowed by law on that site, it was in fact utilising the airspace around the building to its full effect, by drawing valuable attention to the sleek lines of the glass and steel structure. The argument Luckman felt was most compelling was conveyed in the language of economic profit:

> I brought to the meeting only a single sheet of paper on which were three columns of figures. The first column showed the amount of income we would derive if we put stores, shops, and banks at ground level; the second showed how relatively little profit, after taxes, we would make after adding the potential ground-floor income to our regular Lever Brothers company income; the third showed the cost of a page of advertising in various magazines and newspapers.[109]

Though Luckman's figures needed work, his point was clear – that the path towards higher profits was advertising, not income generated from ground level real estate. By advertising, Luckman meant the architecture of the corporate headquarters design. At the meeting, Luckman also declared, 'If you let me do what I want, I will get millions and millions of dollars of free advertising for Lever Brothers from around the world.'[110] The discussion went on for seven hours, ending in the unanimous acceptance of the design.

The secret plan for the construction of a new headquarters in New York City would be revealed only after the Unilever board approved the design. When the approval became official, Luckman planned a comprehensive announcement on Tuesday, 1 October 1949, at 3pm, to 22 sales offices, seven manufacturing plants, all laboratories and subsidiaries, and the headquarters in Boston. To mitigate the shock, Luckman had employee booklets made, offering information about New York and the move itself. These 'guidebooks', as he called them, 'spelled out the reasons, methods, procedures, and arrangements involved in the move'.[111]

Media attention from the *New York Times*, *Time* magazine, and the *New York Herald Tribune* commented on the drama of the secrecy. *Time* magazine reported:

> Charles Luckman, no man to tip his hand to real estate speculators, went about his project with about as much secrecy as if he were making

atom bombs out of soap chips. He set up several dummy corporations in New York, Boston and Chicago, which began negotiating for parcels of land. . . . Lever executives who masterminded the deals used twenty unlisted phones, talked in code words and numbers instead of names and carefully tore up all scribbled notes of phone conversations. . . . Up until press time, no words which might tip off appeared in the text [of the guidebooks]. (Dummy phrases were substituted.) At the last moment, the correct words were inserted, said a Lever executive breathlessly, 'by a single trusted typesetter.'[112]

The design of Lever House was cloaked in the drama of Lever Brothers' reorganisation and move to New York. At the centre of the maelstrom was Charles Luckman, SOM's client. As such, the most significant contribution of the new president was not pecuniary but rather architectural. Meanwhile, the SOM architects continued developing Lever House in their New York office, designing the building's blue-green glass curtain wall facade.

'Thin skin'

The curtain wall of Lever House – its 'thin skin' – was 'the main point of [the] building', according to Bunshaft. 'Thin skin was in the air', and 'doing it at that time' brought recognition to the firm. At mid-century, architects were trying to move beyond the heaviness of masonry facades toward lighter construction, for reasons of both aesthetics and economy.[113] At the time, all-glass skyscrapers such as Mies's 1921 Friedrichstrasse skyscraper were not yet prevalent. To be sure, all-glass curtain walls had been built in the US, with Willis Polk's Hallidie office building in San Francisco, 1917–1918 and Pietro Belluschi's Equitable Building in Portland, 1945–1948. Lever House's curtain wall, along with the UN Secretariat building, were among the early examples of the glass curtain wall.

'We wanted to do a glass building', Bunshaft matter-of-factly stated 'We wanted to be as avant-garde as possible.'[114] In fact, the curtain wall's visual effects were more progressive and stunning than its designers had anticipated. Reflections of the sky and neighbourhood would appear on Lever House's smooth, blank facade. Fellow architects and critics reported being 'dazzled by the technical excellence and implications of material'[115] (Fig. 72).

SOM's administrative partner, William S. Brown, managed the curtain wall design. He later described the experience as 'a major miracle, as far as I'm concerned':

> While the design was indeed a masterpiece of simplicity, the technical problems that had to be solved were new and were viewed with skepticism by the trade. The preparation of the working drawings was accomplished by a comparatively inexperienced and unqualified staff. There was not yet available that hard core of almost fanatically trained technicians whom we now [in 1970] have and often take for granted![116]

SOM designed a 'homemade version of spandrel' because, according to Bunshaft, there was 'nothing on the market'.[117] The curtain wall created a complete glass envelope, which was achieved by glazing over the spandrel, or area between the ceiling of one storey and the floor of the storey above. The spandrel glass was designed as 'wired glass', a type of glass traditionally used for fireproofing, at the largest size available at the time.[118] These spandrel panes appear as a slightly darker blue-green shade than the windows, as they were painted black from the inside to hide the cinder block firewalls behind them. The architects created a three-inch pocket of air behind the curtain wall because, as Bunshaft points out, 'you also had to have air movement in there'.[119] The double spandrel panels, coupled in the pattern of two rectangles, covered a doubled firewall that masked the floor slabs, radiators, and the suspended ceiling, with its mechanical and electrical ducts. Because it was custom-made, the glass pane 'sizes were odd'.[120] The darker, opaque green-blue glass was held in place by steel mullions with stainless steel trim. Another custom-made aspect of the curtain wall was the design of flaps over the weep holes. These were needed to prevent rainwater from entering.

Lever House was one of the earliest buildings that achieved a complete glass skin, with Wallace

77   Lever House window-washing equipment.

Harrison's contemporaneous United Nations Secretariat building nearby being another one. The UN, Bunshaft stated, was 'designed with blue glass and a homemade spandrel' – the same coloured and heat-resistant Thermopane glass that he would use on Lever House.[121] Aesthetically, the delicate yet striking blue-green colour of Lever House's curtain wall (one of the few tints in which heat-absorbing glass was then available) made the tower memorable.

To present a clean, shiny surface of glass necessary to adequately represent a soap company, the facade would require a high degree of maintenance. SOM assigned architect Kenneth M. Young to specify an existing exterior window-washing machine capable of this scale of operation, but none was available. As a result, SOM designed the mechanical exterior cleaning apparatus, in collaboration with mechanical engineers Jaros, Baum, & Bolles and the Otis Elevator Company.[122] A 10½-foot T-crane suspending a motor-driven gondola ran around the periphery of the roof on railroad tracks. The gondola moved up and down the facade, holding two human window washers (Fig.77). This would become a standard feature of curtain-walled buildings. Washing the facade could be completed in 116 man-hours.[123] Behind the squeaky clean, blue-green, glass facade, Raymond Loewy used colour in his branding strategy for Lever House's interior design.

Merchandised Interiors

Raymond Loewy, the self-proclaimed father of industrial design, possessed the unique skill of designing for commercial appeal. Loewy's collaboration as interior designer of Lever House was preceded by a history of design work for Charles Luckman, both when he was president at Pepsodent and at Lever Brothers in the Cambridge, Massachusetts office. What began as a new package design for the Pepsodent toothpaste carton turned into a long-standing collaboration, engaging Loewy's skills as a graphic, package, and interior designer.[124]

As his client, Luckman described Loewy's approach as two pronged: 'Loewy keeps one eye on the imagination and one eye on the cash register.'[125] Operating from his design principle 'MAYA', an acronym for Most Advanced Yet Acceptable, Loewy sought 'the most advanced product that research can develop and technology can produce'.[126] He explained that his experience with consumers' reactions showed that extreme modern design did not always sell well: 'There seems to be for each individual product (or service, or store, or package, etc.) a critical area at which the consumer's desire for novelty reaches what I might call the shock-zone.'[127]

For Pepsodent, Loewy applied MAYA in his designs for Breeze laundry detergent packaging and a DuPont-made toothbrush. In 1938, when Loewy redesigned the Pepsodent toothpaste package, the design was clean, with an ascetic white exterior and modest script lettering. His design contrasted with the garish red graphics and bold black print of competing toothpaste packages. Through what Loewy called 'streamlining', his marketing strategy gave the product an image of luxury and good taste.[128] Loewy's streamlined aesthetic was just the trend that Frank Lloyd Wright belittled but at the same time incorporated into his design for Johnson Wax in 1936. In the realm of industrial design

for corporate clients, Loewy's streamlining was effective and profitable. His streamlining designs undoubtedly contributed to Pepsodent increasing its sales by 17 per cent during that quarter.[129]

For Lever House's interior design, Loewy used colour as a branding technique. He had learned about the potency of colour in appealing to consumers through his core practice of package design and advertising, anticipating what would later become one of the fundamental components of brand identity. For Loewy, colour was a sales stimulant. For Lever House, he sought to establish a custom all-over background colour, which was aptly named 'Lever House beige'.[130] The greyish beige colour was used for all stock furniture in the general spaces, Venetian blinds, and acoustical ceilings. Loewy chose this particular colour for a number of reasons: it neutralised the cold tone of the light admitted by the blue-green glass windows; it enabled the interiors to read as a uniform tone from the outside; it created less glare and reflection; and it soothed employees' eyes. In his *New Yorker* article, historian of technology, sociologist, and literary critic Lewis Mumford picked up on Loewy's branding colour scheme, noting that even the elevator operators were dressed in dark beige, and he applauded its coherence in identifying the corporation.

Against the neutral Lever House beige, Loewy specified 31 vibrant and contrasting colours throughout the building.[131] He skilfully deployed these colours to give identity to each of the brands housed in Lever Brothers' new offices: these included Lux Soap, Swan, Lifebuoy, Rinso, Silver Dust, Breeze, Surf, Pepsodent, Chlorodent, Harriet Hubbard Ayer Cosmetics, and Good Luck Margarine. The colour schemes of each product brand and their packaging correlated with those of the interior design. As the staff writer explained in an article in *Interiors* magazine, 'Walls, elevator doors and corridors utilized 31 colors, arranged in special identifying schemes for each floor, and matched, when possible, with the particular product schemes to which the floor is devoted.'[132] Mumford also described the appealing effect of the intra-company colour scheme: 'Each floor has its own color scheme, from brisk yellows and delicate hues to a combination – on the floor devoted to the firm's cosmetics – of boudoir pink and eyeshadow lavender . . . I don't know any other building in the city in which so much color has been used with such skill and charm over such a large area.'[133] The heterogeneous mix of interior colours offered a humanising effect. Loewy designed Lever House interiors with a colour-based branding strategy that communicated each product's personality in an effective way.

Unlike PSFS and Johnson Wax, Lever House was not a total work of art, designed consistently from the largest to the smallest scale. Instead, Lever House was realised as a distinct division of labour between architecture and interior design, signalling the specialisation of design professions. In some ways, Loewy's interior design, which featured openness of space and workplace flexibility, synchronised with the modern character of SOM's architectural design. In other ways, the two were at odds.

This was perhaps most apparent in the building's Raymond Loewy-designed lobby. During construction, Loewy designed three glass display units located in the lobby.[134] Each month, a different product from the family of Lever products would be displayed as a 'dramatic' feature. These popular displays were even recommended by taxi drivers to out-of-towners as must-see sites of interest.[135] One Christmas display featured a carousel loaded with 'jolly figures' and various Lever products. These displays encapsulated Loewy's expertise: his design approach was aimed at encouraging consumerism. While it diverged from the abstract modernism of SOM's design, Loewy's carnivalesque displays brought Park Avenue down to earth, to the level of the proverbial American Main Street. Advertising experts considered the lobby displays a great success, providing a cordial welcome to visitors of the building.[136]

Even though Lever House was not consistently designed across all of its different scales, it offers important issues of architectural branding. SOM's sleek, modern design expressed Lever Brothers as progressive and aloof, while Loewy's interior design was colourful and friendly, creating a familiar, even folksy, personality that humanised Lever Brothers. Through a symbiotic relationship, Lever House's architecture restrained while its interiors divulged. The duality of Lever House suggests an example of branding in which architectural form fully represents the corporate client, while at the same time revealing the realities of interdisciplinary collaboration. After ten months, the design team submitted working drawings on 1 July 1950. Construction lasted a year and four months. The building was completed in December 1951 and opened in April 1952. The ground floor plaza design – with elements of sculpture and landscaping, also designed by SOM – would not be executed until 1953.[137]

When its new headquarters opened in April 1952, Lever Brothers' move to New York was complete. Lever House stood out because of its striking forms, as well as its brazen modernity amongst the mostly traditional architecture of Park Avenue; although modernisation of Park Avenue was already underway as a number of speculative office buildings designed by architecture firm Emery Roth & Sons had been constructed there in the late 1940s and early 1950s.[138] Devoid of setbacks, the horizontal and vertical slabs stood out among most high-rise buildings in Manhattan.[139] The building stood 21 storeys (or 302 feet) high, housing 1,200 transferred and new employees. Lever House was the result of a corporate impulse, the pooling of individual skills, and the collaboration of architecture, interior design, and business.

'House of Glass'

When it opened in 1952, 'Lever House turned out to be news', and most of it good.[140] This proved Charles Luckman's convictions that architecture would serve as effective advertising for the company. Nathaniel Owings claimed he did not understand 'why Lever House caused such a stir'.[141] To him, the success of architecture was inexplicable. 'Unlike painting, sculpture or even musical composition', Owings reasoned, 'design is the sum total of often unpredictable events . . . If the outcome is successful, that is a miracle.'[142] William Brown, in contrast, credited Lever House's great success to its unique design and to the favourable publicity it generated.

In the three months after the building opened, Lever Brothers' public relations agents peppered

That blue-green glass building is Lever House...

Perhaps you may have wondered about this building... the slim tower with glass walls...with the deep setback and landscaped terrace...the inner court, with its garden and willow tree, the spacious open ground floor.... We'd like to tell you how Lever House came to be the building it is...

Lever House is the new business home of Lever Brothers Company.

Many architects have told us that Lever House is the finest modern office building in Manhattan. It wasn't our intention, however, just to have an unusual building or an architectural showplace. Lever House was built to work in!

A good factory is planned around the necessary machinery and processes, and to make the work easier for the people who have to do it. An office building, to our way of thinking, deserves the same functional planning.

This building was not erected to fill a site, or bring in rent. We asked our architects for the best possible working quarters for 1280 people doing certain kinds of jobs. Lever House is the building that grew out of our requirements.

Naturally we wanted a convenient location. The site on Park Avenue, between Fifty-third and Fifty-fourth Streets, is removed from the more congested Manhattan areas. Lever House is near two subways and surface transportation, and close to Grand Central.

Everybody likes an office with a window. Why not an office that is all windows? When you turn windows into walls, every worker can have natural light, if the floor is small enough.

Above the ground floor, we needed only one large floor for a number of service departments. So above the second floor, the building was set back—became a tower of small floors. This tower was walled with glass.

Glass, we found, had many advantages. Glass is cheaper than the common types of wall construction, and easier to replace. Of all solid materials, glass is the easiest to clean. The entire outside of Lever House, top to bottom, can be washed by two men in a week, and at less expense than washing the windows of a conventional building of comparable size.

The blue-green glass lets in the sunlight, but shuts out about one-third of the sun's heat, helps the building's air-conditioning.

And our glass tower is sealed tight against dust and grime, keeps cleaner inside.

The offices in Lever House are quiet. Ceilings are soundproofed. Elevators, washrooms, pipes and ducts have been placed on the West side, and leave four-fifths of the floor relatively free from movement and traffic. The mail conveyor system makes frequent trips from floor to floor unnecessary.

Reducing distractions and noise raises efficiency and lowers fatigue.

Inside Lever House, color has been used not merely for appearance, but to establish a better working environment.

Desks and office fixtures are finished in Lever beige, a warm tan-gray. The aluminum chairs have colorful seat coverings. Walls are tinted in soft, gay pastels. Each floor has its color scheme. The office atmosphere *is* relaxed and tranquil, helps people to feel at ease and to concentrate better. We think every office is a pleasant place to be, and a better place to work.

In our offices, special consideration has been given to our women workers. Their desks have light glareproof tops to lessen eyestrain, rounded

standards that spare nylons. The desk height can be adjusted. Fluorescents recessed in the ceilings give better light than is found in most offices. Women were consulted in the arrangements of the restrooms.

The workers in Lever House need not leave the building at noontime. A spacious, well-equipped cafeteria on the terrace floor serves a variety of lunches at low prices. Outside the restaurant is the landscaped deck for noontime leisure and recreation. An attractive lounge for employees is situated on the floor below.

On the first floor we have test kitchens for our food products, and a small auditorium to be used for Company meetings. The reception room is intended to make our visitors more comfortable. Even though the decorations are still unfinished, we think you will find the lobby and court of interest. And as you become accustomed to Lever House, we believe you will like it as well as we do.

Because Lever House is a better place to work, it is our hope to serve better the thousands of distributors and dealers, and the millions of customers whose support built this Company... and made this building possible.

Lever Brothers Company

Makers of... Lux Toilet Soap, Swan, Lifebuoy...Lux Flakes, Rinso, Silver Dust, Breeze, Surf... Pepsodent, Chlorodent & Rayve Products...Shadow Wave Home Permanent... Harriet Hubbard Ayer Cosmetics...Spry, Good Luck Margarine, bulk shortening, glycerine

ARCHITECTS: *Skidmore, Owings & Merrill*
INTERIORS *by Raymond Loewy Associates*
CONTRACTORS: *George A. Fuller Company*

78   'That blue-green glass building is Lever House . . .', Lever Brothers advertisement, *New York Times*, 29 April 1952.

the popular media with publicity. Images and stories on Lever House appeared in Sunday supplements, full-page newspaper advertisements, and popular magazines. Lever Brothers promoted its new headquarters with a full-page advertisement in the *New York Times*, the headline of which read, 'That blue-green glass building is Lever House', and the ad answered the question then piquing the curiosity of many New Yorkers (Fig.78). Other businesses rode on the coattails of Lever House: Gimbels department store, for example, ran an ad illustrating the glass skyscraper outfitted with frilly curtains behind its sleek curtain wall (Fig.79). The public relations force cast SOM's design not as 'avant-garde Architecture', as Bunshaft would have liked, but rather as 'the product of such universal values as efficiency, economy, mechanization, and financial foresight, and civic leadership'.[143] Lever's PR team aimed publicity about Lever House at the mass-market, and hit its mark.

Lever Brothers marketed to the masses not only through print advertising but also through radio and television. At this postwar moment, television sets had become widely available, marketed, and owned. In 1949 American consumers bought 250,000 sets a month and watched four to five hours of television a day. Americans of all ages became exposed to increasingly sophisticated advertisements for products marketed as necessary for living the good life. Lever Brothers was one of the first major TV advertisers, paying $7.2 million to sponsor two seasons of 'Top 5' prime-time programmes – Lux Radio Theater and Bob Hope's Pepsodent show – as well as two daytime soap operas.

Lever House also appealed to the architectural community. In the years following the opening of its new building, architectural critics Aline Loucheim and Ada Louise Huxtable praised Lever House's architectural achievements; according to Bunshaft, they were 'dazzled by the technical excellence and the implications and possibilities of the material'.[144] In her 1952 review, Loucheim claimed that Lever House took the steel skeletons and glass curtain walls of Le Corbusier and Mies van der Rohe to a new level, calling the building 'coloristic and poetic', and 'the most handsome and best example of modern architecture in New York'.[145] Huxtable's 1957 article, 'The Park Avenue School of Architecture',

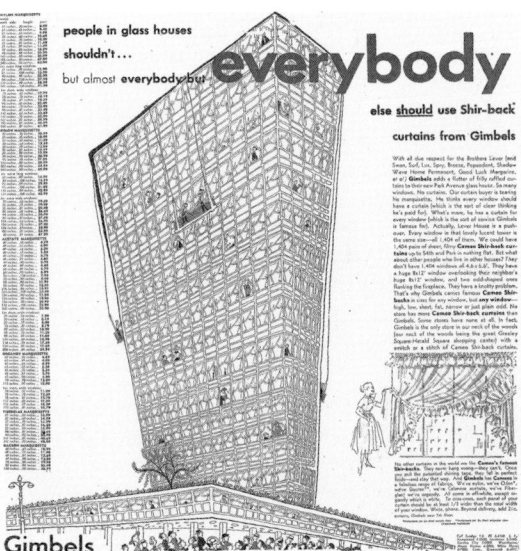

79 'People in glass houses shouldn't . . .', Gimbels advertisement, *New York Times*, 21 September 1952.

published in *The New York Times Magazine*, touted the 'sleek towers of steel-framed blue, green, or gray-tinted glass' as giving Park Avenue 'a glamorous and glittering new look'.[146]

The 'top-notch architectural criticism' most appreciated by Bunshaft, however, was that of Lewis Mumford.[147] In his essay titled 'House of Glass', featured in his Skyline column of the *New Yorker* in 1952, Mumford waxed ecstatic about Lever House, extolling it as 'the eighth wonder of the world'.[148] Mumford promoted Lever House as a new example in corporate architecture. An astute city dweller, Mumford recognised the building's clever use of architecture to advertise – by not advertising. He pointed out, 'This whole structure is chastely free of advertisement.' But he continued, 'The building itself is a showcase and an advertisement.' He perceptively noted that, 'in its very avoidance of vulgar forms of publicity, it has become one of the most valuable pieces of advertising a big commercial enterprise could conceive.'[149]

Mumford found the lean proportions of Lever House refreshing in comparison to previous office buildings, which were 'swaggering in specious dimensions'.[150] 'For years', he wrote, 'businessmen vied with each other in the attempt to put up the tallest building in the city; thus the Metropolitan Life capped the Singer and the Empire State capped the Chrysler in the effort to make the sky the limit.'[151] Lever House chose a better way – a revitalising and humanising way for corporations to declare their identity through architecture. He suggested the building would play a pioneering role: 'Possibly Lever House has pointed the way for a new kind of competition – a competition to provide open spaces and a return to the human scale.'[152]

Lever House's distinctive form was a major, evolutional leap in how buildings served as brands, within the 20th-century case studies of this book, as well as within the company, considering Port Sunlight, Lever Brothers' early attempt at a nostalgic version of architectural branding. Lever House stood as a brand for both Lever Brothers and SOM. For Lever Brothers, the architecture of Lever House expressed and communicated the characteristics and value of the corporation: modern, clean, and hygienic. For SOM, Lever House set the prototype for an inventory of corporate modernism in the years to come.

'Everyone knows it's Lever House'

As critics praised Lever House's striking corporate modernism, Gordon Bunshaft recalled how the client was 'proud of that building'.[153] He pointed out that 'Unilever never tied their name into a product prior to Lever House. But after the building was completed, they would tie their name/logo into their products.'[154] He also enjoyed mentioning that the corporation's president felt that the headquarters was their monument.[155]

J.E. Drew, Lever Brothers' head of public relations, boasted that if Lever House's publicity were to be evaluated in inches of newspaper columns, the advertising value would more than match the price paid to build it.[156] He even quantified the building as 'four million dollars' worth of free advertising'.[157] In a speech delivered to the AIA in 1970, he explained how Lever House's powerful advertising worked:

Corporations throughout the country have for many years been working earnestly on what some of them call institutional advertising, or that which establishes good public relations for business. . . . Each company approaches this goal in their own way. You will recall seeing any magnificent structures topped by flamboyant, ugly electric signs or neon displays which proclaimed to the world that this is the 'Whozit Building'. . . . The same purpose can be accomplished much better by *distinctive building design*. There are no signs on the top of Lever House nor do they appear anywhere else in the building. *Everyone knows it's Lever House.*[158]

The name of the building, 'Lever House', appeared only in discreet metal letters on the lobby's glass wall. Lever Brothers launched the building advertising simultaneously with its opening, and even leveraged the building's success as a recruitment and retention tool.[159] Instead of a sign, which was one of the ways the PSFS Building provided branding, Lever House's architectural form was its branding mechanism. As such, architectural form functioned like a distinctive signature or trademark for the client, as well as for the architects.

SOM's Signature Design

In a 1968 interview with *Time* magazine, Owings discussed the signature design style of about a dozen famous architects. The press, he pointed out, emphasised famous architects. He explained, 'They [the press] need a handle to their stories, an identifiable individual. They need a hero or a villain – they can't talk about the faceless masses.'[160] Owings understood that great architects publicised themselves. 'Masters of self-publicization', Owings pointed out, 'such as Mies van der Rohe, whose "Less is more" and "God is in the details" are quotable and memorable and almost alone would have gained him immortality.'[161]

Owings also cited Philip Johnson, Walter Gropius, Minoru Yamasaki, Paul Rudolph, I.M. Pei, and Edward Durell Stone as 'masters of self-publicization'. Each of these architects had developed a unique identity or architectural signature. For example, Yamasaki was 'clearly identified by his multiple-arched structures', and Rudolph was known 'by his nervous cookie-cutter shapes which he strives to establish as a new architectural idiom'.[162] Owings pointed out that 'Each of those featured architects has his own trademark, his own way of not only capturing the essential quality of architecture as he sees it, but also gaining the essential quality of public relations and national business-getting fame.'[163] His client had learned the value of trademarks long ago in the trademarking of Sunlight soap, which had led to its first success.

Despite SOM's collective nature, Owings's theory of architectural trademarks was applied to his own firm. SOM's architecture possessed an identifiable image that had value as a tool of public relations. SOM's architectural trademark was the modern skyscraper and slab. An extension of Owings's list of famous architects was the roster of talented architects he had cultivated: Gordon Bunshaft, Walter Netsch, Bruce Graham, Charles Bassett, and Myron Goldsmith. Although the work of these five architects was bolstered by the framework provided by SOM, each was given latitude to bring a unique approach to their projects. For example, Owings described partner Myron Goldsmith as the 'quiet, meticulous' engineer; he was known at SOM as 'the professor'.[164] He described partner Chuck Bassett as 'tweedy, informal, [and] a creative designer of humane proportions'.[165]

In the role of catalyst, Owings established SOM's division of labour that enabled these design partners to flourish. 'While we could not claim to be geniuses at finding people', he recalled, 'perhaps we had been able to provide the natural climate with soil, water, sun and shade necessary to bring out the genius in the people we had.'[166] Thus, Owings claimed that SOM produced homegrown signature architects who worked within the SOM collective or framework to create variations on a modern theme.

Lever House proved to be the breakthrough commission that put SOM 'on the map of the world'.[167] The firm's systematic design process enabled them to build up a set of core themes and continually improve their architecture over time. Three subsequent corporate headquarters by SOM – Inland Steel, Crown Zellerbach, and Union Carbide – displayed elements first established by the design of Lever House in 1952. The sleek glass and steel slab became synonymous with the firm, and by the late 1950s it had become internationally renowned for its corporate modernism.

As the first SOM corporate headquarters design, Lever House displayed key modern characteristics: a sleek curtain wall, purity of form, and an open plaza. These three attributes became the quintessential modern architectural symbols of corporations, and thus corporate architecture. While all three previously mentioned SOM corporate headquarters were designed from principles established in Lever House, each possessed its own idiosyncrasies.[168] However, with their drastic break from the stepped skyscraper forms of past decades, they pioneered a new typological form.

The Lever House project offered SOM the opportunity to establish its organisational process and develop the roles played by specialist architects, from the salesman architect to the administrative partner to the genius designer. Whereas Howe and Lescaze at PSFS and Wright at Johnson Wax managed the entire scope of work, designing total environments in their buildings, SOM contributed only a part – the architectural design – pointing to the growth of interdisciplinary collaboration, as professional design services became more and more subdivided in the second half of the 20th century. As we will see in the next case study, the Röhm and Haas Building, such specialisation and collaboration would continue to develop through later expressions of corporate modernism.

Lever House Brand

From its early days, Lever Brothers carefully cultivated its image and ultimately its brand, as evidenced not only by the modern architecture of Lever House but also by the nostalgic company village Port Sunlight before it. Both design projects, regardless of the specific design language, aimed to make connections with people. With Lever House, the multinational corporation achieved the unique architectural combination of modern and monumental qualities that stood as a symbol of an era: that of the rise of the large corporation. Lever House, like the Johnson Wax Building, demonstrated the role of architects as salesmen.

Usually, selling is seen more as a business concern and less as an architectural one, but as these case studies show, architects possessing salesmanship were both necessary and effective. Lever Brothers hired a relatively unknown company (rather than a famous architect such as Frank Lloyd Wright) and ended up with a distinctive modern building. Through a series of key decisions, aided by the client Charles Luckman, SOM created a striking modern design for Lever Brothers' headquarters

that stood apart, urbanistically and architecturally, from its context. As a result, Lever House's unique architectural form spoke to the public, thus enhancing its client's corporate branding.

In the three 20th-century case studies discussed so far, architecture served as the medium of branding. Each corporation communicated its message through architectural branding: the PSFS with its sign, S.C. Johnson & Son with Frank Lloyd Wright's fame, and Lever Brothers with Lever House's distinctive architectural form. The next case study of Röhm and Haas will add approach of material display to the collection of strategies of architectural branding studied in this book.

5 MATERIAL

Plexiglas and the Röhm and Haas Building

After World War II, American business boomed. Industries which developed during the war repurposed their products, and consumerism became a way of life. As more and more middle-class Americans chose to live the 'good life' in the suburbs, urban renewal advocates denigrated downtown districts as areas of crime and dilapidated building stock. Active land redevelopment through the federal urban renewal programme played a significant role in the changing face of American cities. This controversial programme instigated social and racial unrest, while creating opportunities for private corporations. The Röhm and Haas chemical company was one of those corporations who benefited from urban renewal by building a new headquarters in downtown Philadelphia.

In the 1960s, corporations became increasingly concerned with communications management within the context of increasing globalisation of trade and the growth of multinational corporations.[1] Also at this time, corporate identity, the precursor to branding, was developed by a number of large enterprises including IBM, the Olivetti Company, and the Container Corporation of America. Through corporate identity programmes, companies considered the design of all mediums that represented themselves, from office buildings and retail shops to vehicles, stationery, and staff uniforms. Like their peers, Röhm and Haas would develop a corporate identity programme, understanding that the architecture of their corporate headquarters was an opportunity to advertise and showcase their revolutionary product, Plexiglas. As the brand movement revolutionised advertising, it would also fully implicate architecture.

The Röhm and Haas headquarters was designed at a moment when architects were exploring new

forms, materials, and meanings. By the late 1950s, the paradigm of the modern glass box corporate headquarters such as Lever House and the Seagram Building had come under scrutiny by architects and critics. Some critics claimed that the curtain wall was not only an isolating force in society but possessed malicious intent. Colin Rowe's 1956 essay 'Chicago Frame' re-cast the modern glass curtain wall as the 'nakedly irresponsible agent of a too ruthless commercialism'.[2] The building that consultant architect Pietro Belluschi, together with associated architect Alexander Ewing and his team, would design as the Röhm and Haas headquarters from 1962 to 1964 brought forth a re-evaluated vision of corporate modernism – one that sought both continuity with early 20th-century modern architecture and forward-looking change. Most importantly, the material exploration of the design created strong connections with occupants, thus making the Röhm and Haas Building an example of architectural branding.

The Bulldozer and the Modern Building

In 1961, when the design for the Röhm and Haas headquarters began, the PSFS Building had been standing for three decades and was still one of the most conspicuous examples of modern architecture in Philadelphia (Fig.80). Modernism had had an uneasy time in a city that appreciates its colonial and Beaux-Arts architecture far more than its modern ones. In the 1950s and 1960s, urban renewal offered modern architecture its greatest opportunity, and Röhm and Haas became the city's first private corporation to seize it. At

80   The Röhm and Haas Building with the PSFS Building down the street (looking up Market Street), photograph c.1965.

this time, Philadelphia, like many American cities, suffered from neglect, ageing infrastructure, and overcrowding. Philadelphia's particular urban blight resulted from structural deterioration, with half of its housing stock built in the 19th century, as well as social deterioration driven by racism. These forces ultimately led to urban decentralisation and suburbanisation. Planning commissions were revived and soon, a cadre of urbanists mobilised to solve housing, zoning, and crime problems and to build highways.[3]

In 1947, urban optimism was stoked by the *Better Philadelphia* exhibition, designed and installed by architect Oscar Stonorov and planner Edmund Bacon. Inspired by Norman Bel Geddes's Futurama exhibit at the 1939 New York World's Fair, the exhibition lent drama to the new ideas in modern form that would reinvent Philadelphia after years of depression and world war. The exhibition also paved the way for Bacon to become executive director of the Philadelphia City Planning Commission in 1949. In this position, which he would occupy until 1970, Bacon took advantage of post-World War II hope to build a better future for Philadelphia, with the design of comprehensive plans that would eliminate blight and obsolete industrial infrastructure. The Housing Act, also of 1949, jump-started the 'urban renewal' programme, providing the federal funding which cities needed to cover the cost of acquiring areas perceived to be 'slums'. Those sites were then given to private developers to construct new housing in response to the post-World War II housing shortage.

In Philadelphia, Society Hill stood in stark contrast to most urban renewal projects. It provides an exemplary case study of rehabilitation. Bacon's idea was to empower private citizens to restore their own homes, with particular emphasis on the house's public street front. Through the restoration of existing housing stock, which consisted of 18th-century row homes and grand houses, bulldozing of the entire area could be avoided. In 1958, a design by the developer-architect team of Webb & Knapp and Chinese American architect I.M. Pei was selected to design what would become Society Hill Towers for the eastern portion of the redevelopment area. While the goal of providing low-income housing was not achieved in the district, the Society Hill Redevelopment was a successful result of urban renewal. Architecturally, Society Hill's redevelopment championed historic preservation and building new greenways. It also boldly promoted designing new construction as contemporaneous, and therefore distinct from historical structures.[4] The future Röhm and Haas Building, a few blocks away from Society Hill, aligned with the idea that its design would be new for its time, yet would respect its context of history and site.

The federal urban renewal programme funded improvements in Philadelphia in the years leading up to the 1976 Bicentennial and Philadelphia World's Fair, the latter of which did not come to fruition. Independence Hall was projected as the main focus of the event, and the Röhm and Haas Building would stand cater-corner to it during the festivities. A number of existing fair buildings and transportation systems were intended to remain and enhance Philadelphia's urban experience.[5] While Ed Bacon's original plan was for a Bicentennial merged with a World's Fair, the latter portion never happened.

Growing criticism of urban renewal came from those who lived in the path of the bulldozer, as well as from both political extremes. It was attacked from the Left as a reactionary effort to force African American and other minority groups out of the city.[6] At the same time, it was attacked from the Right as a Communist or Socialist give-away. Ultimately, the private sector played a critical role in much of the city's redevelopment.[7] Since the 1940s, keeping private corporate headquarters and offices in cities had posed both a challenge and an opportunity for urban renewal advocates like the Philadelphia City Planning Commission. Despite the exodus of many headquarters to the suburbs, it was just these corporations that urban renewal advocates targeted to fill cleared land. Private corporations and developers were vitally necessary to make the final stage of urban renewal work. From Penn Center to Market East to Society Hill, Bacon's plans found support from powerful local business organisations, private investors, and developers.[8]

From a developer's point of view, urban renewal provided a unique opportunity for exponential profits with relatively small capital investment: while the risk was high, the potential payoff would also be high. Developers who had anticipated good capital gains found that, in reality urban renewal was not as profitable or as easy to carry out as expected. The programme was slow in producing tangible results. By the 1960s, developers like William Zeckendorf and Herbert Greenwald had sold off most of their urban renewal projects. This harkened the entry of large corporations into the urban renewal field.

According to economist Martin Anderson, in his 1964 book *The Federal Bulldozer: A Critical Analysis of Urban Renewal, 1942–1962*, large corporations saw several advantages to investing in urban renewal properties. First, it afforded the corporation an opportunity to sell their products in prime locations. Second, it provided a showplace where corporations could demonstrate the variety of uses to which its products could be put. Third, urban renewal projects permitted the company to experiment with the use of its materials. And fourth, urban renewal promised good profits.[9] The case study in this chapter, the Röhm and Haas Company, recognised all of these as reasons for involvement – prime location, showcasing its product, and profits. Its headquarters became the first private-investor urban renewal project in Philadelphia.

The Client

As Röhm and Haas transitioned its products from wartime to post-World War II civilian and domestic use, it put forth a new architectural identity in participating in urban renewal development. As a company, Röhm and Haas was made up of scientists, researchers, and salesmen who invented and experimented with chemicals in order to produce useful and marketable products. It had effectively promoted the use of its product Plexiglas in fighter planes during World War II: one of its wartime ads read, 'From nose to tail . . . it's Plexiglas.' In the post-World War II period, the company reinvented Plexiglas for the building market. In ads imploring commercial clients to '[Put] your best fascia forward', Röhm and Haas portrayed their polymethyl methacrylate material as a particularly mutable substance that offered endless possibilities of form, colour, and texture.[10] Although

Plexiglas was only one of Röhm and Haas's products, it was one that could be easily tailored to market desire. Because of its synthetic nature and absolute flexibility, it was quickly dubbed a miracle material. Finding the right market, however, was not always easy.

The Röhm and Haas Company had been founded in 1909 as a partnership between two German nationals, Otto Röhm and Otto Haas. Haas was an entrepreneur who came to America to make his fortune. His childhood friend, Röhm, was a talented chemist. The company operated between two cities: Röhm, in Darmstadt, led the chemical innovation and technology, and Haas, in Philadelphia, took the chemical goods to market. This arrangement proved advantageous. Philadelphia – the 19th-century 'Workshop of the World' – was at this time the global centre for the production of glazed kid, a soft, pliable goatskin used to make shoes and gloves. Germany, from the last third of the 19th century on, had been recognised around the world for its advances in chemistry. German trademarks on chemical products represented excellence. Thus, in America, Haas was backed by the power of a German brand. Oropon, a bating agent for animal skins and fur, was Röhm and Haas's first trademarked product. Because of its German origins, it found acceptance from manufacturers, who felt confident the product was of consistently high quality. The importance of trademarks and brands was new in the 1910s, and it was crucial for businesses establishing their reputation. Brand names and trademarks gave consumers the confidence to try out new projects. Brands also served to establish trust between the maker and the consumer, cementing their relationship to build a devoted consumer base.

While experimenting with applications for acrylic resins, Röhm and his chemists found a way to make automotive safety glass from a rubbery adhesive called Plexigum. Patented in 1928 as Luglas®, Röhm and Haas's new type of safety glass for windshields was its first plastic product. It was distributed by the American Window Glass Company, who announced it as 'the New Glass'. The Luglas® windshield possessed similar qualities to glass – it was transparent and mouldable – yet it had advantages in its lightness and safety in accidents. Soon after, Röhm and his company

PLEXIGLAS*

THIS acrylic plastic, outstanding in color-
less transparency, aging stability, impact
strength, and ability to be formed, is
used in the windows, turret, and cockpit
enclosure of the Consolidated XPB2Y-1.

*Trade Mark Reg. U. S. Pat. Office

RÖHM & HAAS COMPANY, INC.
222 West Washington Square, PHILADELPHIA, PA.

JUNE 1938   33

81 With rising military
need for plastic windshields
in planes, Röhm and Haas
entered a new phase of
business with the outbreak of
World War II. This Röhm and
Haas Plexiglas advertisement
announced the material's use
in the war effort. 'Plexiglas
is being used in the cockpit
enclosures of the Curtiss-
Wright P-36 and X P-40
pursuit planes.' March 1939.

scientists developed a method for polymerising methyl-methacrylate resulting in Plexiglas®. The new material quickly enjoyed widespread use in pre-war applications such as instrument covers and watch glasses. Plexiglas was initially disparaged in some instances as an ersatz glass, but as a product that could be formed into virtually anything, it soon came into its own. Although the company (like many) experienced a downturn during the Depression, this proved to be but a temporary setback. Don Frederick, Röhm and Haas's chemist-turned-salesman, worked successfully to educate customers from big businesses to small, family-owned mould shops on the advantage of acrylic

plastics. Signage provided a key industrial outlet before World War II. At the 1939 World's Fair, Röhm and Haas supplied and manufactured Plexiglas for a number of exhibits, including General Motors' Plymouth 'X-ray' sedan, the Public Health Building's larger-than-life-sized Plexiglas Man (with its visible organs), and the Home Center's full-scale Plexiglas House. Designers experimented with Plexiglas with stunning success.

The promises of Plexiglas were put on hold as the world moved into World War II in September 1939 (Fig.81). Three years earlier, Frederick had introduced Plexiglas to the Army Air Corps. At that point, in early 1936, no plastic had filled aviation's needs for transparency, non-flammability, and impact resistance. With rising military need for plastic windshields in planes, Röhm and Haas entered a new phase of business. In 1937, sales of Röhm and Haas Plexiglas rose tenfold from the prior year – from 13,000 to 119,000 units. In March 1941, when Congress passed the Lend Lease Act authorising President Franklin Delano Roosevelt to supply material to the Allies, Plexiglas sales increased exponentially, reaching $8.9 million. In 1941, the United States built more than 18,000 military aircraft, 85 per cent of which were built with Röhm and Haas plastics. For seven years, Röhm and Haas supplied Plexiglas for the U.S. Army and continued to develop other products for better visibility. The Army gave high praise to Röhm and Haas for improving 'the eyes of aviation' with Plexiglas and awarded the company an Army–Navy Excellence Award in 1943 and a number of other commendations.[11]

On 14 August 1945, Japan surrendered, and this brought Röhm and Haas's wartime business to an abrupt end, as orders for Plexiglas were cancelled and Plexiglas sheet sales plummeted. The commitment of company resources to acrylics was so great that the company's survival now hung in the balance. Later that year, it closed its Plexiglas fabrication facility in Bristol, Pennsylvania, while Haas and Frederick grappled with how to re-cast Plexiglas for the post-World War II consumer landscape.

The company used advertising and promotion to fill the void. It cleverly pitched Plexiglas as a glamorous, progressive design material for the future, in stark contrast to the military applications of its recent past. One of the first markets in which it found success was in the booming industry of automobile design. Plexiglas had originally only been produced in clear, colourless sheets. But with Röhm and Haas chemist Stanton Kelton Jr's discovery of new methods for adding pigments to the plastic, coupled with consumer demand for coloured sheets, Plexiglas became available in vibrant colours. Plexiglas's acrylic moulding powder, Crystalite, was adopted by the resurgent automobile industry in 1946 and as a result, Plexiglas tail lights became the industry standard. Plexiglas became the indispensable material for forming the dramatic red, rocket-shaped tailfins

characteristic of the period. Röhm and Haas entered the market with high-concept car designs like the Explorer III, the result of collaboration with car designer William M. Schmidt Associates.[12] Plexiglas became established as the coloured, weatherproof material for headlights, hood ornaments, nameplates, steering-wheel medallions, speedometer dials, instrument panels, and interior lighting, in addition to its signature tail lights (Fig.82).

Like the car, the suburban home emerged as a major preoccupation of postwar American culture. In collaboration with *House and Garden* magazine, Röhm and Haas developed and constructed the 'Dream Suite', casting Plexiglas as a desired material for the home. First introduced in 1945 at the John Wanamaker department store in Philadelphia, the three-room Dream Suite exhibit travelled to 14 high-end department stores demonstrating how Plexiglas would enable consumers to live 'the good life'. This term referred to postwar America's consumer culture in which the production, marketing, and acquisition of the material symbols of 'the good life' shaped society and its values. The 'Dream Suite' promised 'to sweep away traditional styling in interior architecture'.[13] It presented a sequence of spaces for bathing, dressing, and sleeping that showcased new applications of Plexiglas, including edge-lit decorative mirrors, revolving hat racks, a curved shower enclosure, transparent room dividers, and an expansive back-lit mural.[14]

Looking Ahead Through Rohm & Haas Plexiglas, a short promotional film produced by Röhm and Haas in 1947, offered a closer look at the Dream Suite. As the film opens, a robe-clad woman leisurely demonstrates the interior amenities while a male narrator speaks. The camera pans through the space, showcasing how Plexiglas has been designed to store and display personal belongings as well as divide and enclose interior spaces. The Plexiglas of the Dream Suite is portrayed as luxurious, warm, and inviting, suitable for the most intimate areas of the home.

The Dream Suite also served to persuade consumers to choose Plexiglas over glass. Like glass, Plexiglas could 'lend an air of spaciousness to a room quite small. Sweeping transparency removes all feeling of confinement.'[15] But Plexiglas was 'amazingly light in weight yet strong and

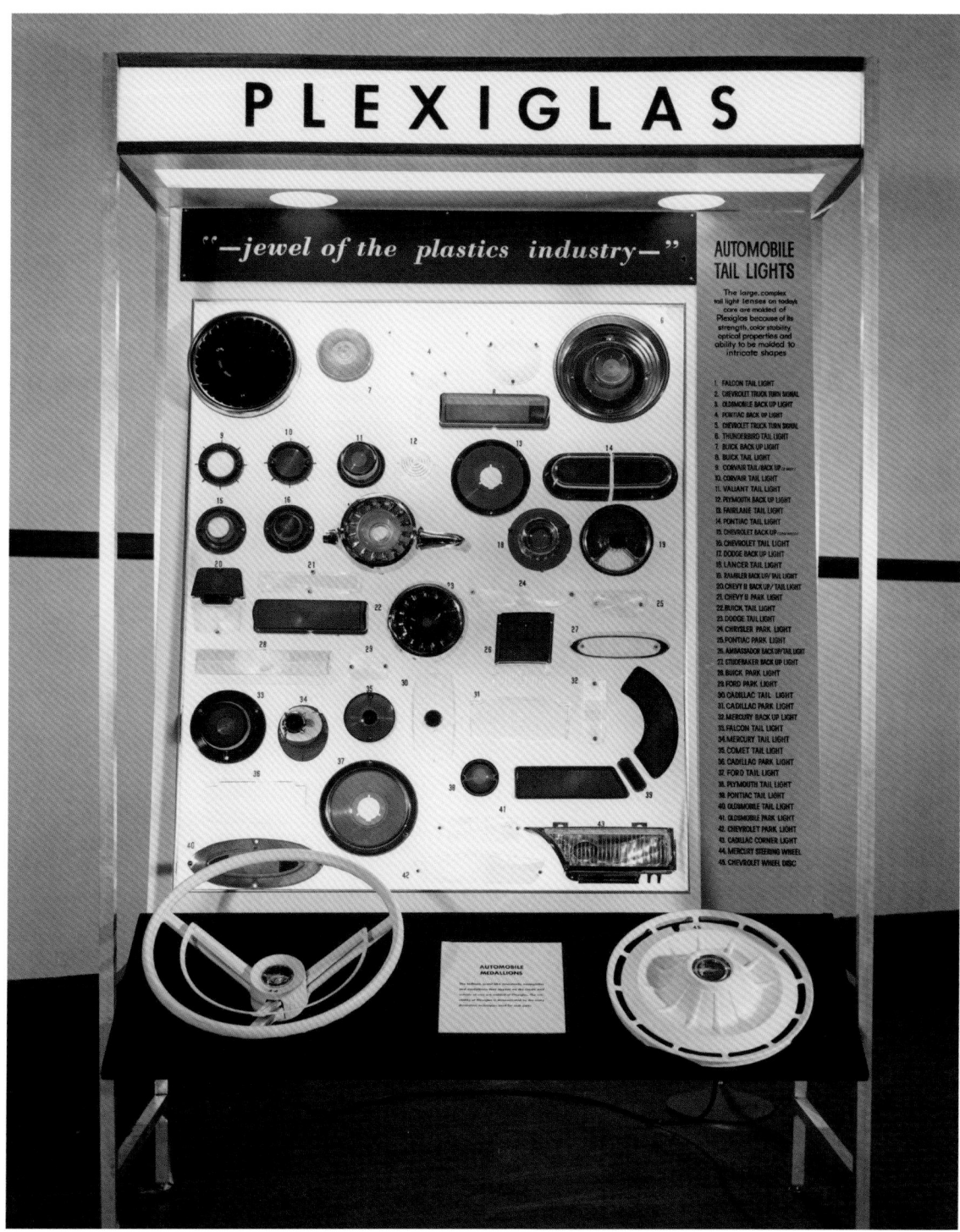

82　The discovery of adding coloured pigment to clear Plexiglas, became indispensable for forming a number of parts, from dramatic red, rocket-shaped tailfins to speedometer dials. This Röhm and Haas trade exhibit displays the tagline, '– jewel of the plastics industry –' for numerous examples of automobile tail lights. 'The large, complex tail light lenses on today's cars are molded of Plexiglas because of the strength, color-stability, optical properties, and ability to be molded to intricate shapes.'

shatter resistant', which were positive qualities that glass did not possess.[16] Through the design of the exhibit, Röhm and Haas touted Plexiglas as 'the most glamourous glass of all'.[17] The firm marketed the project to 'architects, designers, and home owners', as demonstrating 'just how Plexiglas can add to the beauty and comfort of the home'.[18] While glamorous, the material was also down-to-earth: by seizing the do-it-yourself spirit of the times, Röhm and Haas hoped the Dream Suite would spur demand for Plexiglas in suburban homes.

In 1946 Plexiglas sheet unexpectedly started selling again. Aircraft makers used Plexiglas sheet in the manufacture of small civilian airplanes, for which they anticipated a growing market as pilots returned home from war. In addition, returning veterans used Plexiglas to start new businesses. Pigment options encouraged the use of Plexiglas in novelties and giftware, such as cigarette boxes, doll furniture, umbrella handles, and jewellery. The volume of sheet sold in 1946 actually matched that of 1945. Yet demand for Plexiglas proved short-lived; after October of 1946, sheet sales died as quickly as they had revived. Despite their initial appeal, Plexiglas novelties failed to hold consumer interest. Once gold and silver became available again after the war, Plexiglas novelties fell out of favour. Similarly, the predicted boom in civilian aircraft did not occur. In 1947 the largest single market for Plexiglas sheet was jukeboxes: three manufacturers collectively purchased three-quarters of a million dollars' worth of Plexiglas for use as music machine covers. This outlet collapsed the next year. Ultimately, decorative trinkets and jukeboxes could not sustain Plexiglas's market and keep Röhm and Haas's giant plants in Bristol, Pennsylvania and Knoxville, Tennessee running.

Analysing the company's missteps, Frederick surmised that Röhm and Haas 'spent too much time with small customers with questionable futures when we should have been concentrating our efforts on developing stable industrial outlets'.[19] Röhm and Haas had a long record of technical sales development in industries such as leather, textiles, and aircraft, and it was in such industrial outlets that the future success of Plexiglas would be found. Frederick already knew, from limited work done before the war, where these markets might lie: with sign builders,

lighting fixture manufacturers, architects, and railroad car designers. These were the markets where the product could be sold for its unique performance advantages rather than for its novelty.

Röhm and Haas chemist Stanton Kelton Jr's newfound coloured pigment knowledge also helped Plexiglas sheet find its first major civilian market in illuminated signage (Fig.83). Before the war, standard signs were illuminated at night either by shining an external light source on the sign or by outlining the sign with neon tubes. The PSFS sign of 1932 is an example of this. Plexiglas sheet offered a better way. Fabricated in three dimensions, hollow signs were evenly lit from within. Sign production required a wide palette of coloured sheet, so that customers could replicate their well-known signs in acrylic. Sales representatives in the plastics department would sell a company like Sun Oil on Plexiglas signs, and then give the task of duplicating Sun's yellow and blue colours in translucent Plexiglas to Kelton's lab. With signs leading the way, Plexiglas sheet sales began to recover, reaching $10.3 million in 1949 and $12.8 million in 1950.[20]

Outdoor, illuminated commercial signage was an important growth market for Plexiglas. Businesses populating the suburban landscape used Plexiglas signs to identify themselves to customers moving at a fast pace in their cars. Sunoco and Shell gas stations were the first to install signs made of this material; by 1953, 15,000 service stations displayed them.[21] The auto industry embraced Plexiglas signage for auto dealerships; by the late 1960s, the three largest American automakers – Ford Motor Company, General Motors, and Chrysler – would use Plexiglas signs in their nationwide corporate identity programmes. Fast-food restaurants lining the suburban strip competed for the patronage of hungry customers by creating distinctive Plexiglas signs, such as McDonald's iconic 'golden arches'.

Although signs constituted the largest civilian market for Plexiglas sheet, architecture and building became important. To explore architectural possibilities, Röhm and Haas approached experts. 'We worked a lot with industrial designers like Walter Dorwin Teague and Raymond Loewy and Gilbert Rhode and

83   Röhm and Haas trade exhibit displaying Plexiglas signage fabricated
as a hollow, three-dimensional construction, evenly lit from within.

Henry Dreyfuss, and all that crowd', Don Frederick
recalled. 'We even hired Walter Gropius, the
founder of the Bauhaus.'[22] Gropius led a research
team tasked with articulating the advantages of
Plexiglas to architects. Touted as lightweight,
bendable, available in a variety of forms and
colours, and characterised by low thermal
conductivity, the material was promoted as
offering unlimited flexibility. Gropius pointed out
its potential for use in curved walls, novel lighting
effects, and decorative treatments.[23] This research
led Röhm and Haas to broader markets in the

building industry as Plexiglas was subsequently
used in many architectural applications.

   Plexiglas's protean material qualities were at
the core of its appeal to diverse markets. Once
valued merely as a substitute for glass, it became
recognised as a material possessing its own unique
nature. When combined with artificial light,
Plexiglas proved to be a potent application – one
still common today in the artificial fluorescent
light fixtures of the commercial and institutional
interior landscape and in the back-lit signage of
the commercial strip. As the company entered a

new phase in its development, it would look for additional ways to expand its market share. In doing so, it would also pioneer a new relationship between architecture and the brand.

Planning for the Corporate Headquarters

In 1959, 87-year-old founder Otto Haas stepped down as president and chief executive officer of his company due to his declining health. Soon afterward, he passed away. Two days before his death, the board ratified the appointment of his eldest son, Fritz Otto Haas, as his successor, with the company's research director, Ralph Connor, as chairman of the board. Connor's appointment was meant to provide counsel and guidance to Fritz Otto during the transition. The climate of the company during this time changed. As Connor put it, 'Mr. Haas had been a strong character, and with him gone what was it going to be like? People needed a little reassurance that there wasn't going to be an upheaval.' Furthermore, he explained, 'It was a difficult time in the history of the company, not only because of economic conditions but because we had to do something about office space.'[24] The company was sprawled out in 11 different buildings around downtown Philadelphia, in various rented office spaces.[25] 'This was a very inefficient way of operating', said Connor, 'and we couldn't go on just renting . . . different buildings.' Röhm and Haas had to do something to solve their 'space problems'.[26]

The Röhm and Haas Company was not unlike other corporations in the late 1950s and early 1960s that recognised the value in hiring architectural firms that were structured like efficient corporations and that provided comprehensive services – large firms such as Emery Roth & Sons in New York and Smith, Hinchman, & Grylls in Detroit. These types of firms worked on large commercial buildings and speculative developer projects and frequently served as associated architects for other firms tasked with design. On the other end of the spectrum, companies such as S.C. Johnson & Son, as we have seen, hired iconoclasts like Frank Lloyd Wright who would provide innovative

design and instant visibility to their project. In their architect selection, Röhm and Haas would hire an architectural team that encompassed both worlds.[27]

Before his death, Otto Haas Sr hosted preliminary discussions about expanding the headquarters office at 222 West Washington Square with George M. Ewing, Co., a Philadelphia-based architecture and engineering firm. Alexander Ewing (known as Alec), son of the firm's founder and partner in the firm, recalled that Otto Haas Sr, 'in a very brief meeting made it plain to me that Röhm and Haas does not spend construction dollars on headquarters. The message [was] . . . keep it simple and economical.'[28] But during this transitional time for the company, a new attitude about the headquarters emerged. 'Between the death of Otto Haas Sr and the appointment of Otto Haas Jr as CEO', wrote Ewing, 'it became clear that the Washington Square buildings were too limited to accommodate the growth of the Röhm and Haas administration group': the existing site could not satisfy the growing needs of the company, and another site would need to be found and acquired to allow the project to go forward.[29]

Whereas the elder Haas was tight-fisted when it came to spending on workspace and building projects, the younger Haas saw value in investing in a new headquarters. He recognised that this was an opportunity to elevate the company's visibility through a larger scope of design and a prominent location, at a time when advertising and branding were becoming important aspects of business. Ewing was initially asked by Röhm and Haas to design an addition. The project evolved quickly, however, into a full-blown building on a new site.

After considering a move to a suburban location for their new headquarters, Röhm and Haas opted for a prominent urban location.[30] The new site was part of Philadelphia's postwar urban renewal effort and would form one of the crucial borders defining the new Independence Mall. Work on the Mall began in 1950 and would continue until 1967. Connor explained, 'The City wanted to develop Independence Mall . . . and there was a desire on their part for us to build there and we didn't want to pay much of a premium for that, but we thought if we could essentially swap the area that we owned on Washington Square for a site on the mall, we'd be justified in doing this. That was the way it got

84   Röhm and Haas's prominent site had clear sight lines to the colonial landmark, Independence Hall, on the lower left.

started and it looked like a good proposition in which we did not pay much of a penalty for a better location.'[31]

The proposed Röhm and Haas Building was part of the first phase of Independence Mall's redevelopment (Fig.84). Its site was located on the first block facing Independence Hall, once the most distinguished building in 18th-century Philadelphia. Begun in 1731, Independence Hall served as the statehouse from which the colony was governed. The Second Continental Congress met there in

1776, and the Declaration of Independence was ratified there on 4 July. Modelled on a grand mansion in the region, the brick building with stone and wood trim was designed with a centre hall plan, expanded to nine bays. The Georgian-style statehouse also featured a tower, influenced by the church steeples of British architect Christopher Wren. As Independence Hall became the focus of this new mall plan, historical significance inspired and infused Philadelphia's urban renewal efforts. This part of the city – Old City and Society Hill, where colonial Philadelphians had lived and worked – had fallen into decay as westerly parts of the city developed in the 19th century. The urban renewal project would test how modern and 18th-century architecture might co-exist as parts of an urban mall design.

From the city's perspective, having the Röhm and Haas corporate headquarters on Independence Mall was a huge coup. In the formative stages of the project, Alec Ewing let his clients know about the opportunity with the Old Philadelphia Development Corporation and the Philadelphia Redevelopment Authority, which were anxious to expedite the growth of their plan to redevelop properties on Independence Mall.[32] Röhm and Haas chief financial officer William McClintock negotiated the move to Sixth Street and Market Street.[33] The company's former office on Washington Square was sold to the Redevelopment Authority and the company bought the new site; both transactions were part of the federally funded, urban renewal project. The process involved two property sales – an unusual move in urban renewal practice.[34] The new building at Sixth and Market Streets, Röhm and Haas projected, would provide about 400,000 square feet, which was enough space to meet the company's requirements for the next 20 years. The result was a win-win situation for both Röhm and Haas and the city of Philadelphia because not only would it ignite quality development of the Mall, but the building itself would be by far the most sophisticated design to be realised there.[35]

As an urban renewal project, the Redevelopment Authority was involved in the design process. Walter D'Alessio, project coordinator for the agency, attended the weekly design meetings at Röhm and Haas's Washington Square office. Two key Röhm and Haas executives were involved in the building project in addition to McClintock. The first was Stanley Cole, who had started at Röhm and Haas as a salesman for Plexiglas. He had studied architecture at Pennsylvania State College and entered World War II as a pilot in the Air Corps, operating B24 fighter planes over the Pacific. After returning from the war, he was hired by Harrison & Abramowitz in New York City, where he worked on the prestigious United Nations project. Cole eventually moved to Bristol, Pennsylvania to work for Röhm and Haas's engineering group. As the

only architect employed by the company, Cole was assigned to serve as a professional aide, what is known as a 'client's representative architect' today.[36] He reported to Röhm and Haas's building committee, which had oversight and management of the building project.

On behalf of Röhm and Haas, Cole reviewed Alexander Ewing's initial design, which met all the programmatic needs of the company, but not the requirements for branding Plexiglas on the building's exterior. Ensuring that the company's 'strong interest' in advertising Plexiglas was met was, in fact, 'one of the reasons [he, Stanley Cole] served on the committee'.[37] As a trained architect with practical experience working at the chemical company, Cole was the important link between architect and client, articulating Röhm and Haas's explicit desire for the new headquarters to serve as a showcase for Plexiglas.

The second Röhm and Haas representative on the project was Richard Lindabury, a chemical engineer. As planning director for design and construction, his role was to ensure that internal space allocation met the company's work requirements.[38] Lindabury also attended weekly meetings between the Röhm and Haas team and the architects and was responsible for decisions on such everyday matters as establishing a coordinated system of wall clocks, which would allow employees to operate on precisely the same time.

William McClintock represented the Haas brothers, Otto Jr and John, and ostensibly served as the client over the course of the building project. In this role, McClintock upheld the Haas brothers' three objectives: 1) that the building should be notable, yet not 'flashy'; 2) that the building should fit Röhm and Haas's reputation for financial prudence; and 3) that a 'design consultant' with both a national and an international reputation should be retained.[39] Thus, while McClintock looked after the interests of the Haas brothers on the headquarters project, Lindabury managed the project, and Cole focused on ensuring that the architectural design incorporated Plexiglas.

The Haas brothers' objectives echo those of another company in the city, the Philadelphia Saving Fund Society, who also sought good architecture for its headquarters but refused its architects the opportunity of designing a monument to themselves.

There were varied public images of the architect at that time, one of which was the designer as an unrelenting style-maker, vividly depicted by the fictionalised account of architect Howard Roark in the book and film *The Fountainhead*. This image of the architect is especially untenable when the design and building process carried out by architects on behalf of corporate clients requires open communication, negotiation, and most importantly, joint decision-making. The other, more mainstream image of the architect was as a part of a large architectural firm, a model which had existed for decades. This included firms like D.H. Burnham & Co.; Graham, Anderson, Probst & White; Smith, Hinchman & Grylls; and Voorhees, Gmelin & Walker, among others. The Röhm and Haas project was based on a hybrid model that utilised the large architectural firm model with George M. Ewing & Co. and Pietro Belluschi as consultant designer. Thus, a hybrid model of efficiency and innovative design would accomplish the dual goals of completing a solid building project and an architectural brand identity for the company.

The Architects

The architectural practice of George Ewing & Co. was undergoing similar generational changes that paralleled that of their client, Röhm and Haas. When the Röhm and Haas project began in 1962, Alec Ewing, son of the firm's founder, had already established his own group within George M. Ewing & Co. known as Division 2. The commission would be important in staking the son's independence from the father. Alec Ewing was not an intellectual architect but instead a pragmatic, no-nonsense one. He graduated from the University of Pennsylvania in 1942. Though Paul Philippe Cret had left his professorship there in 1937, the school was still steeped in the Beaux-Arts tradition, which heavily influenced Ewing's architectural education. Upon graduation, Ewing went to work for his father's firm.

In 1959, after the project scope had expanded to become a new construction, Röhm and Haas asked Ewing to submit a preliminary design. The Redevelopment Authority had established an Advisory Board of Design that dealt with new construction and major rehabilitation projects in Center City Philadelphia. The members of the Advisory Board who reviewed the Röhm and Haas design were: Edmund Bacon, Director of the City Planning Commission; Robert Geddes of the architecture firm Geddes, Brecher, Qualls, Cunningham, known for its modern expression in architectural design; and Sydney Martin of the architecture firm Martin and Kirkpatrick, who was an expert in the Georgian architecture that defined the nearby Society Hill neighbourhood.

Sited on the corner of 6th and Ranstead Streets (Ranstead Street is between Market and Chestnut Streets), Ewing's scheme maintained close proximity to Independence Hall, an effort to 'contain the Mall with the building'.[40] While extant images of Ewing's scheme do not exist, its design can be surmised based on the meeting minutes of 12 June 1962 between the client and architects. Ewing's design is described as a 'tower' with a 'metal curtain wall', located at one end of the site, nearest to Independence Hall.[41] While the Advisory Board of Design agreed that the Ewing firm was quite competent and that the interior design met all the space programming needs of its client, it highly recommended that a design consultant with an international reputation be engaged to work with George M. Ewing and Company, specifically to design the building's exterior facade.[42] Geddes emphasised the need for a design consultant and recommended Pietro Belluschi as the architect that Röhm and Haas should consider.[43]

In early June 1962, McClintock, Lindabury, and Ewing travelled to Cambridge, Massachusetts to meet with Pietro Belluschi – who was dean of the architecture school at Massachusetts Institute of Technology at the time – to discuss the design consultancy role.[44] Belluschi accepted right away, considering the urban renewal programme at Independence Mall to be one of the best civic developments in the country. He was particularly drawn to the commission because it gave him the opportunity to develop new applications for the company's products.[45] After this meeting with Belluschi, the project organisers considered no other architects.[46]

At the time, the architects loosely referred to as the Philadelphia School were just beginning to be known nationally and internationally.[47] These architects included Louis Kahn, Robert Venturi, and Mitchell/Giurgola. In 1960, Kahn began design on the Erdman Hall dormitories at Bryn Mawr College. His design for the Margaret Esherick House, commissioned in 1959, was completed in 1961, as was his design for the Richards Medical Labs on the University of Pennsylvania campus. In the early 1960s, Kahn was beginning to gain national fame among architects as a result of Vincent Scully's monograph and the MoMA catalogue on the Richards Building, as well as coverage in architectural journals. Also at this time, Venturi was designing Mother's House in Chestnut Hill, completing it in 1962. His design for Guild House was built in 1963. Mitchell/Giurgola completed the Wright Brothers National Memorial Visitor Center in Kitty Hawk, North Carolina in 1960. Both Venturi and Giurgola were little known until the second half of the decade; neither one had any experience with large-scale commercial projects in the early 1960s. Though not part of the Philadelphia School, architect I.M. Pei was working in the city as well, on a tower and townhouse complex renewal project in Society Hill, which was completed in 1962. While there was certainly no dearth of talented architects in Philadelphia, Alec Ewing had no interest in working with them: his criticism of the leading Philadelphia architects was that they were prima donnas.[48]

Belluschi was a nationally and internationally respected architect who had recently become the dean at MIT, one of the most prestigious architecture schools in the country. Based in the Pacific Northwest, he was known for his regional and contextual approach to modern architecture, which forged a new direction in the postwar period. While rejecting historicism and following modern principles, practitioners of this style spurned the imported conventions of the International Style. Belluschi, along with William Wurster, Richard Neutra, and Rudolph Schindler on the west coast, Charles Eames, and (to some extent) Frank Lloyd Wright, stood as the movement's leaders – yet each had a strong and distinct design personality. This architecture was built from local materials and based on humanistic concerns. For Belluschi in particular, regionalism was based on an emotional understanding of the natural environment.

Yet Belluschi did not achieve the utmost critical acclaim enjoyed by some of his more celebrated contemporaries. While he was certainly accomplished, what tipped the balance in his favour with clients was his affable personality and ability to work well with collaborators. His persona went against the *enfant terrible* style of an architect like Frank Lloyd Wright, but also against the poetics of an architect like Louis Kahn. The determining factor of who got the job was pragmatic. Cole weighed in on the choice of Belluschi, explaining, 'It was my feeling at that time that the person selected should be someone who had demonstrated an ability to communicate with executives in straightforward language about the design elements of such a major building without letting his personal ego get in the way and was easy to work with.'[49] Alec Ewing and Belluschi shared a down-to-earth, common-sense approach to architecture, and although there is no indication that they personally knew each other before the project began, it led to a collegial and productive collaboration that would continue beyond the Röhm and Haas headquarters project.

Possessing both the right credentials and temperament for the position, Belluschi was hired by Röhm and Haas in May of 1962 to serve as architectural design consultant for their new headquarters building. At this point in his career, Belluschi had enjoyed much professional success, as a practitioner and as an academic. He became an influential juror for some of the most important American commissions from the 1950s to the 1980s, including Boston City Hall (1960) and the Vietnam War Memorial (1981). Even greater was his impact as an advisor for architectural projects. Over the course of his career, he advised: individual patrons, including Phyllis Lambert (on the Seagram Building) and Jacqueline Kennedy (on the Kennedy Library); corporations, such as the Ford Foundation and CBS; and art institutions, such as the National Gallery in Washington; as well as developers, foreign ambassadors, and university leaders.[50] Belluschi's contextual approach, interest in the emotional aspect of modern architecture, natural way with clients, and pioneering role as a consultant are important to the story of the Röhm and Haas Building and its position in the evolution of corporate modernism.

Born in Ancona, Italy in 1899, Belluschi studied engineering at the University of Rome and then immigrated to the United States to study at Cornell University.[51] After an unsuccessful job search in New York and a brief electrical engineering job in Idaho, Belluschi travelled to the West Coast in hopes of finding a better position. In April 1925, he found work at A.E. Doyle & Associates in Portland, Oregon, one of the largest architectural firms in the Pacific Northwest.[52] While there, he decided to become an architect, educating himself on the job and passing the licensing exam. Belluschi's success was due not only to his hard work and determination but also to his charming and diplomatic demeanour: at this early point in his career, his innate talent for dealing well with clients emerged. Belluschi was quickly promoted to head of the design department, and in 1933 he became a partner of the firm.

At the same time, Belluschi's commitment to modern architecture deepened. He travelled to Europe in 1929. In Germany, he was inspired by built examples of modern architecture by Erich Mendelsohn, whose theatre in Lehniner Platz, Berlin was newly completed. At the time, most architects travelled throughout Europe to study Classical, Renaissance, and Baroque architecture, but instead Belluschi travelled to Germany to study modernism, an experience similar to that of William Lescaze, architect of the PSFS Building. The Swiss immigrant Lescaze had also travelled back to Europe after briefly working in the United States. For Lescaze, Mendelsohn's work greatly influenced his subsequent projects, especially the PSFS Building design. For Belluschi, Mendelsohn's work also influenced his design at A.E. Doyle. In 1931 and 1932, Belluschi remodelled a pair of existing two-storey buildings – the Equitable Savings and Loan, and the headquarters for the Commonwealth Trust & Title Company. The first banking hall (not the Equitable Building of 1948) whose clean and crisp, curved double-height massing and corner site, clearly show the influence of both Mendelsohn and of Howe and Lescaze's PSFS Building design.

As Belluschi came into his own as an architect, he became known for his modern regionalist approach. By 1943, he had bought out A.E. Doyle and changed its name to Pietro Belluschi, Architect. His designs for houses of the late 1930s and 1940s and for churches in the 1940s and 1950s responded to their specific environmental contexts and offered material tactility and sensuousness. His regional modernism hit upon some very relevant architectural issues of the moment as curators of the Museum of Modern Art featured two of Belluschi's projects in the *Built in the USA, 1932–1944* exhibition of 1953, and editors of the major architectural journals clamoured to publish his work.

Belluschi's work was fundamentally modernist, yet not overly ideological, and also grew out of specifics of place. In defining himself against traditional modernism, Belluschi stated in 1948, 'Architecture must not be dictated by the machine. It must express an emotional understanding of its environment.'[53] Belluschi defined his own regionalism as 'not a school of thought but simply a recognition within its own sphere of what architecture is to human beings, a deep regard for their emotional demands. This need not be forfeited even in the most practical demands of a project.'[54] His sensitivity to human emotion would make his architecture well suited as branding, which aims to reach customers through emotion.

The high point of Belluschi's West Coast practice was his design for the Equitable Building, built in 1948. Among a number of iconic modern corporate headquarters, the Equitable Building was the earliest: it predated SOM's Lever House, Harrison and Abramovitz's Alcoa Building, and Wallace K. Harrison's United Nations Secretariat, all of which were completed in 1952. The Equitable Building, a modern, slab office headquarters, displayed a smooth, seamless aluminium facade and reinforced concrete structural frame.[55] At the age of 50, Belluschi was at the height of his career and one of the leading spokespeople for modernism.

Belluschi left Portland to start his deanship at MIT in January of 1951. He began a new phase of his career as a tastemaker, removing himself from the day-to-day practice of architecture. A number of large projects were still on the boards or in construction at the firm, and Belluschi's associates were not able to continue running the office. His desire to see these projects through led to a meeting with Nathanial Owings of SOM. Belluschi brokered a deal for his projects to be completed by the SOM office, with Belluschi remaining as design principal. By May of 1951 they had signed

85   Pietro Belluschi (*left*), design architect, F.O. Haas (*centre*), client, and Alec Ewing (*right*), architect of record in front of the Röhm and Haas Building, c.1963.

a five-year contract to form Belluschi/Skidmore, Owings & Merrill (B/SOM).[56] This was not an easy union, and through working together both parties discovered untenable differences in their values. SOM's systematic design process clashed with Belluschi's warmer, sense-driven approach. In a mutual decision, B/SOM disbanded at the end of their contract.[57] B/SOM was the first experiment in Belluschi's career as an architectural consultant; future experiments would prove more fruitful.

Belluschi worked well with clients, quickly eliciting their confidence. A number of his contemporaries also built similar reputations, including Minoru Yamasaki, Eero Saarinen, and SOM. By the 1950s, corporate clients had become the norm, and in turn, more and more architecture firms became corporately organised. Large architectural firms that could provide the scaled-up services that corporate clients needed prospered.[58] But because of their size, these big firms experienced difficulty with design innovation and high-quality design – both creating it and maintaining it.[59] As distinctive designs for corporate clients like Lever House and the Seagram Building demonstrated, good architecture brought with it prestige. As a result, corporate clients looked beyond the bottom line and sought out well-known architects. Hiring a 'design consultant' seemed to offer the perfect solution to increasing the level of design of a large architecture firm.[60] Belluschi created his own version of a corporate consultancy, as he carved out a unique role for himself as a renowned and experienced architect who worked with associated architecture firms.

Belluschi's consultancy was enabled by his fame as an architect – the same kind of fame that motivated clients like S.C. Johnson & Son to hire Frank Lloyd Wright. With his down-to-earth personality, Belluschi was an unlikely 'starchitect', but he had nevertheless attained a high degree of fame. Consultancy allowed corporate clients who were aware that architectural prestige could help their image, to bring a famous architect on board as a collaborator. Belluschi worked in association with a variety of firms, including Carl Koch, Emery Roth, RTKL, and Jung/Brannen. Although the quality of the resulting architecture varied, at the height of his career Belluschi had found a viable way to continue designing high-profile projects while pursuing his

academic career as dean. In the case of the Röhm and Haas Building, Belluschi's association with George M. Ewing & Co would prove to be a success (Fig.85).

At times, Belluschi's vision was at odds with current architectural explorations that reached beyond modernism. Unlike other postwar architects such as Paul Rudolph, Marcel Breuer, Louis Kahn, and Eero Saarinen – who explored issues of form and monumentality – Belluschi remained committed to place-driven modernism.[61] Architectural historian and Belluschi biographer and scholar Meredith Clausen points out that Belluschi's approach to architecture was simply pragmatic and resulted in his championing of client demands.[62] In fact, Belluschi prided himself on his business acumen, stating, 'My later professional success was due not a little to luck, much to a practical business approach coming from my early middle-class influence, and to an ability to deal with people.'[63]

Belluschi's alignment with the client and his belief that 'architecture should be part of its environment' coupled well with an ambitious branding strategy developed by Röhm and Haas. Belluschi's beliefs about the importance of place, people, and emotion in architectural design were ones that easily translated to branding the company's identity.

The Design of the Röhm and Haas Building

With F. Otto Haas Jr at the helm, Röhm and Haas began a new era. Belluschi was hired as lead architect in association with George M. Ewing and Company, and the Röhm and Haas Building design began. The first step was for Belluschi to re-design the initial work done by Ewing's firm. 'The basic plan [by Ewing]', explained Stan Cole, Röhm and Haas architect, 'had been developed earlier in the process, with the uncertainty of the exterior design being the concern, particularly given the company's strong interest in making the building a showcase for the architectural usages of its acrylic material – Plexiglas.'[64]

In June 1962, one month after Belluschi was hired, Alec Ewing and his staff met at the architect's office in Cambridge, Massachusetts. Supplied with renderings of Ewing's current design proposal, and photographs of the existing buildings in the site area, Belluschi worked out the beginnings of a new design for the headquarters building.[65] Belluschi approached the design in response to certain aspects of Ewing's design that he deemed inappropriate – specifically its orientation to the mall, 'tower'-like proportions, and 'metal curtain wall'.[66] First, he disagreed with the siting and orientation of the building, which was on the corner nearest to Independence Hall, and with a perpendicular orientation to the Mall. He felt that Ewing's design unsuccessfully attempted to contain the very large mall with this relationship. As a result, he suggested that the building be turned 90 degrees to stand parallel with the Mall. A discussion about how this orientation would address the street followed. The always-practical Belluschi noted that while the 90-degree turning of the building would present an air-conditioning problem, he would turn this into an advantage with 'some imaginative use of Plexiglas'.[67]

Belluschi also felt Ewing's 'tower'-like, vertical building massing was not the right one. He suggested a longer and wider, more 'pleasing' proportion.[68] A lower building, he argued would give a 'higher net to gross ratio', offering the client more usable space. He cited current trends towards larger floor areas, like his recent design for the Pan Am Building in New York. He proposed a new building massing of 270 feet by 150 feet and eight storeys tall.[69] Finally, Belluschi took issue with the exterior expression of Ewing's design. He reacted to Ewing's 'metal curtain wall' design. He denigrated it as 'non-architecture' because of its 'anonymity'.[70] While Belluschi did not propose a specific design for the building's exterior yet, he planned to incorporate Plexiglas 'in a manner expressive of its inherent qualities and not to duplicate other building materials'.[71] Once Belluschi had established the concepts, he would work with Ewing and his architects to develop the design, meeting regularly in Cambridge or Philadelphia.[72] During design development and construction, weekly meetings were held at the Röhm and Haas offices at Washington Square.[73]

While urban renewal brought modern architecture to cities, it was still a controversial process. Understanding this, Belluschi extended his diplomatic approach to the design: it was envisioned as a respectful and neighbourly response to the context of Independence Mall. A new modern building could be considered a shocking addition to a historic neighbourhood. The Röhm and Haas Building would be a bold but contextual assertion in that context. At the time, modern buildings were not yet constructed in the area. Pei's Society Hill Towers were on track for completion in 1964, but other modern buildings, the Liberty Bell Pavilion and Penn Mutual, both by Mitchell Giurgola, would not appear on the Mall until the 1970s.

By the end of the next month, in July 1962, Belluschi would present the main design features of the headquarters to Röhm and Haas Vice-President William McClintock, and company representatives Richard N. Lindabury and Stanley Cole. At this meeting, the design showed expressive, exposed concrete columns with hyperbolic paraboloid caps supporting the upper six floors. The exterior materials were shown as concrete, Plexiglas, aluminium, and tinted window glass. Belluschi noted that exterior colours would be selected 'within a small range of warm colors to unify the overall design'.[74]

Belluschi also accomplished his desire to incorporate Plexiglas into the building facade. The client's landmark product appeared as Plexiglas sunshades around the upper six floors, Plexiglas spandrels, and a 3-foot-wide catwalk. This was the imaginative use of Plexiglas that Belluschi had mentioned in the last client meeting. Belluschi explained that the balconies and sunshades would eliminate the need for interior window blinds except on the west elevation.[75] The prefabricated Plexiglas window frames, or spandrels, were located above and below the tinted window glass.

At this point, Belluschi's main design elements had been established. From then on, Ewing's team would focus on their realisation, with approval and input from Belluschi. In its final built form, the Röhm and Haas corporate headquarters occupied a prominent 298 feet along the western edge of Independence Mall. Situated northwest of Independence Hall, the site had a direct sight line to the colonial landmark (see Fig.86). Allotted 400,000 square feet, Röhm and Haas had more than enough office space to consolidate their employees and rent out space to other businesses (Fig.87).

86   Rendering of the Röhm and Haas Building with a view of Independence Hall.

NOW RENTING...

SUPERB OFFICE SPACE in the handsome new **ROHM & HAAS BUILDING** under construction where the most exciting urban renewal is going forward . . . □ **INDEPENDENCE MALL WEST** at Market and 6th Streets in Philadelphia □ Approximately 150,000 square feet, including full floors are available for lease. Projected occupancy late 1964. Pencil in your office requirements on the typical floor plan inside. See how the central core construction provides large areas of uninterrupted space to permit complete flexibility of office layout.

87   A leasing brochure boasted 'superb office space in the handsome new Röhm and Haas Building under construction where the most exciting urban renewal is going forward . . .' *c.*1963.

88 View from the Röhm and Haas Building onto Independence Mall through Plexiglas screens.

When the Röhm and Haas Building was completed, it was by far the most sophisticated building on Independence Mall. The building's strong horizontal pattern was articulated by the projecting edges of the floors and the textured sunshades of Plexiglas. The prominent nine-storey-tall, mid-rise building sits on a granite plinth, defined by perimeter landscaping of evergreen shrubs and low growing myrtle.[76] Lifted a few feet above the sidewalk, the headquarters building established a rarefied plane, thus setting an appropriate tone for the chemical company desirous of prestige. At the same time, the building established a respectful and diplomatic relationship to Independence Mall (Fig.88). The Röhm and Haas Building's reinforced concrete structural system rested on a grid of prismoidal cast concrete columns capped by wide, inverted pyramids, also of reinforced concrete. The

building read as a light glass and acrylic mass atop muscular pilotis, with the ground floor stepping back five feet to create a continuous arcade (or 'galleria') around the building. The overhang and prismoidal columns defined the covered walkway around the entire ground floor with 22-foot-tall, vaulted ceilings. This dramatic space would become iconic in the company's real estate brochures.

Broad granite steps led from the wide, Sixth Street sidewalk up to the plinth. The galleria extended around and underneath the building in a 60-foot-wide plaza, which bifurcated the ground floor at its midpoint. Two lobby entrances – one for Röhm and Haas, and the other slated for a branch of the Fidelity-Philadelphia Trust Company bank – occupied this space. Radiant sidewalk heating, a novel technological innovation at the time, was installed on the path leading to the lobbies. Each

89 Construction photograph of
the building's monolithic prismoidal
columns were cast in place and
left exposed, requiring the finest-
possible concrete finish.

prismoidal column supported an inverted pyramid, creating a continuous vertical to horizontal support system, spaced on a 30-foot module. The tapering line of the columns was three feet at the base and four feet at the top. Cast in place, the columns and caps were left exposed, requiring the finest-possible concrete finish work. With the distance from the floor to the highest point in the ceiling, the resultant space was voluminous. The ground floor was enclosed by sections of glazing 30 feet wide by 22 feet high at their highest point, an abstracted pointed arch form resulting from the inverted pyramid and prismoidal column.[77]

The sculptural, first-floor columns supported reinforced concrete diagonal beams. Above that, a grid of square columns extended and supported the eight floors above, resting on the ends of the cantilevers and crossing points of the diagonals. All upper floors were reinforced concrete flat slab, with 30-inch waffle forms.[78] Röhm and Haas asked G. Holmes Perkins, dean of the architecture school at the University of Pennsylvania, to review the project before it went up for approval, on the suggestion of the Redevelopment Authority Advisory Board of Design, as a safety device. In a matter of months, the design was accepted by the client and approved by the Philadelphia Planning Commission, the Redevelopment Authority, and the Art Commission.

At the ground floor – the most public level of the building – the reinforced concrete pilotis were rendered in a muscular and textured brutalism reminiscent of Marcel Breuer's work. The space created by the columns and caps telegraphed monumentality, solidity, materiality, visual dynamism, and patterning. These were elements characteristic of a search for an expression that was more typical of architects such as Saarinen, Breuer, and Kahn than it was for Belluschi himself. This demonstrated the evolving modernism of his architecture. The abstract column and ceiling forms created an arcade of light and shadow, based on a faceted, diagonal geometry (Figs 89, 90).

The Plexiglas sunscreen that enveloped the upper storeys of the Röhm and Haas Building ingeniously displayed the company's product, thus serving as branded architecture in its most explicit sense. It effectively merged branding and architecture, as the company's product made direct connections with all who viewed the building. The building's eight upper floors read as a bronze-tinted glass box. The heat-absorbing glass was fixed in place with bronze-coloured

90   At the entrance to the Röhm and Haas Building, the abstract shapes of the columns create an arcade of light and shadow.

91 Textured Plexiglas sunscreen device on top left, supported by bronze-coloured aluminium structural members

aluminium used for the exterior latticework supporting the sunscreens, spandrel panels, and interior metal frames (Fig.91).[79]

The sunscreens were hung five feet off the building by the aluminium lattice frame. Four-foot-high horizontal ribbons of bronze-coloured Plexiglas began at the top of the second floor and repeated eight times to the top floor. These corrugated sunscreens hung down over the upper portions of the windows on all sides of the building except the north.[80] Brown, opaque, textured Plexiglas spandrel panels provided ornamental contrast with the exposed concrete structure. The panels' slightly pebbly surface pattern (designed to eliminate large areas of reflection) took the form of shallow pans (Fig.92).[81]

By creating a framework around the building, Belluschi aimed to minimise the building's bulk, which in turn respected the scale of Independence Hall.[82] Initially, the client had wanted to showcase the vibrant colours that were available in Plexiglas and suggested a blue colour for the building panels. Belluschi objected, however, successfully arguing his case against the colour:

Pietro and I attended all meetings with our client and much of that related to visual impact issues. It was Pietro's strong recommendation that the color of the Plexiglas be an earth tone, rather than a sky color favored by Röhm & Haas's management. His reasoning made sense . . . he said a 500,000-sf building will overpower the domestic scale of Independence Hall and it would be a mistake to have a bold color competing with Independence Hall. In a matter of minutes Otto and John Haas, along with their Executive Committee, bought Pietro's recommendation. Later they were pleased that they followed Pietro's recommendation.[83]

When questioned about his bronze and brown colour choice for the building, Belluschi reportedly said, 'Go look at the Seagram Building.'[84] By referencing the seminal corporate headquarters, Belluschi signalled an important precedent as well as his continued allegiance to a Miesian model for his work.[85]

Röhm and Haas's Plexiglas sunscreen was a major architectural branding achievement. From the time Belluschi was hired, he embraced the idea of

92 Exterior photo showing window details.

experimentation with Plexiglas: his understanding of the commission resulted in an exciting new identity for his client. At the same time, Belluschi created sunscreens to cover large expanses of glass on the building exterior. Responding to the problems associated with the widespread use of glass curtain walls, architects reasoned that screens cooled the glazed interiors. Because sunscreens provided the function of tempering harsh sunlight into interior space, architects considered them an environmental necessity.

At the same time, there were other implications of sunscreens that can be applied to the Röhm and Haas Plexiglas sunscreen, as explained by *Architectural Forum* editor Douglas Haskell. 'Sunscreens', he wrote, 'would surround their bare walls with sets of louvres and with egg-crate screens, which happened to cast pretty shadows – but these ornamental features were billed as purely functional sunshades.'[86] In his essay 'Ornament Rides Again', published in the April 1958 issue of *Architectural Forum*, Haskell discussed the recent break-out of what had been the 'covert ornamentalism of modern architecture'.[87] Haskell quoted Adolf Loos's assertion that 'The progress of modern man is measured by his removal of ornament from useful objects.'[88] Yet by the mid-1950s, Haskell argued, the 'sly sinners' were designing 'surreptitious decoration'.

The architects to whom he referred included the high priests of modernism who were largely influential to Belluschi. Haskell wrote,

> Mies van der Rohe's steel rails, which ran up the building were decorative but the rails were described as structural stiffening. Le Corbusier made sculpture of ventilation fans and penthouses on roofs, and lifted his building with ornamental effect onto legs called 'pilotis'; but was not all this strictly essential?[89]

Like many architects with long careers, Mies's and Le Corbusier's work had evolved. Reintroducing ornament to modern architecture was no small feat and transitional means were necessary. Le Corbusier's *brise-soleil*, for example, can be considered modern ornament. The device was a means of counteracting the vulnerability of the fully glazed facade to heat gain, without returning to the traditional hole-in-the-wall solid facade.[90] His designs for *brise-soleil* at the Cité de Refuge in Paris (1933), the Unité d'Habitation in Marseille (1952), and the Secretariat Building at Chandigarh (1958), all made of concrete, possessed depth and created subdivisions, giving the facades the modelling and aedicular expression that had been lost with the decline of classical window frames and pilasters. The device created a relationship to the human being as well as to the building as a whole, reintroducing a hierarchy of scales. While Belluschi's Plexiglas and aluminium sunscreen on the Röhm and Haas Building was of an altogether different materiality and construction, it too created a symbolic and functional relationship to the viewer and occupant.

In the narrative of Röhm and Haas branding, the Plexiglas sunscreen functioned as a kind of material signage displaying the company's product on its most conspicuous surface – the facade. Thus, the display of Plexiglas enabled a connection with the public. When the Röhm and Haas Building was being designed, theories on how architecture and the built environment affected the human subject were numerous and influential: these included Reyner Banham's *The New Brutalism* (1957), Jane Jacobs's *The Death and Life of Great American Cities* (1961), Steen Eiler Rasmussen's *Experiencing Architecture* (1964), and Aldo Rossi's *The Architecture of the City* (1966), among others. *Experiencing Architecture*, for example, considered the psychology of art. Universal concepts like spatial relationships, volume, and contrasting effects of solids and cavities, scale and proportion, were the means to achieve empathy in modernism. Aesthetics in this vein was not about style but about how everyone, inclusively, could relate to and experience architecture. This was very much in line with not only Belluschi's convictions about humanistic concerns in architecture, but the emerging practice of branding which aims to make emotional connections with people.

At the time, other corporations also employed architectural devices in their headquarters designs to connect with the public. In fact, the Röhm and Haas design resembled contemporaneous designs by Breuer and Saarinen. Breuer was commissioned by IBM to participate in its branding programme.[91] The German émigré designed IBM's Research Center in La Gaude, France in 1958–1962 (Fig.93).

93   Belluschi's Röhm and Haas design for prismoidal concrete columns resembled Marcel Breuer's column design for IBM's Research Center, La Gaude, France, designed 1958–1962. Construction photograph, detail of column, 1961.

Both office buildings displayed structural muscularity – Breuer's supported on prismoidal, Y-shaped pillars, and Belluschi's on paraboloid columns, both formed in a raw concrete materiality. Both took sun-shading seriously, with Breuer's as a concrete egg-crate facade and Belluschi's as a Plexiglas sunscreen. With the two architects working in close proximity at the time – Belluschi at MIT and Breuer at Harvard University's Graduate School of Design, where he taught under Walter Gropius – it is probable that Belluschi admired Breuer's IBM design, which was completed in the same year as Belluschi began his design for the Röhm and Haas Building.

Like Belluschi, Saarinen also welcomed the corporate client's identity infusing his designs. Although he was criticised for the varied quality of his designs, it was precisely this aspect that defined his corporate work as architectural branding. Saarinen's John Deere & Company corporate headquarters in Moline, Illinois (1961–1964) shares many features with Belluschi's Röhm and Haas design.[92] Both were low, horizontal glass buildings with articulated sunscreens. For John Deere, the sunscreens were formed out of Corten steel and referenced the rusted tractor familiar to the farm equipment of its customers.[93] Analogously, in the Röhm and Haas design, the company's own product, Plexiglas, was used to fabricate sunscreens on the building exterior. The similarities between these projects situate Belluschi within the critical re-evaluation of modernism taking place at the time. With this headquarters design, Belluschi was no longer an outsider. He was part of an important and timely discussion about how modern architecture served corporate clients.

Putting Your Best Fascia Forward

Into the mid-1960s, Plexiglas sales continued to grow, revolutionising the outdoor sign industry. At the same time, Röhm and Haas entered the synthetic fibre industry, with innovations like Amin/8 stretch fibre for clothing and Formell colour-spun hosiery. Unfortunately, the company's arrival into this sector came too late and formidable competition from DuPont could not be overcome. On the other hand, Röhm and Haas's postwar investment in design, consulting architectural leaders like Walter Gropius and marketing the Dream Suite, created success for the company. Plexiglas applications were divided by whether the material was used as a substitute for glass, or as a material of its own unique nature.[94] The ersatz applications provided

94 In photos and descriptions, the Röhm and Haas Company documented the use of curved Plexiglas panels in the design of the State Capital Bank of Oklahoma City.

95 The Röhm and Haas Company documented the Plexiglas dome in the design of the Capp Towers Motor Hotel in Minneapolis, Minnesota.

a large and reliable market for Plexiglas, while those designed in the nature of the material reached a smaller, but important market. The latter applications were pursued by architects and designers.

Röhm and Haas vigorously promoted Plexiglas's use in architecture.[95] The company documented dozens of architectural projects in the 1960s that used Plexiglas in curved storefronts, fascias, domes, and coloured facades.[96] Fascias – coverings positioned at the top of buildings that enclose the ends of internal roof beams – read like signage, especially when viewed from fast-moving cars at far distances. The projects were designed by illustrious architects such as Frank Lloyd Wright, large corporate firms such as SOM, and small-to-medium-sized firms across America. Wright exploited Plexiglas's unique qualities in his design for the V.C. Morris Gift Shop in San Francisco.[97] He chose Plexiglas to create an illuminated ceiling formed with a series of domes over a spiral-ramped space. Plexiglas panels also found successful application in the curved panels of the State Capitol Bank in Oklahoma City, a dome at the Capp Towers Motor Hotel in Minneapolis, and a Mondrian-inspired coloured storefront at the Oak Cliff Savings & Loan, in Dallas (Figs 94, 95, 96).[98] Plexiglas was widely used in interior lighting fixtures, including those at the Equitable Life Assurance Society Building in New York City by SOM (Fig.97). That building used 43,000, 1 × 3-foot light-control lenses injection moulded from Plexiglas moulding powder. Plexiglas's superior qualities over traditional glass were clear: 'The lenses are many times more breakage resistant than glass and less than one-half the weight.'[99]

After the Röhm and Haas headquarters project, one of Alexander Ewing and Associates' first commissions, the Parke Davis District Office and Warehouse in Cherry Hill, New Jersey, used 56 formed panels of Plexiglas in an internally lit fascia that cantilevered over the building interior (Fig.98).[100] At and above the roofline of commercial suburban buildings, fascias were highly visible. Röhm and Haas highlighted other examples of Plexiglas fascia design: the Montgomery Ward Store in the Apache Plaza Shopping Center in Minneapolis (Fig.99), and the Mansfield Shopping Center in Springfield, Ohio.[101]

Perhaps the most architecturally significant Plexiglas project was the Buckminster Fuller-designed icosahedron dome at the 1967 World's Fair Expo in Montreal (Figs 100, 101). Designed as the USA Pavilion, the monumental dome employed more than 200,000 square feet of transparent grey Plexiglas. Nineteen hundred individual dome-shaped panels measuring 10 × 12 feet were used. Three shades of grey Plexiglas, decreasing in degree of light transmittance from the base of the pavilion to the top, provided daylight in the interior, along with effective control of solar heat and glare. Exploiting Plexiglas's materiality, architects and designers embraced its futuristic qualities: transparency, formability, and light transmittance. Unfortunately, Plexiglas lacked in fireproof qualities, as demonstrated by a 1976 fire caused by welders sealing an opening in the shell. Within minutes, the fire destroyed the entire Plexiglas dome, leaving only the steel truss skeleton.

Röhm and Haas's own corporate headquarters would become the ultimate showcase for Plexiglas. The experience of visiting the corporate headquarters in person would serve as the most effective sales tool. 'Röhm & Haas', recalled Alec Ewing, 'wanted their new headquarters to be an example of incorporating their product Plexiglas.' The material was infused throughout the architecture as 'specially-designed Plexiglas doorknobs, bronze-color sunshades of Plexiglas [to] shield windows, lobby chandeliers using Plexiglas rods for unique lighting effects, and lighting fixtures equipped with rectangular lenses and circular diffusers of Plexiglas'.[102] These applications and many others amounted to 130,000 square feet of Plexiglas used throughout the building exterior and interior.[103]

Applications of Plexiglas on the building interior were wide ranging and included such accessories as telephone faceplates, coat rack enclosures, push plates and kick plates on doors, and modesty panels at rest room entrances. Other Röhm and Haas acrylic products were also incorporated in less conspicuous applications: in mortar and caulking compounds for masonry joints, Paraplex plasticisers for vinyl wallcoverings, upholstery fabrics, in the paint on the walls, and polyester resins for tile-like facings (Fig.102).[104] Plexiglas

96 The Röhm and Haas Company documented the coloured Plexiglas facade panels
of the Oak Cliff Savings and Loan in Dallas, Texas.

97 The Röhm and Haas Company documented the Plexiglas use in the interior light lenses
in the SOM-designed Equitable Life Assurance Society Building in New York City.

98   The Röhm and Haas Company documented the use of Plexiglas in the internally lit
fascia of the Parke Davis District Office and Warehouse in Cherry Hill, New Jersey.

99   The Röhm and Haas Company documented the use of Plexiglas on the fascia of the Montgomery Ward Store in Minneapolis, Minnesota.

The largest transparent enclosure ever built—a geodesic dome glazed with Plexiglas acrylic plastic— houses the United States exhibit at Expo 67, the world's fair at Montreal. The giant dome is 250 feet in diameter and 187 feet high. Its glazing required over 200,000 square feet of transparent Plexiglas, formed into nearly 2,000 individual 10 by 12 foot panels. The photograph at right shows one of the panels being hoisted into position.

100   The Röhm and Haas Company advertised the Plexiglas icosahedron dome used in the Buckminster Fuller-designed U.S. Pavilion for Expo '67 in Montreal, Canada.

101   The Röhm and Haas Company highlighted the use of Plexiglas at Expo '67 in a trade exhibit.

Specially-designed Plexiglas doorknobs are used throughout the building.

Telephone instrument face plates are made of Plexiglas.

Bronze-color sunshades of Plexiglas shield windows.

Lobby chandeliers, designed by Professor Gyorgy Kepes of Massachusetts Institute of Technology, use Plexiglas rods for unique lighting effects.

Caulking compounds for masonry joints and window walls use acrylic polymers for permanent flexibility.

Lighting fixtures are equipped with rectangular lenses and circular diffusers of Plexiglas.

Decorative vinyl wall coverings use Paraplex® plasticizers.

Cement blocks in basement have been given a tile-like facing with Paraplex polyester resins.

102   Plexiglas was used throughout the building in a variety of applications which amounted to 130,000 square feet of the material used throughout the interior and exterior, in the pamphlet 'Welcome to the Röhm and Haas Company, A Handbook for Employees'.

was used in much of the lighting systems of the building (Fig.103). These included all of the refractors for fluorescent lights and other fixtures – ranging from coves to incandescent downlights to circular-diffuser installations.[105]

For the lobby spaces of the Röhm and Haas Building, Belluschi envisioned special light fixtures. The client had suggested Altamira-brand lights, which were installed at the nearby Hopkinson House apartment building designed by modernist architect Oskar Stonorov. When he was in town, Belluschi stopped into Hopkinson House to inspect the fixtures. He did not like the design or workmanship of the lighting and felt they were the wrong fixtures for the Röhm and Haas Building. In a memo from C. Van R. Bogert Jr of George M. Ewing and Co. to the Röhm and Haas Company, Belluschi's

suggestion was for 'long, thin rods and tubes which would hang like the prism on the old crystal chandeliers'.[106] He continued, 'If this is not practical, as an alternate, a specially designed chandelier with long, graceful arms supporting the light sources' would be appropriate.[107]

Belluschi approached his friend and MIT colleague, artist György Kepes, to design Plexiglas light sculptures for the Röhm and Haas headquarters' lobby spaces. The result, referred to by Kepes as 'illumination design', formed the pinnacle of showcasing Plexiglas in the building. The 15 chandeliers were 16 × 16 feet each and hung from thin metal rods located at the intersection of four ceiling units (Fig.104). The X form of the chandeliers echoed Belluschi's ceiling joints and added a dynamic, luminous,

103   Plexiglas is used for striking circular light diffusers in the boardroom of the Röhm and Haas Building.

104　György Kepes designed fifteen Plexiglas chandeliers for the Röhm and Haas building.

floating form to the grid of pyramidal caps and prismoidal columns. In each fixture, a light box cast fluorescent light through more than 2,000 clear Plexiglas rods of differing widths and lengths, in a composition that resembled vertical rays of light. The rods served as vehicles for the transfer of light from end to end (Fig.105). The effect of these chandeliers was extraordinary. The fruitful collaboration between art, architecture, and industrial production demonstrated not only how important light was for Plexiglas applications but also how spectacular design could bring distinction to a product and its company.

As an artist, György Kepes worked with industrially constructed media that expressed the modern age. His preferred media were photography and film, both intrinsically involving light. His work at MIT enabled areas of overlap and collaboration between art and science. By 1967 Kepes had founded the Center for Advanced Visual Studies at MIT, a forum for artists and designers to conduct experiments with scientists and engineers. Kepes's experimental and collaborative spirit enabled him to make connections between people in different fields. In his collaboration with architecture and industry, through Belluschi and Röhm and Haas, Kepes took his vision beyond academia, into the commercial world.[108]

Röhm and Haas co-opted the narrative of art and industry to tout Plexiglas as a relevant new material for art. Required by the Redevelopment Authority to spend a substantial amount of money on art installed in the building, the company took the opportunity to commission a number of additional artworks incorporating Plexiglas. A 1966 article in the *Röhm and Haas Reporter* asserted, 'Plexiglas – a product of modern science and industry – has much to offer the artist.' It recognised the great advantage of cultivating this audience: 'The artist has a great deal to contribute to the function, scope and even the status of a material such as Plexiglas.'[109] The company commissioned Mexican sculptor Arturo Cuetara to create a highly polished Plexiglas and stainless-steel piece in the form of an architectural column for the boardroom foyer. It also commissioned artist Freda Koblick and illustrator Sheryl Tattersfield to create colourful and dynamic Plexiglas murals that were placed at the entrances to the lounge and lunchroom areas on the fifth floor. Röhm and Haas also commissioned sculptor Clark B. Fitzgerald to create an outdoor sculpture and fountain entitled *Milkweed Pod*. Through these works, Plexiglas was realised as a 'truly plastic material in an artistic sense' – one that 'not only permits plasticity of design and execution, but plasticity of thought'.[110]

Though Plexiglas possessed distinct characteristics, such as transparency, lightness, colour, and texture, each of these characteristics could be customised in response to a specified need. In short, Plexiglas was not so much an end product as it was a material means to a product end, defined by market demand. Architecture in this sense presented the ideal market for Plexiglas and demonstrated an ideal version of Plexiglas achievement in architecture and art, intended as the inspiration and encouragement for subsequent creativity in architectural applications.

Collaboration in the Röhm and Haas Building occurred not only through the intersection of art and industry but also in its architectural design structure. 'The association was the best we ever had', recalled Alec Ewing. He continued, 'Pietro, during the entire design and construction process was extraordinary. He never insisted on his way or being given all of the credit. He welcomed our input and made us feel that we had a true joint-venture.'[111] Alec Ewing gave credit for the design first to Pietro Belluschi and then to George M. Ewing & Co.

There are very few Pietros in any generation. While he became an academic he never lost sight of what life is like in the trenches of practicing architecture. He fully understood that it takes dozens of well-trained and fully experienced architects and engineers to develop the design of a building like this one. Then it is just as important that hundreds in the building trades constructed it well. A successful architect must have a back-up staff and an extraordinary client.[112]

105   The upper portion of the chandelier was a light box, which cast light through the multitudinous 2,087 Plexiglas rods of differing widths and lengths.

The Röhm and Haas project demonstrates both the proto-starchitect phenomenon and the emerging practice model of collaboration. Belluschi was hired for his fame. However, the collaboration involving Pietro Belluschi as consultant architect, Alec Ewing as associated architect, and Stanley Cole as client representative was what created a productive and fruitful design. Not only would Belluschi and Ewing work together again – on the University Lutheran Center in 1969 – but after completing the Röhm and Haas project Cole would leave the chemical corporation and partner with Alec Ewing in a new architecture firm.[113] In 1979, Belluschi would serve as consultant to the Federal Reserve Bank in Washington, DC: he recommended EwingCole as designers for the new headquarters of the Federal Reserve in Philadelphia, and EwingCole received and completed the commission.[114]

The specialised collaboration that created the Röhm and Haas headquarters represented a shift in architectural practice. Whereas the previous case study, Lever House, was the product of SOM's comprehensive structure, which enabled it to provide both design and production services within the same firm, the Röhm and Haas Building was the result of a specialised structure involving an architectural consultant and an associated firm. Comprehensive and specialised firms would continue to proliferate in and by the 1980s – most architecture firms would be one or the other.[115]

The Röhm and Haas Building was completed in 1964. In the following year, it was awarded first prize for 'Office of the Year' by the editorial board of *Administrative Management* magazine. Editor Walter Kleinschrod cited the building as a 'superb embodiment of administrative efficiency', praising its offices as 'look[ing] ahead 50 years'.[116] An article on the award pointed out that many employee amenities – the fifth floor employee cafeteria, a public cafeteria in the basement, a blast shelter to accommodate 2,250 people, and a 300-car parking garage on an adjoining site – had been incorporated in the scheme.[117] From the business community's point of view, the Röhm and Haas Building was a great success.

The nuanced siting of the Röhm and Haas headquarters building was not lost on *Administrative Management*. The trade journal cited the building's success in upholding its civic responsibility, applauding the company for creating a 'modern building fit into an area steeped in antiquity'.[118] In a role as urban catalyst, the building stood as an example for other corporations to participate in redevelopment. Just as the firm had considered and then rejected a move to the suburbs, other corporations were persuaded to do the same based on the success of the Röhm and Haas project. The urban context of landmarks, historical monuments, parks, and transportation facilities offered a rich experience not matched by the suburbs. These were provisions offered by the city that projected a future for major businesses committed to revitalising the downtown area.[119]

Corporate Identity and Architecture as Brand

By the mid-1960s, a new emphasis on corporate identity and design coordination began to expand the designer's role. In the 1960s, corporations became concerned with communications management as the context in which trade took place expanded to globalised trade with the growing number of multinational corporations.[120] Books such as Henrion and Parkin's *Design Coordination and Corporate Image* (1967) and James Pilditch's *Communication by Design: A Study in Corporate Identity* (1970) detailed corporate identity at the time. The design of corporate identity sought to connect with audiences through presenting a cohesive message through different media.[121]

Henrion and Parkin's *Design Coordination and Corporate Image* offers a look into how corporate identity was defined and developed at this time. The practice of 'corporate identity' encompassed 'the totality of pictures or ideas or reputations of a corporation in the minds of the people who come into contact with it'.[122] As related to corporate identity, the book's authors discussed the term 'image', which they defined from the 1965 *Oxford Modern English Usage* dictionary as the idea or the general impression of some person, or institution, as received by the mind's eye of an outsider. They pointed out that 'image' determines 'whether the person is a good chap or a bad chap, the institution a good show or a bad show'.[123] The public perception of corporations was immensely important: identity emerged as a means of addressing the organisation's need to ensure its overall financial success.[124]

Identities were manifested comprehensively. 'A corporation has many points of contact with various groups of people', explained Henri Kay Henrion, German graphic designer and pioneer of European corporate identity. He defined the scope of corporate identity as having:

> Premises, works, products, packaging, stationery, forms, vehicles, publications, and uniforms, as well as the usual kinds of promotional activities. These things are seen by customers, agents, suppliers, financiers, shareholders, competitors, the press, and the general public, as well as its own staff. The people in these groups build up their idea of the corporation from what they see and experience of it. An image is therefore an intangible and essentially complicated thing, involving the effect of many and varied factors on many and varied people with many and varied interests.[125]

By synthesising the various physical artefacts that represent the company through a consistent trademark (a legally registered name, logo, slogan, and design), identity is given a visual, design-based expression. Companies at this time, including Röhm and Haas, understood the important role of design in crafting their identity.

Röhm and Haas unveiled the company's new corporate identity and its new headquarters building simultaneously in 1964.[126] The company had hired leading American graphic designer Lester Beall to design a new logo as well as other collateral logos. The logo appeared as an abstracted chemical flask outlined with an up-pointing arrow. The flask outline was articulated as a cut-out, against a vertically oriented, orange rectangle. Below the flask, the company name was stacked, in bold black letters.[127] Röhm and Haas's new identity was featured in *Design Coordination and Corporate Image*. In it, company CEO F. Otto Haas was quoted as saying:

> The new corporate symbol we have adopted represents more than just a change and modernization of our long-established mark. It reflects the dynamic spirit of our company, its expanding interests in new and challenging fields, both here and aboard. The proper use of the new mark is essential if we are to make the most of our opportunities to develop a strong public awareness of our corporate identity.[128]

The variety of names under which the company operated around the world had caused a good deal of confusion. With the new trademark, these disparate operations would be unified. 'This new symbol was adopted to give a common corporate identity to members of the Röhm and Haas family, both here and abroad. . . . The symbol is being used in all printed material and advertising prepared by the parent company, its foreign subsidiaries and certain domestic subsidiaries.'[129]

A focus on corporate identity became widespread after World War II, a period characterised by industrial growth and market changes. As corporations faced greater competition, it became imperative to distinguish themselves in the marketplace. A number of enlightened corporations, such as Braun, CBS, Chase Manhattan Bank, Herman Miller, IBM, International Paper, Knoll, Olivetti, and Westinghouse, understood that a new comprehensive design identity programme would be key to their business success. New logotypes and visual identities were designed to define each corporation's particular ethos, in order to stand out among competing corporations and their products.

Lester Beall, together with other modernist American graphic designers such as Paul Rand, Herbert Bayer, and Alvin Lustig, propelled the development of comprehensive corporate identity programmes from the early 1950s until the late 1960s. Beall's most exemplary identity work was for the Connecticut General Life Insurance Company between 1955 and 1958.[130] The identity design programme followed the architectural and interior design project headed up by Gordon Bunshaft and SOM, together with Florence Knoll in Bloomfield, Connecticut. Beall designed not only an iconic, award-winning, trademark but also interior building signage, policy forms,

106　Trade show exhibit displaying Röhm and Haas's Lester Beall-designed corporate identity .

coordinate the many separate items all belonging to the one corporation, to achieve coherent and control results over a long period. This is what we understand by design coordination.'[131] Corporations embraced design and design coordination as a competitive business strategy. A new role for designers in the corporate world emerged.

The Röhm and Haas company achieved corporate identity and design coordination. Lester Beall designed a corporate identity programme that included a trademark, letterhead, and signage for research labs, water towers, and transportation vehicles (Fig.106). Röhm and Haas's three-dimensional corporate identity was defined by the use of Plexiglas in objects, art, lighting fixtures, signage, accessories, interior design, and architecture. Together, the various designs exhibited a coordinated whole (Fig.107).[132] In 1966, the interior designer of the Röhm and Haas Building, Michael Saphier of Saphier, Lerner, Schindler, Inc. of New York, explained the role of office design as a public relations medium. In the trade journal *The Office*, Saphier explained how office design had moved beyond impressing the office visitor to informing him or her about the company. At Röhm and Haas, company-invented materials were on prominent display and integrated into the building (Fig. 108). They demonstrated to personnel the aesthetic possibilities of their company's products and to visitors the desirability of that aesthetic. Saphier emphasised how the office functioned as a communications medium for the corporation.[133]

Previous case studies presented in this book have demonstrated various ways in which architecture communicates a company's brand identity and connects with its consumers through its corporate headquarters design. PSFS's brand was bolstered with the building design, and in particular its rooftop sign; S.C. Johnson & Son leveraged Frank Lloyd Wright's fame and design as its brand identity; and Lever Brothers represented itself with the dramatic formal statement of Lever House. PSFS, S.C. Johnson & Son, and now Röhm and Haas achieved synthesised interiors whose unity of design created strong connections with occupants, thereby reinforcing their client institution's brands.

annual reports, letterheads, advertising, and other promotional material for the large insurance company.

The rapid growth of the corporation and the increased competition for consumers in the postwar era encouraged a level of control over a wide range of things, the appearance of which was affected by design. Corporations sought good design but recognised that in isolation it was not as powerful as it could be: 'Further effort, of a different kind', Henrion pointed out, 'is needed to

107 This trade exhibit shows Röhm and Haas's strategy of architecture as a vehicle to demonstrate and publicise its products. The presentation reads: 'Röhm & Haas products used in the new home office building.'

108   In a series of paste-ups, the Röhm and Haas company's advertising department presented a number of architectural projects that incorporated Plexiglas, including their own Philadelphia headquarters.

In this final study, the Röhm and Haas Building brings this study of architectural brand building to its apogee. The Röhm and Haas Building brought architectural branding to a new level with its material product displayed on the building's exterior as well as throughout its interior spaces, creating a multitude of opportunities for inhabitants to engage with Plexiglas's intrinsic and fascinating material qualities. The three previous case studies did not achieve what the Röhm and Haas headquarters did in branding the corporation through a material. By displaying their product architecturally, the very materiality of the building serves as the medium for the message.

Through architecture, interior design, light fixtures, furniture, and graphics, the Röhm and Haas corporate headquarters reinforced the message that Röhm and Haas was an innovative, technologically advanced chemical company. From the Plexiglas sunscreens to the spectacular chandeliers to the various interior light fixtures to the unique commissioned art pieces, the building created a total Plexiglas environment, thus, creating a myriad of opportunities for material expression. The headquarters represented a new kind of office – one that advertised the corporation's products to the public on the exterior, and infused the everyday work experience of company associates, potential clients, supplier salesmen, and employees on the interior. It was, at the same time, a total work of art and a comprehensively branded environment.

Röhm and Haas was not the only corporation at this time to approach its architecture as a display of its products. Alcoa and Reynolds Metals, both leaders in the aluminium industry, also seized the material potential of their products and displayed them on the facades of their buildings. Alcoa's 1953 Pittsburgh headquarters by Harrison and Abramowitz featured pressed and anodised sheet aluminium panels on its 30-storey skyscraper design. SOM designed aluminium sun louvres and a plethora of aluminium applications, interior partitions, and hardware for Reynolds Metals' 1958 Executive Office Building in Richmond, Virginia. Minoru Yamasaki designed a regional headquarters for Reynolds Metals in Southfield, Michigan; the 1959 design featured a spectacular display of intricately fused, extruded aluminium that formed a sunscreen over the glass facade.[134] An abundance of aluminium was also used on the interior. The power

of architectural branding becomes amplified with material display, which activates human connection through the senses.

Röhm and Haas's promotional material sang the praises of Plexiglas and demonstrated how it provided colour, texture, and patterning on buildings.[135] Don T. Brophy, sales manager of the Plastics Department, launched an Authorized Plexiglas Distributors programme in an effort to mutually enhance the company's sales and distribution income.[136] '[Put] Your Best Fascia Forward', urged Brophy's letter to distributors. Plexiglas's malleability made it an ideal material to form fascias. It was used in suburban retail buildings throughout the country. In educating distributors on how to pitch Plexiglas to architects and building owners, Brophy referenced the tag line, 'It's what's up front that counts', explaining that an 'economical yet custom designed fascia doubles as an advertisement'.[137] Brophy also advertised Plexiglas in numerous magazines, signage and retail trade journals, and architectural journals, for example, *Signs of the Times*, *Chain Store Age*, *Modern Stores*, *Architectural Forum*, *Architectural Record*, *House and Home*, and *Progressive Architecture*. Together, Röhm and Haas and authorised Plexiglas distributors marketed to a segmented audience of architects and building owners. Plexiglas proved to be an effective material for commercial buildings in urban and suburban settings.

Röhm and Haas's post-World War II advertising was also an example of motivational research, based on an understanding of what elicits emotions and motivates human behaviour. An ad for Plexiglas aimed to bolster the ego of its customers: 'How to sign your name with confidence – use Plexiglas.' 'Plexiglas for lighting that stands out and stands up' (Figs 109, 110). There were also ads that patted the consumer on the back for using Plexiglas: 'Do it with Plexiglas and You've Done it Right.' Ads linked customers of Plexiglas to specific character traits, implying that the choice of Plexiglas signalled intelligence, assertiveness, and self-confidence.

Like its ads for Plexiglas building applications, Röhm and Haas's corporate headquarters' architecture also spoke to human emotion and the senses. Brands, by definition, offer audiences a gut feeling about a product, service, or company. It is a

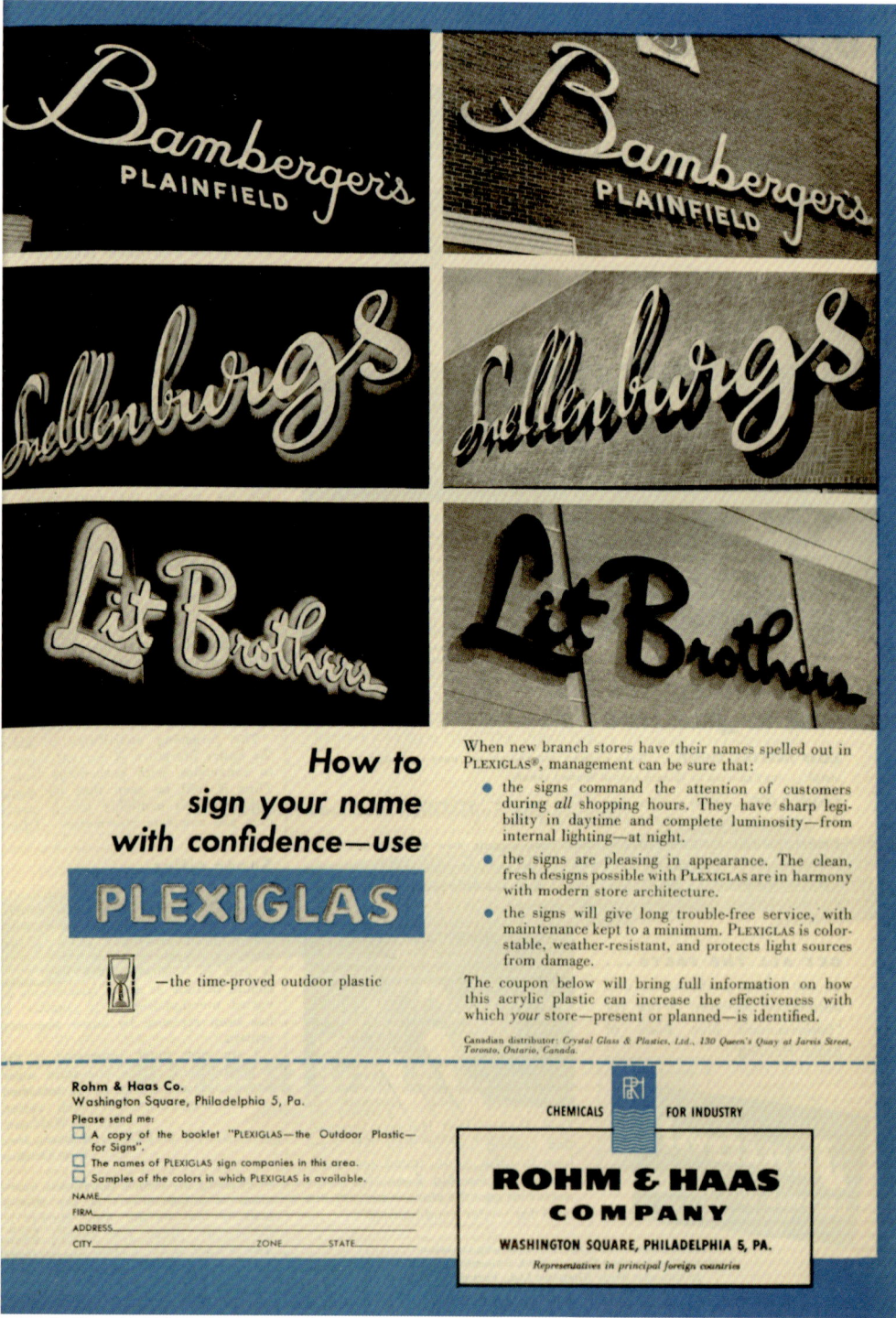

109 Mid-twentieth-century ad for Plexiglas: 'How to sign your name with confidence – use Plexiglas.' The ad implies that Plexiglas can impart confidence. *Chain Store Age*, January 1955.

PLEXIGLAS

...for lighting that stands out and stands up

Sixteen 4' x 4' pan-type diffusers of white translucent PLEXIGLAS are used to light the striking new branch office of Mechanics National Bank in Levittown, N. J. Architect: Clifford Garner.

Handsome buildings deserve the *best* in lighting, and they get it when lighting equipment includes diffusers or lenses made of PLEXIGLAS® acrylic plastic. PLEXIGLAS provides highest efficiency in transmission and diffusion. It is rigid, with a smooth, easily cleaned surface. Above all, it is a *durable* material—highly resistant to breakage, and free from discoloration even after years of exposure to fluorescent light.

We will be pleased to send you the names of manufacturers whose lighting equipment is based on the use of PLEXIGLAS.

Chemicals for Industry

ROHM & HAAS
COMPANY
WASHINGTON SQUARE, PHILADELPHIA 5, PA.

In Canada: *Rohm & Haas Company of Canada, Ltd., West Hill, Ontario*

110   Another mid-twentieth-century ad for Plexiglas: 'Plexiglas . . . for lighting that stands out and stands up'. The material is given an outgoing and exceptional character. *Architectural Record*, October 1959.

111   The Röhm and Haas Building on completion, 1964.

promise, a guarantee of the emotional payoff on our investment, be it in an object, a place, an individual, or even an experience. A strong brand makes and maintains an emotional connection with the consumer and consistently delivers that emotion. The incorporation of Plexiglas throughout the building, inside and out, and as sunshades on the building elevations offered a visceral and interactive medium through which occupants could engage with the company. Additionally, the nuanced modernism that Belluschi offered to the project also addressed human emotion, further connecting the Röhm and Haas design with the public. Thus, these elements which constituted the architectural branding offered an emotional element that spoke to all who experienced the building. For the client, Röhm and Haas, this aspect of the architecture would activate and reinforce its brand.

While Plexiglas transformed the commercial landscape of postwar America, it also offered architects an opportunity to re-think materiality.

The tenets of modernism did not fully accept non-traditional building materials, those other than glass, concrete, steel, and wood. On the other hand, new building materials such as aluminium, and other synthetic and chemically enhanced materials were being introduced. Plexiglas offers a telling material metaphor: if glass is a modern material, then Plexiglas is a postmodern one. In a bold turn against modernism, the Röhm and Haas Building unabashedly displayed its antithesis – through the synthetic material of Plexiglas, as a potent and meaningful symbol of its client. As a total work of art, the Röhm and Haas Building is at the summit of architectural branding (Fig.111). The building is a foil to the glass box corporate headquarters – it delivered idiosyncrasy, while glass boxes were uniform; it communicated, while glass boxes were mute. In the place of generic corporate architecture, the Röhm and Haas Building connects with occupants as a precise integration of materials and mission, tailored to the corporation's branding strategies.

6 CONCLUSION

Connecting with Society and the Future of Architectural Branding

The case studies in this book – the headquarters of the Philadelphia Saving Fund Society, S.C. Johnson & Son, Lever Brothers, and Röhm and Haas – offered rich histories of how modern American architecture in urban environments provided branding for its clients. Architects took these opportunities to collaborate with business clients, and as a result, experimented with design strategies to reach, connect with, and engage with audiences. These strategies – signs and textual communication, the architect's fame, form and shape, and material display – as well as their gesamtkunstwerk conditions – have prospered and evolved in a rapidly changing society.

The last case study of the Röhm and Haas headquarters brought us to the late 1960s, the chronological end of this book. During the subsequent decades in the 1970s and 1980s, architectural branding entered a decidedly clear yet complicated phase of late modern and postmodern design which lay outside this book's modernist scope. What began as a re-evaluation of orthodox modernism expanded into its outright rejection. Relentless mirrored facades, imposing slabs, and abstracted ornament became languages for architectural branding. Examples include Eero Saarinen's Bell Labs (1959–1962), Walter Gropius and Pietro Belluschi's Pan Am Building (1960–1963), and Philip Johnson's AT&T Building (1984). Architectural branding with buildings such as Richard Rogers's Lloyd's of London (1978–1986) and Norman Foster's Hong Kong and Shanghai Bank Headquarters (1979–1986) offered powerful messages that reinforced the rational and technological legacy of the modern movement. Not surprisingly, 'high tech' expressions reinforced corporate, top-down tendencies.[1] By the 21st century, we had reached a breaking point. The postmodern language that had branded corporations would be deemed too exclusive and not democratic enough in the emerging milieu.[2] However, architectural branding based on the lessons of the modern movement offers an alternative.

This book has re-examined corporate modernism through the lenses of social, cultural, and business histories and discovered a much richer, humanistic design at its core. The four case study narratives cast the modern architecture of corporations not as ruthless and indifferent, but as designs that engage with people in meaningful ways. The relevance of this new interpretation of corporate modernism as architectural branding is significant. If we understand corporate headquarters architecture not as imposing symbols of power, but instead as mediums of communication, then the inversion of messaging from top down to bottom up could be achieved. As corporations listen intently to what consumers want, we must seize the opportunity to express what is important to society. As a new generation of architects approaches the design of branded environments and architecture for the future, this interpretation of corporate modernism as branding will provide a catalyst for a crucial flipping of the script. In the following sections, the relevance of each modern case study of architectural branding to contemporary projects will be examined.

Sign

While the PSFS Building's expressionist massing and its gesamtkunstwerk certainly contributed to the company's brand identity, its rooftop sign was the design's unique contribution to the history of architectural branding. Relative to other communication mediums, language provides the utmost clarity. Design of the sign gives language specific ways of engaging its audience. The way the text is designed, its typography, and the words themselves speak volumes to what the corporation stands for and, as a result, determines how they connect with their stockholders and customers. For example, the sans serif typeface of the PSFS sign communicated progressiveness and a clean and rational image to the public. As such, texts and signs can accomplish much more than merely announcing the company's name. The medium of what the corporation has to say is as important as the message.

In *Complexity and Contradiction in Architecture*, Robert Venturi observed how the PSFS Building's 'big sign sits on top of the building yet it is invisible from below'.[3] Forty years after the PSFS Building was completed, Robert Venturi and Denise Scott Brown developed architectural communication through the language of text with designs like Best Products and BASCO showrooms which featured overscaled signs in a suburban landscape. Venturi and Scott Brown's decorated shed – a 'dumb' box with an identifying sign – would become propagated as a widespread solution for commercial construction in the form of big box

112   BASCO showroom, Philadelphia, Pennsylvania.
Venturi, Scott Brown and Associates, 1976.

tubes to today's LED technology, night illumination offers sensorial urban experiences. Today, the PSFS sign's legacy has continued to provide a powerful form of architectural branding in cities.

Fame

While the Johnson Wax Building design offered architectural branding, it was Frank Lloyd Wright, the person behind the design, who uniquely contributes to this book's narrative on branding. Influential individuals serve as powerful mediums for branding. Wright's persona, for example, was as charismatic as it was difficult. Frank Lloyd Wright was a 'starchitect' more than half a century before the term was coined. His swagger and his bold design for S.C. Johnson & Son gave the company a strong brand identity. Certainly, his fame waxed and waned, but he was consistently well known and at the time of this commission, his renown was at a high point. At the same time, a relevant question arose: how to discern between the identity of Wright and of the corporation? In this building, Wright's and his client's identity were one and the same. S.C. Johnson & Son benefited from Wright's fame and his innovative design.

Since the 2000s, similar collaborations between starchitects and corporations have proven to be a formidable architectural branding strategy in our media-fixated and celebrity-focused world. Aware of the benefits, corporations receive good design, high visibility, and a co-existing brand identity through the commission of famed architects. The currency of an architect's fame has become even more valuable to clients in the age of digital media. Recent high-profile corporation and architect couplings have included Apple and Norman Foster, Facebook and Frank Gehry, and Google and Bjarke Ingels Group and Thomas Heatherwick.

Despite the persistence of the starchitect phenomenon, architects have largely ridiculed it based on its perpetuation of celebrity adulation and a perceived lack of substance. Further, that

stores, fast-food restaurants, and speculative office parks (Fig.112). Additionally, memorable signs like McDonald's golden arches and gas station signs like Gulf and Shell Oil have ubiquitously lined highways and roadways since the 1950s. Internally lit, these signs become even more conspicuous at night.

After sundown, the PSFS sign gives off a red neon glow on the Philadelphia skyline. Amongst a context of architectural night lighting, the PSFS sign's legacy has urban implications and global reach. From the Great White Way on Broadway in New York to contemporary locations like the Las Vegas strip, the Shibuya district in Tokyo, and Manhattan's Times Square, the accumulation of contemporary signage at night formed saturated media environments. From the PSFS sign's neon

113   Illustration from Nicolai Ourousoff's *New York Times* article, 'Let the "Starchitects" Work All the Angles',
16 December 2007. Original caption reads: 'A roster of celebrity architects: clockwise from center, Rem Koolhaas,
Jean Nouvel, Santiago Calatrava and Frank Gehry.'

one lead architect would take credit for what was in truth a team effort was a flagrantly inequitable model. The term 'starchitects', coined in the 2000s by then-*New York Times* architecture critic Nicolai Ourousoff, has become pejorative (Fig.113). Instead, the growth of collaborative architectural practices demonstrates the rise of a more equitable model. In addition, how these architects design has also changed. For example, Frank Gehry's ebullient form-making has literally gone underground in his recent design for an expansion of the Philadelphia Museum of Art. Also, his 2015 design for the Facebook campus in Silicon Valley is strikingly unassuming and anonymous. Its single-level, 40,000-square-foot open plan office features a large rooftop park.

Google's Silicon Valley headquarters design also shows evidence of a change in the role of starchitects. Google's decision to hire not one but two esteemed architecture firms, Bjarke Ingels Group and Heatherwick Studio, shows that the corporation sought a collaborative design over a single architect's vision. At the same time, an architect's fame will always draw public interest and is not necessarily negative in and of itself. A crucial element will be that the architects who serve in a branding capacity take their responsibility seriously as influencers who represent the company's identity. Thus, their models of practice, values, and social causes will carry the weight of the public's perception of the company. In addition to collaborative studios, innovative models of practice and the diversity of architects is starting to re-define the 'starchitect' landscape. Prominent contemporary architectural practices of this kind include the female duo-led Grafton Architects, non-profit MASS Design Group, female-led Studio Gang, and British-Ghanaian-led Adjaye Associates.

Form

When Lever House was completed, the clients were extremely pleased that the modern architectural form of their headquarters did not rely on a sign to let New Yorkers know that it was owned by Lever Brothers. Its abstract, rectangular shapes served as powerful visual communicators for their brand.

Charles Jencks discussed the effects of spectacular and iconic architectural form in his 2005 essay 'The Bilbao Effect'.[4] He cited Gehry's 1997 Guggenheim Bilbao, Saarinen's 1962 TWA terminal, and Utzon's 1973 Sydney Opera House as the kinds of iconic and expressive architecture that elicit a new scale of public interest (Fig.114). Jencks found these singular forms capable of instigating positive change. For example, the spectacular form of the Guggenheim Bilbao was the first of a series of recent projects that catalysed new growth and a service and tourism industry in a post-industrial city in need of new sources of economic growth. Similarly, Lever House led the change of that stretch of Park Avenue from a residential to a commercial neighbourhood. It was the first modern glass office building in a neighbourhood defined by masonry apartment buildings that led future commercial development, including the Mies van der Rohe-designed Seagram Building sited cater-corner from Lever House.

Jencks credited the enigmatic nature of architectural form and its powerful effect on viewers and occupants. Today we witness this in such contemporary designs as Apple's and Amazon's new headquarters. Both are bold and memorable trademark visions. Dubbed 'the spaceship', Norman Foster's design for Apple Campus 2 is a sleek, circular ring of offices, sited within a nature reserve. Amazon's headquarters in downtown Seattle also follows Lever House's form-based branding precedent. Designed by global architecture firm NBBJ, the design consists of three interconnected biospheres, housing plant-filled meeting and workplaces and a six-building office complex. The biospheres elicit attention both for their unorthodox and striking forms and the progressive message they impart about nature and urban refuge, work/life balance, and human wellness. Amazon's biospheres are not merely form for form's sake but possess an important sustainability message and function. Today, nature, ecology, and wellness are among society's utmost concerns – which corporations have, in turn, also championed in their architectural branding.

As Lever House has demonstrated, modern architectural form can effectively connect the public to corporations. Today, the formal palette has expanded beyond the simple geometric shapes of modern architecture to idiosyncratic

114   Guggenheim Bilbao Museum, Gehry Partners LLP, Bilbao, Spain, 1993–1997.

and irregular forms like those of Aqua Tower by Studio Gang and Guggenheim Bilbao by Frank Gehry. Architectural shapes and forms continue to engage the public. At the same time, architectural branding should also consider shape and form from a marketing perspective. Consumer behaviour research has shown that people associate meaning with shapes that, in turn, offer powerful psychological responses. For example, rectangles, like those of Lever House's massing, communicate proportion, balance, and professionalism. These qualities inspire trust in an audience searching for strength and security. On the other hand, circles or organic shapes, with their soft edges, offer positive, warm emotional messages. By instilling marketing research when designing buildings, architects can cultivate an interdisciplinary research collaboration, a productive practice model for architectural branding.

Material

The Röhm and Haas Building brings the evolution of architectural branding to an engagement with material display. To architecturally brand the Röhm and Haas company, Pietro Belluschi explored the material characteristics of Plexiglas as well as concrete to rich and multi-dimensional effect. As materials are primarily experienced by the whole body rather than chiefly with the eyes, it is an exceptional medium for branding. Material tactility communicates directly with the bodily senses, especially touch. Its legacy can be found in the contemporary architectural preoccupation of materiality.

The work of contemporary Swiss architects Herzog and de Meuron demonstrates an affinity with the Röhm and Haas Building's use of material display. Innovative methods of materiality and exterior screening are explored in a number of their projects, including the Ricola Factory (1993), the Eberswalde Library (1999), and the de Young Museum (2005).

Herzog and de Meuron designed a layered glass and polycarbonate facade, in which the latter was silkscreened with a series of grainy black and white photographs of a stone bas-relief plant form,

for Ricola, a manufacturer of herbal, plant-based products in Mulhouse-Brunstatt, France (Fig.115). Offering different material effects depending on the time of day, the photo-facade architecturally brands Ricola. The textured image of the photo-facade offers a visceral effect to the viewer. The Ricola photo-facade is similar to the brown-tinted and textured Plexiglas screens of the Röhm and Haas Building. Both use specific materials to create architectural brand identities for their clients.

In Herzog and de Meuron's 2005 de Young Museum in San Francisco, a thin veneer of perforated copper layered over a glass curtain wall gives a layered effect while offering sunshade. At the observation level, the copper screen gives way to a clear view of scenic Golden Gate Park and beyond. Similarly, the brown-tinted Plexiglas screen of the Röhm and Haas Building is layered over a glass curtain wall and at eye level offers clear views over Philadelphia's Independence Mall. Both projects use material layering to mediate the relationship between occupant and site. The Röhm and Haas Building's legacy of materiality engenders connections with its audiences through bodily senses.

Designing architectural branding with an interest in exploring materiality is a powerful way to connect with audiences. However, we must navigate future material experimentation with environmental and safety precautions. An unfortunate episode in Röhm and Haas's history occurred when the company did not properly protect its employees from the toxicity of Plexiglas production and, as a result, 14 employees who worked at their production facility in Spring House, Pennsylvania died of brain cancer.

Finally, another legacy of Röhm and Haas's material display branding is the company's Plexiglas for commercial signage. From the one-off neon PSFS sign to mass-produced signage, signs as branding bookend the case studies. Starting and ending the case studies in Philadelphia is an opportunity to compare, in a space of 12 blocks and 60 years, how modern architecture for corporate clients evolved. PSFS was built in the years immediately following the stock market crash, and Röhm and Haas, in the years of industrial decline and urban renewal. While both projects grew out of very different times, they share historical contexts that were both tumultuous – PSFS, economically, and Röhm and Haas, socially (see Fig.80, page 146). In a single, juxtaposed view up Market Street, modern architectural branding evolved from PSFS's rooftop sign atop a skyscraper to Röhm and Haas's complete integration of brand identity, design, and architecture.

The ultimate gesamtkunstwerk condition was achieved in the Röhm and Haas Building, but at the same time, the company's most profitable application of Plexiglas was commercial signage – the most rudimentary of branding strategies. The quintessential architectural brand triumphed as a total work of art, while other clients preferred to simply mount a sign on their buildings. Ironically, the same market that created the Röhm and Haas Building failed to sustain its high level of architecture and design. The legacies of the 20th-century case studies of architectural branding are abundant. The strategies have persisted, but not without necessary adjustments. After 1968, the four strategies that emerged in the case studies would continue in architectural branding with a renewed sense of social consciousness. This informs how we will approach architectural branding in the future.

In the 21st century, cities have again become the preferred site for corporate headquarters. After the postwar migration to the suburbs, American corporations have moved back into multi-level buildings and high rises in central business districts. Major cities have revitalised and now attract millennial and Gen Z professionals. Cities provide fertile environments, as Rem Koolhaas's concept of 'Manhattanism' and Saskia Sassen's global cities have shown. Within what Koolhaas calls the 'culture of congestion', architectural branding boldly announces client identities. With the growing virtual nature of corporate identities today, architectural branding of physical buildings and spaces is even more important precisely because of the material presence of place – that which the digital realm denies its inhabitants. As sense of place becomes more and more scarce, the task of architects and designers will be to create buildings and spaces that are meaningful and connect to people. Thus, architectural branding will be more necessary than ever.

115   Ricola-Europe SA, Production and Storage Building, Herzog and de Meuron, Mulhouse-Brunstatt, France, 1992–1993.

The return of corporate headquarters into cities signals a counterpoise of suburban isolation. Downtown projects such as Uber's headquarters in San Francisco – designed by boutique architecture firm SHoP – and Amazon's headquarters in Seattle – designed by global architecture, planning, and design firm NBBJ – show the new trajectory. In addition to Amazon and Zappos, who have moved their headquarters to downtown Seattle and Las Vegas respectively, blue chip companies like General Electric, Weyerhaeuser, and ConAgra are also moving into cities from the suburbs.

The importance of collaboration amongst a variety of professionals, from designers to brand managers, underscores the location of headquarters offices in dense cities. Just as chance social encounters in Manhattan were an essential urban ingredient for Jane Jacobs, dense cities of today offer potential collaboration that a suburban office does not. Architecturally, urban headquarters offer a number of socially beneficial, place-specific qualities including green spaces, adaptive reuse practices, and urban revitalisation. Silicon Valley is the exception to the turn towards urban headquarters. Tech giants like Apple, Google, and Facebook have commissioned important architects to design what amounts to isolated microcosms that spur internal innovation yet turn their backs on the rest of the world. Considering today's suburbs that have become littered with abandoned campuses of corporate giants, Silicon Valley corporations should re-think these reclusive and anti-social strategies.

Today, branding has come under attack from activists who have been suspicious of advertising since the 1960s. Anti-branding sentiment has leveraged against corporations who now must address these concerns in order to survive. The voices of 'crowd culture', everyday people rather than brands, are heard and taken seriously.[5] Thus, ideologies based on social change, inclusion, human equity, and diversity, among many others, are able to incubate and become mass cultural phenomena. Traditional branding has been turned upside down, and as a result, authenticity and transparency have defined the new crop of architectural branding for corporate headquarters.[6]

These qualities are not so different than the spirit of the modern movement which sought to design for the needs of the current milieu and worked towards the social aspiration of offering good design to all. The coupling of modernism and branding evinces the alignment of shared characteristics: both emerged out of industrialisation and mass production, both addressed mass media and audiences, and both designed with the essential and simplified in mind. While the modern ethos defined architectural branding of the case study buildings, today's corporate identities have built upon it. If 20th-century corporate brands communicated modern concepts like efficiency and progressiveness, 21st-century corporations are about transparency and societal responsibilities. The modernist spirit has not been lost in today's zeitgeist. The qualities of modern architecture, in fact, achieved the objectives of branding. At the same time, branding brought out the underlying emotional and human qualities of modern architecture.

Architecture and design play a more important role than ever in cultivating corporate character in quickly proliferating modes of expression. As today's synthesised brand identities have expanded into the digital realm, they have become all encompassing. Since the inception of branding, engaging human emotion has been its defining element. Analogously, this is true of architectural branding as well. To be sure, architectural branding going forward will not leave 20th-century strategies behind. The legacies of this book's case studies – signs, media environments, fame, architects as influencers, engaging forms, and materiality – will continue to thrive and evolve. Twenty-first century architects will brand corporations through these strategies while cultivating community, reclaiming nature, and championing sustainability and human wellness. Society will inform corporations, not the other way around, of critical issues in building architectural brands for the future.

ACKNOWLEDGEMENTS

Many people and institutions contributed to the making of this book. In bringing it to its published form, I am deeply indebted to my academic institution, Thomas Jefferson University for awarding me the Faculty Research and Creative Scholarship Grant. I thank my supportive colleagues in the College of Architecture and the Built Environment: Dean Barbara Klinkhammer, Lauren Baumbach, Suzanne Singletary, David Breiner, and everyone at the Office of Applied Research, particularly Dean Ronald Kander and Andrea Echeverri.

This book originated as my doctoral dissertation, 'Architecture, Advertising, and Corporations, 1929–1959', at the University of Pennsylvania. I was fortunate to have the support of the academic community at the School of Design, University of Pennsylvania. David Leatherbarrow and Detlef Mertins provided me with intellectual and pedagogical opportunities to hone my architectural history and theory knowledge. I owe David Brownlee, who supervised my dissertation, a debt of gratitude for his support of my topic, meticulous editing, and kind mentorship. Committee member, Walter Licht offered economic and business history insights. I received helpful advice from Jonathan Lipman, Kathryn Smith, and Nicholas Adams. In presenting my scholarship at Yale University School of Architecture, Bard Graduate Center, Frank Lloyd Wright Building Conservancy, and DocomomoUS-Greater Philadelphia, I benefited from the comments of colleagues, students, and members of the public.

Archival materials of corporations and architects are at the core of this book. I appreciate the assistance offered to me at the following institutions: Hagley Museum and Library, Syracuse University Special Collections Research Center, Science History Institute, S.C. Johnson & Son Archives, Library of Congress, Frank Lloyd Wright Foundation at Getty Research Institute, Avery Architectural and Fine Arts Library at Columbia University, Philadelphia Museum of Art, Athenaeum of Philadelphia, and the Architectural Archives at the University of Pennsylvania. Through interviews, a number of individuals offered key experiences of Röhm and Haas: Andy Jarvis of EwingCole, Robert Geddes, Walter D'Alessio, and Nadine Cole.

I am very grateful for the insights and suggestions of colleagues who read all or part of my manuscript: Richard Longstreth, Meredith Clausen, Susan Solomon, and Jennifer Wilson. I owe Nancy Later a special gratitude for her keen editorial eye, and consistent enthusiasm for this manuscript. Colleagues and friends from near and far offered wisdom and support: Janet Antich, Halee Bouchehrian, Rosemarie Buchanan, DocomomoPHL board members, Alexander Eisenschmidt, Rafaella Fabiani Giannetto, Gabriel Hernandez, Amy Holtman, Peter Laurence, Mark Karlen, Sonja Pacho, Tania Calovi Pereira, David Raizman, John Sadar, Esra Sahin, Laura Keenan Spero, Patrick Spero, Franca Trubiano, Liz Waytkus, and William Whitaker. My mentor and friend, Martha Thorne has been a tireless supporter of me and my success.

The team at Lund Humphries, Valerie Rose, Rochelle Roberts, Sarah Thorowgood, Anna Norman, Victoria Benjamin, Meris Ryan-Goff, Victoria Benjamin, Jacqui Cornish, Pamela Bertram, and Sophie Hartley have earned my profound gratitude for their expertise and professionalism in bringing this project to fruition.

Most importantly, I could not have realized this book without the love and encouragement of my husband Albert, and our daughters Lucy and Evelyn. They have cheered me on, served as sounding boards, tolerated my long hours of writing, continued to have faith in me in getting this book published, and above all, inspired me to find my voice. This book is dedicated to them.

NOTES

Abbreviations and Archives

ATH   PSFS Collection, The Athenaeum of Philadelphia

GHAV   George Howe, 1886–1955, Avery Architectural and Fine Arts Library, Columbia University Libraries

GBAV   Gordon Bunshaft, 1909–1990, Drawing & Archives, Avery Architectural and Fine Arts Library, Columbia University

GRI   Frank Lloyd Wright Foundation at the Getty Research Institute, Los Angeles

HFJ   H.F. Johnson Museum Archives, Cornell University

HML   Philadelphia Saving Fund Society Archive, Manuscripts and Archives, Hagley Museum and Library

LH   Lever House Architectural Drawings, Avery Architectural and Fine Arts Library, Drawing & Archives

LOC   Papers of Nathaniel Alexander Owings, The Library of Congress

PMA   PSFS Papers, American Art Department, Philadelphia Museum of Art

RLA   Raymond Loewy Archive, Hagley Library and Archives

CURB   S.C. Johnson & Son Alumni Records, Cornell University, Rare Books and Manuscripts

SCJ   S.C. Johnson & Son Archives, Racine, WI

SYR   William Lescaze Papers, Special Collections Research Center, Syracuse University Library

1 INTRODUCTION Communicating Messages through Business and Architecture

1 American Marketing Association.

2 Marty Neumeier defines branding, brand experience, and other relevant terms in Marty Neumeier, *Brand Gap: How to Bridge the Distance Between Business Strategy and Design* (New Riders, Berkeley, CA, 2006), pp 1–2, p.161.

3 For a comprehensive history of corporate branding, see John M.T. Balmer and Stephen A. Greyser (eds), *Revealing the Corporation: Perspectives on Identity, Image, Reputation, Corporate Branding, and Corporate-Level Marketing* (Routledge, London, 2003).

4 Patrizio Bertelli, Rem Koolhaas, Jens Hommert and Michael Kubo, *Projects for Prada, Part 1* (Fondazione Prada Edizioni, Milan, 2001), p.2.

5 The case study topics were chosen based on the accessibility of primary research materials, and the quality and abundance of existing scholarship. Half of the corporations are now defunct. Studying defunct corporations was preferable because their archives were publicly accessible. This was the case for the PSFS and Röhm and Haas archives. My research on the extant corporations, Unilever and S.C. Johnson & Son, was supported by thorough corporate histories and permission to access company archives. For all the case studies, existing scholarship was invaluable as it allowed me to situate my own discoveries and arguments within and against an existing body of knowledge of thought. I offer important alternate histories of these particular modern buildings, and a new way of analysing the corporate headquarters type, demonstrating that their clients played a paramount role in shaping architectural branding.

6 Books such as Louise Mozingo, *Pastoral Capitalism: A History of Suburban Corporate Landscapes* (MIT Press, Cambridge, MA, 2014), focus on postwar suburban corporate headquarters.

7   A number of recent books study skyscrapers; see, for example, Benjamin Flowers, *The Politics and Power of Building New York City in the Twentieth Century* (University of Pennsylvania Press, Philadelphia, PA, 2009), and Adnan Morshed, *Impossible Heights: Skyscrapers, Flight, and the Master Builder* (University of Minnesota, Minneapolis, MN, 2015). Another recent book focusing on one skyscraper and which discusses client involvement is Phyllis Lambert, *Building Seagram* (Yale University Press, New Haven, CT, 2013).

8   The study of other 19th- and 20th-century building types such as department stores, hotels, or university campuses has been productive in examining branding; superb examples include Meredith Clausen and Richard Longstreth on department stores and Annabel Wharton on hotels. Architectural historian and preservationist Richard Longstreth's important and innovative book, *The American Department Store Transformed, 1920–1960* (Yale University Press, New Haven, CT, 2010), analyses the development and evolution of American urban and suburban department stores as they were shaped by the complexities of economic and urban change. Meredith L. Clausen illuminates and details the history of the Parisian department store type in 'The Department Store – Development of the Type', *Journal of Architectural Education*, vol.39, no.1 (1985), pp 20–29.

9   Historians such as Joanna Merwood-Salisbury, Gail Fenske, Katherine Solomonson, and Daniel Abramson have superbly established these 19th-century contributions to corporate architecture as aesthetically and culturally significant. Other excellent books on nineteenth-century corporate architecture include the following: Gail Fenske, *The Skyscraper and the City: The Woolworth Building and the Making of Modern New York* (University of Chicago Press, Chicago, 2008); Katherine Solomonson, *The Chicago Tribune Tower Competition: Skyscraper Design and Cultural Change in the 1920s* (Cambridge University Press, New York, 2001); Joanna Merwood-Salisbury, *Chicago 1890: The Skyscraper and the Modern City* (University of Chicago Press, Chicago, 2009); Daniel M. Abramson, *Skyscraper Rivals: The AIG Building and the Architecture of Wall Street* (Princeton Architectural Press, New York, 2001).

10   While there is currently little research on the modernist era of architectural branding, there are publications on the related topic of product placement. John Jakle and Keith Sculle have studied the impact of signs and roadside architecture, such as gas stations, motels, and franchise restaurants. Their work was a productive development towards architectural branding that laid a foundation for my studies. Some books have also explored the topic of modern corporate headquarters including *Gordon Bunshaft of Skidmore, Owings & Merrill* by Carol Krinsky which discussed the architect's corporate realities and his clients, and *Form Follows Finance: Skyscrapers and Skylines in New York and Chicago* by Carol Willis which cast the city and its buildings as a complex commercial environment. My book offers a fresh interpretation of corporate modernism as branding, built upon the perspectives of the clients – the company presidents, CEOs, and executives who shaped the image of their corporations.

11   Architectural historian, Kenneth Frampton underscored the fact that modern architecture was viewed negatively in comparison to the classical tradition, in which communication was a central goal. See Kenneth Frampton, *Modern Architecture: A Critical History* (Thames & Hudson, London, 1980), pp 9–10. See also Manfredo Tafuri and Francesco dal Co, *Modern Architecture* (Harry Abrams, New York, 1980).

12   Architectural historians and critics of the 1950s and 1960s such as Peter Blake, Vincent Scully, and Lewis Mumford wrote derisive commentary on the modern curtain wall. Manfredo Tafuri criticised the Seagram Building as 'aloof'; Manfredo Tafuri and Francesco Dal Co, *Modern Architecture*, trans. Robert Erich Wolfe (1976; reprint, H.N. Abrams, New York, 1979), pp 340–41. More recently, the scholarship of historians Reinhold Martin and Timothy Rohan has also focused on theoretical interpretations of the modern curtain wall of the 1950s; see Reinhold Martin, *The Organizational Complex: Architecture, Media, and Corporate Space* (MIT Press, Cambridge, MA, 2003), and Timothy M. Rohan, 'Challenging the Curtain Wall: Paul Rudolph's Blue Cross and Blue Shield Building', *Journal of the Society of Architectural Historians*, vol.66, no.1 (March 2007), pp 84–109.

13   Vincent Scully and Lewis Mumford, among others, identified the curtain wall and its repetitive panes as a source of contemporary alienation. This viewpoint was expressed in other cultural forms, such as Jacques Tati's 1967 film, *Playtime*.

14   For a history of American business development, see Walter Licht, *Industrializing America: The Nineteenth Century* (Johns Hopkins University Press, Baltimore, 1995).

15 The terms 'sales' and 'advertising' do not share a definition. A sale is the exchange of a commodity for money or service in return for money, or the action of selling something. Although advertising is not selling, it is related. Advertising calls the public's attention to and stimulates interest in a product or service in the hope that a sale will follow. Advertising assumes its form in many different media, including newspapers, radio, television, and, today, digital media, in order to achieve its goal.

16 Susan Strasser, *Satisfaction Guaranteed: The Making of the American Mass Market* (Smithsonian Books, Washington, DC, 2004), p.28.

17 For an excellent history of the development of the American department store, see Longstreth.

18 Roland Marchand, *Advertising the American Dream: Making Way for Modernity, 1920–1940* (University of California Press, Berkeley, CA, 1986), p.2. Other sources of this type of history of advertising analysis include Strasser's *Satisfaction Guaranteed*, Jackson T. Lears, *Fables of Abundance: A Cultural History of Advertising in America* (Basic Books, New York, 1995), William Leach, *Land of Desire: Merchants, Power, and the Rise of a New American Culture* (Vintage, New York, 1994).

19 Marchand, *Advertising the American Dream*, p.2. Edward Bernays was a key figure in early public relations and advertising in America. His influential book, *Propaganda*, was published in 1928.

20 This paradox is described by economic historian Lizbeth Cohen in *A Consumer's Republic: The Politics of Mass Consumption in Postwar America* (Vintage, New York, 2003).

21 Marchand, *Advertising the American Dream*, p.300. Marchand makes reference to *Printers Ink Monthly*, May 1932, p.38.

22 *Fortune*, September 1931, p.85, illustrated in Marchand, *Advertising the American Dream*, p.301.

23 ibid.

24 ibid., p. 288.

25 Donald J. Bush, *The Streamlined Decade* (George Braziller, New York, 1975).

26 According to historian Elaine Tyler May, Americans won the Cold War through consumerism. See Elaine Tyler May, *Homeward Bound: American Families in the Cold War Era*. (Basic Books, New York, 1988). With the start of the Korean and Vietnam wars (1950 and 1955, respectively), defence spending also rose, further strengthening the American economy.

27 Ernest Dichter (1907–1991) pioneered the application of Freudian psychoanalytic concepts and techniques to business: in particular, to the study of consumer behaviour in the marketplace. Ideas he established significantly influenced the practices of the advertising industry in the 20th century. See Ernest Dichter, *The Strategy of Desire* (Facsimiles-Garl, New York, 1960).

28 F.H.K. Henrion and Alan Parkin, *Design Coordination and Corporate Image* (Studio Vista, London, 1967), p.7. The study of corporate identity is found in the discipline of Design History, which is defined as the examination of objects of design in their historic and stylistic contexts. Emerging in England in the 1960s, Design History studies all designed objects including those of architecture, fashion, crafts, interiors, textiles, graphic design, industrial design, and product design. Leading scholarship in this field includes Jonathan Woodham, *Twentieth-Century Design* (Oxford University Press, Oxford, 1997), and Dennis Doordan, *Design History: An Anthology* (MIT Press, Cambridge, MA, 1996).

29 What we understand as branding today echoes what Wally Olins stated about corporate identity in the 1980s, as multinational corporations and global products proliferated: 'We are entering an epoch in which only those corporations making highly competitive products will survive', pronounced Olins. 'This means, in the longer term, that products from major companies around the world will become the most significant factor in making a choice between one company and its products and another.' Woodham, *Twentieth-Century Design*, p.143.

30 Reyner Banham and Penny Sparke (eds), *Design by Choice* (Rizzoli, New York, 1981).

31 When the Baby Boomer generation came of age, almost 50 per cent of the US population was under the age of 25.

32 Launched in 1959, Volkswagen's campaign to promote its tiny Beetle came at a time when Americans were mesmerised by large, tail-finned automobiles. The campaign depended on honesty and a devoted minority: Volkswagen buyers were nonconformists who avoided extravagance and took pride in simplicity and practicality. Considered one of the great advertisements of the 20th century, the Volkswagen campaign led to segmentation marketing: Daniel Pope, 'Making Sense of Advertisements', in *The Making of Modern Advertising* (Basic Books, New York, 1983), p.4.

33   Stephen King, 'Brand-Building in the 1990s', *Journal of Marketing Management*, vol.7, no.1 (1991), pp 3–13. King is to corporate branding what Wally Olins was to corporate identity. This article was one of the earliest commentaries on corporate branding and as such was ahead of its time.

34   B. Joseph Pine II, and James H. Gilmore, *The Experience Economy: Work Is Theatre & Every Business a Stage* (Harvard Business Review Press, Boston, 1999).

35   Disney is a pioneer of the experience economy, staging compelling and memorable experiences, distinct from the normally uneventful world of goods and services. Pine and Gilmore, p.43.

36   On the office building in the context of England and the United States, see Henry-Russell Hitchcock, *Architecture: Nineteenth and Twentieth Centuries* (Penguin Books, Harmondsworth, 1958).

37   See Fenske on the Woolworth Building, for example.

38   Roberta Moudry (ed.), *The American Skyscraper: Cultural Histories* (Cambridge University Press, Cambridge, 2005), p.128.

39   ibid., p.128.

40   George Gaston, cited in Roland Marchand, *Creating the Corporate Soul: The Rise of Public Relations and Corporate Imagery in American Big Business* (University of California Press, Berkeley, CA, 2001), p.184.

41   Haley Fiske, cited in Marchand, *Creating the Corporate Soul*, p.185.

42   Haley Fiske, cited in Moudry. Haley Fiske, 'The Light that Never Fails', address given at the Triennial Conventions of 1909–1910, in Addresses Delivered at the Triennial Conventions and Managers' Annual Banquets of the Metropolitan Life Insurance Company, vol.1 (The Company, New York, 1923), pp 9–10.

43   Louis J. Horowitz and Boyden Sparkes, *The Towers of New York: The Memoirs of a Master Builder* (New York: Simon & Schuster, 1937), p.2.

44   Fenske, p.25.

45   Solomonson, p.103, analyses how certain corporate headquarters functioned like trademarks.

46   Alfred Barr Jr, in the preface to Henry-Russell Hitchcock and Philip Johnson, *The International Style: Architecture since 1922* (W.W. Norton, New York, 1932), p.14, published following the *Modern Architecture* exhibition held at MoMA between 16 January 1932 and 19 March 1932.

47   Seagram printed 25,000 copies of an eight-page tour brochure, approved by Philip Johnson, in 1958. Seagram Museum collection 1682–1996, bulk 1930–1990, Hagley Museum and Library, Wilmington, Delaware.

48   'Buildings for Business and Government on View at Museum', Press Release, 27 February 1959, MoMA Archives.

49   ibid.

50   My goal in this book is to offer a new scholarly history of corporate modernism and its architectural legacy as branding – as well as the first in-depth historical study of architectural branding. This book differs from Anna Klingmann's *Brandscapes: Architecture in the Experience Economy* in style, methodology, and audience. While both books address the topic of architectural branding, my book (revised from a dissertation) is based on a historical methodology that is based in archival research.

51   The methodology of *Building Brands* is historical and based on primary resource archival materials. Other books that employ a similar approach on the topic include *American Glamour and the Evolution of Modern Architecture* by Alice T. Friedman and *Building Seagram* by Phyllis Lambert. Other books such as *The Interface* by John Harwood and *The Organizational Complex* by Reinhold Martin have certainly contributed valuable insight to the topic of corporate modernism, but their critical theory methodologies are in contrast to *Building Brands*.

2   SIGN The PSFS Building

1   At its inception, the company's name was the 'Philadelphia Saving Fund Society'. After merging with Western Savings Fund Society in 1982, an 's' was added to 'Saving'. The name 'Philadelphia Savings Fund Society' maintained continuity with the former business, yet also distinguished it as new.

2   Two prominent examples of Beaux-Arts architecture in Philadelphia include the 1924 Elverson Building for the *Philadelphia Inquirer* newspaper, designed by the prolific architecture firm Rankin and Kellogg, and the 1926 *Public Ledger* headquarters, designed by architect Horace Trumbauer.

3   Sam Warner Bass Jr, *The Private City: Philadelphia in Three Periods of Its Growth* (University of Pennsylvania Press, Philadelphia, PA, 1968), p.161.

4   Savings banks had existed in Europe for years and in the early 1810s had grown rapidly

throughout Great Britain. As a 'saving fund' rather than a commercial bank, PSFS was modelled after savings banks in Scotland. These institutions were known in Philadelphia through English journals and pamphlets that had circulated to the United States. The main difference between commercial banks and savings funds lies in the services they offer and the clientele they attract: commercial banks cater to large corporations and governments, while savings funds cater to individuals focusing on mortgages and other consumer loans. James M. Willcox, *A History of the Philadelphia Saving Fund Society, 1816–1916* (J.B. Lippincott Co., Philadelphia, PA, 1916), p.11.

5   ibid., pp 25–6.

6   ibid., p.26.

7   George Alter, Claudia Goldin and Elyce Rotella, 'The Savings of Ordinary Americans: The Philadelphia Saving Fund Society in the Mid-Nineteenth Century', *Journal of Economic History* vol.54, no.4 (December 1994), p.740.

8   ibid., p.740.

9   ibid., p.739.

10   Willcox, p.41.

11   ibid., p.64.

12   The first PSFS accommodations were humble: its early banking rooms operated out of houses converted to offices. Willcox, p.57.

13   PSFS, Annual Report, 1850. As footnoted in Alter, Goldin and Rotella.

14   Willcox, p.145.

15   ibid., p.146.

16   ibid., p.64.

17   ibid.

18   ibid., p.65.

19   ibid., p.79.

20   ibid., pp 68–9. Willcox details the Randall mansion's distinguished guests that were reported on in the local *Sunday Dispatch*.

21   ibid., p.79. In explaining the Saving Fund's Washington Square location, Willcox wrote, 'standing at about the place where the Philadelphia of a century ago looked westwardly on the unbuilded (*sic*) waste places which have since become a great city, the present building affords a dignified and befitting Office for the Society.'

22   ibid., p.78.

23   The PSFS's 19th-century advertising was direct and straightforward. An early PSFS advertisement stated its mission was 'to promote and encourage [the] habit of industry and saving in the laboring classes'. It advertised itself as thrift personified, in Willcox. Mass 'consumerism' emerged in the 1880s as a result of the mass production of saleable goods. See David A. Houndshell, *From the American System to Mass Production, 1800–1932: The Development of Manufacturing Technology in the United States* (Johns Hopkins University Press, Baltimore, 1984), William Leach, *Land of Desire: Merchants, Power, and the Rise of a New American Culture* (Vintage, New York, 1994), Jackson Lears, *Fables of Abundance: A Cultural History of Advertising in America* (Basic Books, New York, 1995), and Roland Marchand, *Advertising the American Dream: Making Way for Modernity* (University of California Press, Berkeley, CA, 1986).

24   Roland Marchand, *Advertising the American Dream*, pp 9–13.

25   ibid., p.9.

26   PSFS brochure, September 1927, Box 48/Folder RFII/3, PSFS Collection (Acc. 2062), HML.

27   The programmes were based on consumer research studies on children and teenagers. Record Group II Banking, Box 48/Folder RFII/3, PSFS Collection (Acc. 2062), HML.

28   By 1913, Allen Evans offered the 27-year-old Howe a partnership. For three years, Howe worked at Furness, Evans and Company 'with the avowed intent of infusing life into its outworn Victorian traditions. [But] finding the arteries of these traditions so hardened by age as to be sensitive to no artificial stimulus, either external or internal', he decided 'to pulsate in freer channels'. Robert A.M. Stern, *George Howe: Towards a Modern American Architecture* (Yale University Press, New Haven, CT, 1975), p.30. According to Richard Longstreth, much of Mellor and Meigs's best work looked to post-medieval manors in northern France.

29   George Howe, 'Philadelphia Savings Fund Society Branch Offices', *Architectural Forum*, vol.48 (June 1928), pp 881–6.

30   ibid.

31   ibid.

32   David Brownlee points out that once Paul Cret arrived in the US (he joined the faculty at the University of Pennsylvania in 1903), he advocated for a new form of classicism that later evinced some alignment with the radical ideas of the Swiss modernist, Le Corbusier. David Brownlee, *Building The*

City Beautiful: The Benjamin Franklin Parkway and the Philadelphia Museum of Art (Philadelphia Museum of Art, Philadelphia, PA, 1989).

33   Letter from Paul Cret to George Howe, 28 March 1931, printed in Stern, p.131. This is just one example of how Cret was supportive of Howe's architecture. In this letter, Cret compliments the PSFS design, calling it a 'beautiful work'.

34   George Howe, 'Philadelphia Savings Fund Society Branch Offices', *Architectural Forum*, vol.48 (June 1928), pp 881–6.

35   ibid.

36   ibid.

37   Lescaze was born on 27 March 1896, in Onex, near Geneva, Switzerland, and was ten years younger than his partner George Howe. Lorraine Welling Lanmon, *William Lescaze, Architect* (Art Alliance Press, Philadelphia, PA; Associated University Presses, London, 1987), p.16.

38   Henry-Russell Hitchcock, *Modern Architecture: Romanticism and Reintegration* (Payson & Clarke Ltd, New York, 1929), p.204. Hitchcock refers to the limited number of European architects working in the modern manner as the New Pioneers of America. He includes Austrian émigrés Richard Neutra and Rudolph Schindler in Los Angeles, the Danish architect Lönberg-Holm in Detroit, and the Swiss architect William Lescaze in New York.

39   Hubbell and Benes, and at the Bureau of Design for the Cleveland Board of Education.

40   Lescaze travelled in Berlin in 1922–1923. Lanmon, p.27. At the time, Lescaze would have seen Erich Mendelsohn's expressionist design, Mossehaus, constructed in 1923.

41   Lescaze's solo projects at this time included Capital Bus Terminal on West 51st Street, New York, 1927; Loeser and Co. Showroom, Brooklyn, New York, 1928; Macy's International Exposition Penthouse, 1928; and the S.T. Meyers Foyer, 1928.

42   Hitchcock, p.205.

43   Lescaze's work was a favourite topic of writer and art critic Sheldon Cheney: see Sheldon Cheney and Martha Cheney, *Art and the Machine: An Account of Industrial Design in 20th-Century America* (McGraw Hill, New York, 1936).

44   Lescaze dedicated his career to championing modern architecture. He saw himself as a European modernist who could educate American architects on modern architecture.

45   Lescaze explained his design philosophy in an article for *Home Furnishings Daily*, a supplement to *Women's Wear Daily*, on 28 May 1928.

46   Lescaze uses the term 'entity' in 'A Professional Biographical Essay', 18 February 1929, 'Writings', Box 66, William Lescaze Papers, SYR.

47   George Howe and William Lescaze, 'Architectural Analysis of the Proposed Building for the Philadelphia Saving Fund Society', 26 September 1930, Box 56, Folder 'Correspondence', William Lescaze Papers, SYR.

48   Helen Howe West, *George Howe, Architect, 1886–1955: Recollections of My Beloved Father* (W. Nunn Co., Philadelphia, PA, 1973), p.37.

49   William H. Jordy, 'PSFS: Its Development and Its Significance in Modern Architecture', *Journal of the Society of Architectural Historians*, vol.21, no.2 (May 1962), p.50.

50   'Excerpts-Board Minutes', PSFS Collection (Acc. 2062), Box 84, HML.

51   Alfred Blossom, 'Requirements of a Modern Bank Building', *Journal of the American Bankers Association*, June 1920, p.705. In Charles Belfoure, *Monuments to Money: The Architecture of American Banks* (McFarland & Co., Jefferson, NC, 2005), p.164.

52   'A New Shelter for Savings: George Howe and William Lescaze, Architects', *Architectural Forum*, vol.57 (December 1932), pp 483–98.

53   ibid.

54   ibid.

55   George Howe to James M. Willcox, 25 July 1932, HML.

56   The design has been linked to European sources including Otto Wagner's well-known Postal Saving Bank of 1904–1906 and Josef Maria Olbrich's Secession Gallery of 1899, both in Vienna. Jordy, p.58.

57   George Howe's design for the Sinkler House in West Chester, PA (1928–1930) is an example of how his other work anticipated the PSFS Building design. The Sinkler House represented a transitional modern design in which Howe began to 'hit his stride as a modernist'. The house featured a modern massing, large window openings, and an interior designed with rounded Art Deco furniture and textiles. Stern, p.86.

58   Reyner Banham, 'Machine Aesthetic', *Architectural Review*, vol.117 (April 1955), pp 225–8.

59   Mellor and Meigs's 1929 scheme is an altogether different scheme than the 1926 design

executed by Howe while still a partner at Mellor, Meigs & Howe. ibid.

60   Jordy, p.60.

61   Horizontal expression was considered a stabilising form in a chaotic metropolis, as can be seen in Erich Mendelsohn's Chemnitz Store. See Kathleen James, *Erich Mendelsohn and the Architecture of German Modernism: Modern Architecture and Cultural Identity* (Cambridge University Press, Cambridge, 1997).

62   Jordy, p.59.

63   'Monumental' was used to describe the kind of work that Lescaze sought, in a hand-written letter of recommendation by Karl C. Moser; see his 'Recommendation', 3 June 1920, Correspondence folder, Box 58, SYR.

64   Building Committee Meeting Minutes, 14 August 1929, Record Group 1: Office of the Corporate Secretary, PSFS Collection (Acc. 2062), HML.

65   R. Daniel Wadhwani, 'Soothing the People's Panic: The Banking Crisis of the 1930s in Philadelphia', *Pennsylvania Legacies*, vol.11, no.1 (May 2011), pp 24–31.

66   '[I]t is our opinion, as well as that of the Fuller Company, that the present is a very good time to buy building material.' George Howe to Stacy B. Lloyd, Esq., 29 April 1930, 2, HML.

67   'Memo, M. Todd Cooke, Jr, President of PSFS, Reported by Earle Bolton in an Interview with Todd Cooke, Vice Chairman of PSFS/Meritor Financial Group', 8 April 1969, HML.

68   Isaac W. Roberts, one of the PSFS board members, stated that it was the bankers who originally brought up the idea of the second-floor banking room; William Lescaze believed that the decision to raise the banking floor was promoted by the architects. See Jordy, p.50. The innovative idea of the second-floor banking space had already been executed by architects Ritter and Shay for the 1931 Market Street National Bank, sited a block away from the PSFS Building. This bank was under construction when PSFS was being designed.

69   Robert A.M. Stern attributes PSFS's innovations to William Lescaze as his 'dramatic renderings of the building show – the excitement, in a sense the showmanship, necessary to attract attention to the building in 1932'. Meanwhile Stern attributes concepts that have their based in a logic of rational expression to George Howe. Robert

A.M. Stern, 'PSFS: Beaux-Arts Theory and Rational Expressionism', *Journal of the Society of Architectural Historians*, vol.21 (1962), pp 94–5.

70   Correspondence from J.J.P. Oud to William Lescaze, 7 August 1929, and from William Lescaze to J.J.P. Oud, 11 July 1929, Box 56, William Lescaze Papers, SYR.

71   William Jordy compared the PSFS Building with Mendelsohn's work, arguing that 'the base of PSFS is, in fact, virtually a compressed version of [the Schocken Store at Chemnitz].' Jordy, p.76.

72   Extravagant ornamentation was removed in order to 'purify' the surface. Modern architecture, by contrast, was intended to promote a structure's bare face, without an extra mask. Janet Ward, *Weimar Surfaces: Urban Visual Culture in 1920s Germany* (University of California Press, Berkeley, CA, 2001), p.48.

73   James, p.93.

74   Howe and Lescaze themselves described the PSFS design as 'functional', which meant the design was specialised and resulted in unique forms. To put the term in its historical context, Adolf Behne attempted to define functionalism: 'As the functionalist looks for the greatest possible adaptation to the most specialised purpose, the rationalist looks for the most appropriate solution for many cases.' In Alan Colquhoun, *Modern Architecture* (Oxford University Press, Oxford, 2002), p.169.

75   Howe stated that the architects had already presented a scheme based on these items. He wanted to know for sure if there would be an office building and a store. (The offices were definite at this point, while the store was not.) Howe requested a resolution of the issue by June 1930, in order to finish the design in time. George Howe to Stacy B. Lloyd, PSFS, 29 April 1930, Record Group 8 PSFS Offices and Buildings, PSFS Collection (Acc. 2062), HML.

76   Willcox and Howe had a face-to-face conversation on the hospital roof about this matter – this was mentioned in correspondence. Willcox repeated his request in a 3 June 1930 letter to Howe. James M. Willcox to George Howe, 3 June 1930, PSFS Collection (Acc. 2062), HML.

77   George Howe to James M. Willcox, 26 May 1930, PSFS Collection (Acc. 2062), HML. Negative accounts of prospective tenant reactions to the design were reported by rental agent, Richard Seltzer.

78   Jordy, p.59.

79   ibid.; and Howe to Willcox, 25 July 1930, PSFS Collection (Acc. 2062) Box 83, Howe & Lescaze Correspondence, HML.

80   Howe to Willcox, 26 May 1930, PSFS Collection (Acc. 2062) Box 83, Howe & Lescaze Correspondence, HML.

81   Howe to Willcox, 25 July 1930, PSFS Collection (Acc. 2062) Box 83, Howe & Lescaze Correspondence, HML.

82   Willcox asked the contractor, George Fuller, to look at an article in the *Architectural Record* April 1930 issue, 'The Economic Design of Office Buildings', by R.H. Shreve of Shreve, Lamb, and Harmon, Architects. See George Fuller to James M. Willcox, 7 November 1930, HML.

83   Douglas Haskell, 'Building or Sculpture? The Architecture of "Mass"', *Architectural Record* (April 1930), p.368.

84   ibid., p.367.

85   Louis Sullivan, 'The Tall Office Building Artistically Considered', *Lippincott's Monthly Magazine*, vol.339 (March 1896), pp 403–9.

86   James M. Willcox to George Howe, 3 June 1930, PSFS Collection (Acc. 2062) Box 83, Howe & Lescaze Correspondence, HML.

87   Donald Friedman, 'Hidden Intricacies: The Development of Modern Building Skeletons', *APT Bulletin: The Journal of Preservation Technology*, vol.43, no.4 (2012), p.18.

88   Willcox is here referring to the comment by Seltzer, the rental agent, that people think the design is ugly and that it looks like a loft building. Willcox to Howe, 3 June 1930, PSFS Collection (Acc. 2062) Box 83, Howe & Lescaze Correspondence, HML. The letter from the renting agent to Willcox: Clarke Dailey, President of the Alliance Reality Company of New York, to James M. Willcox, 12 September 1930, PSFS Collection (Acc. 2062), HML.

89   Richard Seltzer, Rental Agent, to James M. Willcox, 12 September 1930, PSFS Collection (Acc. 2062), HML.

90   James M. Willcox to George Howe, 3 June 1930, PSFS Collection (Acc. 2062), HML.

91   ibid.

92   During the late 1920s, Kiesler and Lescaze both developed book proposals comparing modern architecture and design in Europe vs. America. Throughout the 1920s, Lescaze conducted research on modern buildings coupled with their architects' writings. Although the book did not come to fruition, it served as a lens onto Lescaze's particular approach to modern architecture. His research included work by J.J.P. Oud, Auguste Perret, and Robert Mallet-Stevens, among others. He referred to the book as 'a sort of *Etude Comparée* between European and American Work'. William Lescaze Collection, Box 56, SYR. Correspondence between Lescaze and Kiesler of 12 July 1929 and 8 August 1929 documents the use of some photographs of Jan Buijs's Coöperatie de Volderharding and J.J.P. Oud's Hoek van Holland projects that Lescaze loaned to Kiesler. The images appear in Frederick Kiesler's book *Contemporary Art Applied to the Store and Its Display* (Brentano's, New York, 1930), in which store window displays supply the case studies.

93   Kiesler, p.66.

94   ibid.

95   Anecdote, recounted by William H. Jordy, interview with Louis McAllister. Jordy, pp 49–50. Jordy, p.48.

96   James M. Willcox to George Howe, 30 July 1930, p.1, PSFS Collection (Acc. 2062) Box 83, Howe & Lescaze Correspondence, HML.

97   Howe writes, 'the design depended on purely decorative elements, such as the great globe at the summit of the tower, and on a use of set-backs.' In his argument to convince Willcox away from his prior scheme, Howe describes it in terms of its inadequacies. George Howe to James M. Willcox, 25 July 1930, p.2, PSFS Collection (Acc. 2062) Box 83, Howe & Lescaze Correspondence, HML.

98   George Howe to James M. Willcox, 25 July 1930, p.3, PSFS Collection (Acc. 2062), Box 83, HML.

99   ibid., p.5.

100   Kiesler, p.107.

101   James M. Willcox to George Howe, 30 July 1930, p.1, PSFS Collection (Acc. 2062) Box 83, Howe & Lescaze Correspondence, HML.

102   'Architectural Analysis of the Proposed Building for the Philadelphia Saving Fund Society at 12th & Market Streets', 26 September 1930, William Lescaze Collection, Box 6, Folder 284, SYR.

103   Jordy calls Howe's design for the PSFS 1926 branch banks 'Beaux-Arts semi-modernism', in Jordy, p.68.

104   12 November 1930, Board Meeting Minutes, PSFS Collection (Acc. 2062), HML.

105   George Howe to James M. Willcox, 26 May 1930, PSFS Collection (Acc. 2062), Box 83, HML.

106   The bankers feared that an initialled 'PSFS' sign lacked dignity. Up to the very end of the design process, the architects had to convince their clients that the full name of the bank would be all but illegible from the street. Jordy, p.64.

107   Based on examining the drawings and photographs of study models, the full name signs corresponded to the even numbered schemes and the initialled signs with the odd numbered schemes. Drawings and Photographs from the PSFS Collection, Hagley Museum and Library.

108   Originally the building committee had decided to air-condition only the banking floors, but a particularly stifling summer convinced the business-savvy client that office space would be more desirable if 'manufactured air' were installed throughout the entire tower. The PSFS Building was only the second in the nation to offer occupants this luxury. The 20 September 1931 drawing was entitled 'Steel drawing for a roof sign'. 'Correspondence', PSFS Collection (Acc. 2062), HML. 'Manufactured air' was the term used for air-conditioning in the PSFS *Nothing More Modern* brochure. PSFS Collection (Acc. 2062), HML.

109   Mr Roberts, Vice-President of PSFS, cited this statistic in Building Committee Meeting Minutes, PSFS Collection (Acc. 2062), HML.

110   Sign Design Studies, Box 20, SYR.

111   In typography, tracking, or letter-spacing, refers to the amount of space between a group of letters to affect density in a line of block of text. 'Phila Saving Fund' had also been considered, according to a drawing by William Lescaze dated 3 February 1932, Box 20, SYR.

112   In the description of the Bauhaus Building, designed by Walter Gropius, the following is stated: 'Lettering was executed by the printing workshop.' The printing workshop was led by Herbert Bayer. Herbert Bayer, Walter Gropius and Ise Gropius, *Bauhaus 1919–1928* (Museum of Modern Art, New York), p.103.

113   Mike Mills, 'Herbert Bayer's University Type and in Its Historical Contexts', in Ellen Lupton and J. Abbott Miller, *The ABC's of [triangle] [circle] [square]: The Bauhaus and Design Theory* (Princeton Architectural Press, New York, 1991), pp 38–45.

114   Herbert Bayer, 'On Typography', in Arthur Cohen and Herbert Bayer (eds), *Herbert Bayer: The Complete Work* (MIT Press, Cambridge, MA, 1984), p.350.

115   Ellen Lupton, 'Herbert Bayer, Designs for "Universal" Lettering, 1923 and 1927', in Barry Bergdoll et al., *Bauhaus 1919–1933: Workshops for Modernity* (Museum of Modern Art, New York, 2009), pp 200–205.

116   The architects reportedly visited the exposition separately. See Lanmon, p.30, on Lescaze; and Stern, *George Howe*, p.63.

117   Le Corbusier described it as a 'Façade laterale aveugle avec polychromie: blanc, noir, gris clair, gris foncé, ocre jaune, et terre de Sienne brulée.' Le Corbusier, *Almanach d'architecture moderne*, Collection de 'L'Esprit Nouveau' (G. Cráes et Cie, Paris, 1925), p.153.

118   Nicolete Gray, *Lettering on Buildings: 270 Illustrations* (Architectural Press, London, 1960), p.182.

119   Christoph Ribbat, *Flickering Light: A History of Neon* (Reaktion, London, 2011) p.34.

120   ibid., p.35.

121   William Lescaze to A. Sage, *Art & Industrie*, 21 June 1929, 'Correspondence', Box 56, SYR. Lescaze was familiar with the Dutch architect Jan Brinkman, co-designer of the Van Nelle Factory, as he had interviewed him in 1929 for his unpublished book on the comparison between European and American modern architecture. See n.92.

122   The Delaware River Bridge (now known as the Benjamin Franklin Bridge) was designed by Howe's friend Cret and completed in 1926. The idea that the angled sign directly faces the bridge was first mentioned to me in conversation with David Leatherbarrow, who writes about this phenomenon in his book, *Architecture Otherwise Oriented* (Princeton Architectural Press, New York, 2009).

123   See Jordy, p.64, n55.

124   'Minutes of Thirty-fourth General Meeting on the 1200 Market Street Building', 20 April 1932, p.10, PSFS Collection, HML.

125   Burton Harrington, *The Essentials of Poster Design* (Poster Advertising Association Inc., Chicago, 1925), pp 13–15.

126   62,126 people included 30,486 passengers by 1,810 buses, 31,205 passengers by 13,687 automobiles, and 435 pedestrians. Delaware River Joint Commission of Pennsylvania and New Jersey, *Report of the Delaware River Joint Commission of Pennsylvania and New Jersey* (The Commission, Camden, NJ, 1931), p.2.

127   Visitors there were enthralled by the eight-storey-high and block long Wrigley gum advertisement of brilliantly coloured tropical fish (made up of 18,000

electric bulbs) gliding through the waves of sea-green lights. Adjacent to Times Square was New York's 'Great White Way' – named for the fantastic quantity of electric bulb-adorned signs along Broadway and 42nd Street in the theatre district. Catherine Gudis, *Buyways: Billboards, Automobiles, and the American Landscape* (London, Routledge, 2004), p. 129-130.

128   Working drawing for sign, SYR, reproduced in 'The PSFS Building: Philadelphia, Pennsylvania, 1929–1932', *Perspecta*, vol.25 (1989), p.133.

129   Paddy Rowell Sr, current owner of Flexlume Sign Corporation, Buffalo, New York. Telephone interview with the author, 13 January 2010.

130   'The PSFS Sign, A Study of the Design and Significance', Tony Atkin & Associates, ATH.

131   The engineers regarded the fact that the sign's legible distance at night was actually greater than during the day as one of their greatest achievements.

132   Modern typography was a manifesto of a larger modern movement, which advocated for the conception of a new society. Jan Tschichold, *The New Typography: A Handbook for Modern Designers. Weimar and Now*: *German Cultural Criticism* (University of California Press, Berkeley, CA, 1995).

133   J.J.P. Oud, 'Een café' in *Bouwkundig Weekblad*, vol.46, no.31 (1925), p.399, quoted in Ed Taverne, Cor Wagenaar and Martien de Vletter, *J.J.P. Oud: Poetic Functionalist, 1890–1963: The Complete Works* (NAi Publishers, Rotterdam, 2001), p.342.

134   Taverne, Wagenaar and de Vletter, p.335.

135   Douglas C. McMurtrie, *Modern Typography & Layout* (Eyncourt Press, Chicago, 1929), p.65.

136   ibid.

137   Robin Kinross, *Modern Typography: An Essay in Critical History* (Hyphen Press, London, 2004), pp 133–4.

138   Steven Heller, 'Commercial Modern: American Design Style, 1925–1933', *Print*, vol.49, no.5 (September–October 1995), pp 58–122.

139   Henry-Russell Hitchcock and Philip Johnson, *The International Style: Architecture since 1922* (W.W. Norton, New York, 1932), p.74.

140   ibid.

141   ibid.

142   For example, a typographer would have made the upper part of the 'S' smaller than the bottom to stop the letterform from looking top-heavy.

143   Author interview with typographer, Roger Whitehouse, 8 January 2010.

144   ibid.

145   ibid.

146   Marchand, *Advertising The American Dream*, p.9.

147   'A Sign Erection Based on Scientific Tests', *Signs of the Times: The National Journal of Display Advertising*, November 1932, p.18, PSFS Collection (Acc. 2062), HML.

148   For a published collection of the PSFS drawings, see *Perspecta*, vol.25, pp 78–141.

149   Carol Willis, *Form Follows Finance: Skyscrapers and Skylines in New York and Chicago* (Princeton Architectural Press, New York, 1995), pp 7–16.

150   William Lescaze to Bauhaus, 18 June 1929, Box 55, Folder Heading: 'Correspondence', SYR.

151   Josef Albers to William Lescaze, 2 July 1929, Box 55, Folder Heading: 'Correspondence', SYR.

152   Penny Sparke, *The Modern Interior* (Reaktion Books, London, 2008), p.159.

153   The Garland Furniture Company and E.F. Hauserman fabricated the tubular furniture and the metal partitions, respectively, among many other items for the bank and tenant spaces. Jordy, p.73, n75.

154   While neither Howe nor Lescaze had time or interest to execute good detailing, two young German designers working for the firm possessed exceptional detailing skills. Alfred Clauss was a disciple of Mies van der Rohe, and Walter Baermann was an architect trained in Munich. Baermann played a major role in the design of the banking room, the 12th Street entrance lobby, the main elevator lobbies, and other interiors. He was also especially instrumental in the design of metal office partitions, which were subsequently influential in the development of modern ideas in office partitioning. In 1962, Jordy discussed the building's integration of industrial design and architecture, calling it an 'ideal comprehensive space'. Jordy, p.73.

155   'A Professional Biographical Essay', 18 February 1929, Writings, Box 66, SYR.

156   William Lescaze, *On Being an Architect* (New York, G.P. Putnam's Sons, 1942), p.102.

157   ibid.

158   ibid., p.14.

159   'A Professional Biographical Essay', 18 February 1929, Writings, Box 66, SYR.

160   Lescaze's entity, especially in the S.T. Meyers Company design, resembles El Lissitsky's Proun installations. Though it was not confirmed by the Lescaze archive directly, Lescaze's attention to

European currents in the 1920s and his trip to Berlin in the same time period demonstrate that he would have likely had knowledge of El Lissitsky's work and possibly been influenced by it. See 'A Professional Biographical Essay', 18 February 1929, 'Writings', Box 66, SYR.

161   The Cheneys were among the first to closely examine the historical influences and aesthetic impact of streamlined shapes and curvilinear geometry in the fields of industrial design, architecture, and decoration, all before the popularisation of the term 'Art Deco'. Cheney and Cheney, p.217.

162   'A Professional Biographical Essay'.

163   Cheney and Cheney, p.200.

164   'A Professional Biographical Essay'.

165   'Electricity and the Architect: What They Have Produced at 1200 Market Street', p.33, PSFS Collection (Acc. 2062), HML.

166   ibid.

167   ibid. Consulting engineer Leslie S. Tarleton, described the lighting of PSFS as an example of how 'new types of lamps, new methods of lighting control, and the slowly opening door of television, must undoubtedly furnish many architects with those materials of which dreams are made.'

168   'Electricity and the Architect'.

169   'Light in Architecture and Decoration', *Illuminating Engineering Society*, 1934, p.91, PSFS Collection (Acc. 2062), HML.

170   Jerome B. Gray, 'An Ultra-Modern Campaign to Let an Ultra-Modern Building', *Printed Salesmanship* (Chicago), October 1932, pp 132–5, pp 175–6, p.181. Trade Publications, PSFS Collection (Acc. 2062), HML.

171   ibid., p.134.

172   Heller, p.58.

173   'Nothing More Modern' advertising campaign, PSFS Collection (Acc. 2062), HML.

174   ibid.

175   Gray, pp 132–135, 175–176, 181.

176   PSFS Newspaper Ad, in *Public Ledger*, 13 June 1932, PSFS Collection (Acc. 2062), HML.

177   In Stern's book on Howe, he describes the favourable public opinion on the banking hall, based on men hired by PSFS stationed in the banking room to listen to the conversations of visitors. Stern, *George Howe*, p.131. Meanwhile, the newspapers' opinions of the overall building were negative.

178   ibid.

179   In a letter dated 3 May 1933, H.C.L. Miller, Inc., producers of veneer, described the finishes on the 33rd floor: boardroom furniture and vestibule 2 clad in Macassar ebony; the main dining room and vestibule 1 in rosewood; the walls of the committee room, hudoke wood veneer. Sources of the woodwork on a world map by the architects: rosewood from India and Brazil, rotary walnut from Indiana, Macassar ebony from the Island of Celebes, oriental walnut from Australia, laurel from India, hudoke and imbuya from Brazil, travertine from Italy. Variety in materials was a consistent theme throughout the design, from the exterior to the interior. PSFS Collection (Acc. 2062), HML.

180   'A New Shelter for Savings', p.488.

181   ibid.

182   Jordy, p.72.

183   'A New Shelter for Savings', p.490.

184   See Jordy, pp 52–3.

185   Douglas Haskell, 'The Filing-Cabinet Building', *Creative Art*, vol.10 (June 1932), p.448.

186   'Does Modern Architecture Pay?', *Architectural Forum*, vol.83, no.9 (September 1943), p.74.

187   ibid.

188   ibid., p.78.

189   Willcox, cited in ibid., p.74.

190   ibid.

191   Report of the Building and Property Committee, 1 May 1933, PSFS Collection (Acc. 2062), HML.

192   Cheney and Cheney, p.241.

3   FAME Frank Lloyd Wright and the Johnson Wax Building

1   'The World's Most Modern Office' was coined by the Metal Office Furniture Co. (later to become Steelcase) in an advertisement, 1939, S.C. Johnson & Son Archives.

2   *Life* magazine, vol.6, no.19, 8 May 1939, p.15.

3   Samuel C. Johnson, *The Essence of a Family Enterprise: Doing Business the Johnson Way* (The Curtis Publishing Company, Indianapolis, 1988), p.42.

4   ibid., p.42.

5   ibid., p.44.

6   ibid., p.3: Samuel Johnson's poker game anecdote about the advantages of being a private company.

7   For a detailed account of the historical development of welfare capitalism, see Richard Edwards, *Contested Terrain: The Transformation of the*

Workplace in the Twentieth Century (Basic Books, New York, 1979). Edwards presents the various methods of worker control in a capitalist environment as three typologies: simple, technical, and bureaucratic. I would argue that the architecture of corporations, including housing and offices, is a combination of technical and bureaucratic control.

8   For histories of labour strikes in America, see Samuel Yellen, *American Labor Struggles* (Amo, New York, 1969).

9   Profit sharing was established and developed by William Cooper Proctor at Procter & Gamble in Cincinnati in the mid-1880s. Proctor articulated its important role in resolving the conflict between labour and capital of industrial relations.

10   Johnson, p.24.

11   During this volatile time, S.C. Johnson & Son continued its welfare capitalist practices for employees by adding a pension plan in 1934 and hospitalisation coverage in 1939. After World War II, S.C. Johnson & Son built and managed the Lighthouse Resort, a retreat for employees at a minimal cost; in 1951 they provided deferred profit sharing, and major medical insurance in 1953. They also built and maintained Armstrong Park, a recreation centre for employees, in 1957, and added vision care benefits in 1978. In 1980, the JMBA Recreation Center for Fitness and Wellness was built; in 1985, a Child Care Center was provided; and finally, an Aquatic Center was added to the JMBA in 1987. ibid., p.116.

12   'The History of Johnson Advertising', p.1, S.C. Johnson & Son Archives, and noted in Johnson.

13   1918 Johnson Wax ad from Domestic Advertisements Collection, J. Walter Thompson Company Collection, John W. Hartman Center for Sales, Advertising, and Marketing History, Duke University, cited in Jessamyn Neuhaus, *Housework and Housewives in American Advertising: Married to the Mop* (Palgrave Macmillan, New York, 2011), p.177.

14   1930s ad, Advertising Archives.

15   Juliann Sivulka, *Soap, Sex, and Cigarettes: A Cultural History of American Advertising* (Wadsworth Publishing, Belmont, CA, 1998), p.219.

16   S.C. Johnson & Son, Inc., *JONWAX Journal*, Special 75th Anniversary Issue, March 1961, p.19. Tony Won's radio show is described in 'The History of Johnson Advertising', p.2, S.C. Johnson & Son Archives.

17   Barbara Campbell, 'H.F. Johnson Dies; Led Wax Company', *The New York Times*, 14 December 1978.

18   Herbert F. Johnson was Frank Lloyd Wright's great client of the 1930s. Johnson has been compared to two other great Wright clients, Darwin Martin and Edgar Kaufmann.

19   'The Story of Johnson Wax', S.C. Johnson & Son Archives.

20   'The History of Johnson Advertising', p.2, S.C. Johnson & Son Archives. Consumer products of other companies, such as Jell-O, Lucky Strike, Ovaltine, and Pepsi-Cola, likewise came to be identified and purchased because of their association with network broadcasting.

21   ibid.

22   ibid.

23   Herbert Johnson, interviewed by Edward Wilder, 1940, in Jonathan Lipman, *Frank Lloyd Wright and the Johnson Wax Buildings* (Rizzoli, New York, 1986). Lipman curated the 1986 exhibition *Frank Lloyd Wright and the Johnson Wax Buildings: Creating a Corporate Cathedral* organised by the Herbert F. Johnson Museum of Art, Cornell University. The exhibition travelled to 11 locations, with the first at the Renwick Gallery of the National Museum of American Art, Smithsonian Institution, Washington, DC.

24   Johnson, p.137.

25   Lipman, p.1.

26   ibid., p.184.

27   ibid., p.1.

28   Wright designed a number of buildings and homes in Racine including residences for the Miles family (1901), the Hardy family (1905), and Monolith Homes (1919). He also designed Wingspread, a residence for company president Herbert F. Johnson Jr, the year after the administration building was completed (1937), and a residence for Johnson's daughter, Karen, in 1954. See Mark Hertzberg, *Wright in Racine: The Architect's Vision for One American City* (Pomegranate, Petaluma, CA, 2004).

29   The years from 1910 to 1922 were considered Wright's 'lost years'. He travelled to Europe to pursue publication of his work. Wright designed his home, Taliesin, in Spring Green, Wisconsin, which was built in 1911. Three years later it burned to the ground in a tragic fire, preceded by the murder of his lover, Mamah Borthwick, and six others. In the mid- to late 1920s, Wright designed the Graycliff House (1926–1931) for long-time client Darwin Martin, a house for his cousin, Richard Lloyd Jones, in Tulsa, Oklahoma (1928–1929), and Octatilla, a temporary camp for himself in

the Arizona desert (1929). Frank Lloyd Wright, *An Autobiography* (Pomegranate, San Francisco, 2005; first published by Duell, Sloan and Pearce, New York, 1943), p.496.

30   Neil Levine, *The Architecture of Frank Lloyd Wright* (Princeton University Press, Princeton, NJ, 1996), p.192.

31   Letter from Jack Ramsey to Herbert Johnson, 19 July 1936. The Frank Lloyd Wright Foundation.

32   ibid.

33   *Inland Architect*, August/September 1969, p.18, cited in Lipman, p.5.

34   ibid.

35   Jonathan Lipman, interview with Henrietta Louis, 27 May 1981, cited in Lipman, p.13, p.184.

36   *Inland Architect*, August/September 1969, p.18, cited in Lipman, p.5. Wright also gives an account of this visit in *An Autobiography*.

37   Wright, p.468.

38   Needham, Louis & Brorby of Chicago worked for S.C. Johnson & Son from 1929 to 1953. Preceding Needham, Louis & Brorby was the Western Advertising Agency of Racine. After 1953, Foote, Cone & Belding was selected as their second agency, and in 1955 Benton and Bowles of New York also came on their team. Herbert Johnson did not attend this first meeting, despite Wright's recollection. He came to Taliesin at a later date.

39   *Inland Architect*, August/September, 1969, p.18.

40   Edgar Tafel, interviewed by Jonathan Lipman, 16 June 1979.

41   While I maintain that Frank Lloyd Wright was anti-urban with his design of the S.C. Johnson & Son Administration Building, other scholars disagree. The long-accepted notion that Wright disliked the city has been challenged in the following books: Neil Levine, *The Urbanism of Frank Lloyd Wright* (Princeton University Press, Princeton, NJ, 2015), and Herbert Muschamp, *Man About Town* (MIT Press, Cambridge, MA, 1973).

42   Brendan Gill, *Many Masks: A Life of Frank Lloyd Wright* (G.P. Putnam's Sons, New York, 1987), p.357.

43   Letter from Jack Ramsey to Herbert Johnson, 19 July 1936, The Frank Lloyd Wright Foundation, 1990.

44   Lipman writes that Taliesin apprentice John Howe recalled this fact about Wright's one-on-one meetings with potential clients.

45   Wright calling the prior headquarters design a 'fancy crematorium' is also mentioned in *An Autobiography*, p.268.

46   Olgivanna Wright, interviewed by Jonathan Lipman, 19 January 1980, in Lipman, p.13.

47   ibid., p.13.

48   ibid., p.41.

49   Edgar Tafel, interviewed by Jonathan Lipman, 5 February 1982, in Lipman, p.14.

50   Karen Boyd, interviewed by Jonathan Lipman, 23 September 1981.

51   Frank Lloyd Wright, 'An Organic Architecture, 1939', in Edgar Kaufmann and Ben Raeburn (eds), *Frank Lloyd Wright: Writings & Buildings* (New American Library, New York, 1960), p.281.

52   'Co-branding' is a term used by Naomi Klein in *No Logo* (Picador, New York, 2000), p.30. Examples are Michael Jordan and Nike, as well as Martha Stewart and Kmart.

53   Lipman, p.15.

54   Olgivanna Wright, interviewed by Jonathan Lipman, 19 January 1980, in Lipman.

55   Jack Quinan, *Frank Lloyd Wright's Larkin Building: Myth and Fact* (University of Chicago Press, Chicago, 1987), p.100.

56   ibid., p.108.

57   Wright, p.469.

58   ibid.

59   Wright's theories are well known among scholars. An early source is H. Allen Brooks, 'Frank Lloyd Wright and the Destruction of the Box', *Journal of the Society of Architectural Historians*, vol.38, no.1 (1979), pp 7–14.

60   An edited transcript of an address to the Junior Chapter of the AIA, New York City, 1952, in Kaufmann and Raeburn, pp 284–96.

61   ibid.

62   ibid.

63   ibid.

64   Wright's reference to the administration building as 'streamlined' has been quoted in a number of places. This quote is from Wright, p.471.

65   John Howe, Edgar Tafel, and Wes Peters were the main apprentices who worked on the S.C. Johnson & Son Administration Building. Jonathan Lipman pointed out this pattern in Wright's work. Also, Lipman has speculated that if Wright had been considering the building as advertising, adopting his own version of streamlining would have been a good way to do achieve it. Lipman, p.31.

66   Frank Lloyd Wright, Foreword, *Architectural Forum* (January 1938).

67   Levine, p.303.

68   Wes Peters, interviewed by Jonathan Lipman, 22 April 1979, cited in Lipman, p.31.

69   ibid.

70   Wright selected a maroon-orange brick manufactured by the Streator Brick Company in Streator, Illinois. The brick's particular tint was dubbed 'Cherokee red' by Wright. ibid., p.38.

71   Wright referred to the upper level executive's offices as a 'penthouse', as a leftover convention from the Capital Journal project, in which there were two upper levels of apartments which were called 'penthouses'.

72   Frank Lloyd Wright to Mr H.F. Johnson Jr, 20 August 1936, The Frank Lloyd Wright Foundation, 1990.

73   ibid.

74   Lipman, p.43.

75   Frank Lloyd Wright, typed statement in S.C. Johnson & Son, dated 11 October 1936, cited in Lipman, p.43, p.185.

76   John Howe, interviewed by Jonathan Lipman, 27 September 1985.

77   Ramsey to Wright, 5 October 1936, The Frank Lloyd Wright Foundation, 1990.

78   Frank Lloyd Wright, 'The New Building for S. C. Johnson & Son, Inc.', 11 October 1936. Lipman, Appendix 2, p.182.

79   Lipman, p.46. In November 1936, J.M. Richards, assistant editor of *Architectural Review*, wrote to Wright directly, asking for the privilege of publishing the new building.

80   Johnson, p.137.

81   Wright, as quoted by Lipman in Robert McCarter, *Frank Lloyd Wright* (London, Phaidon, 1999) p. 193.

82   ibid., p.472.

83   Kenneth Frampton, 'Introduction, The Johnson Wax Buildings and The Angel of History', in Jonathan Lipman, *Frank Lloyd Wright and the Johnson Wax Buildings* (New York, Rizzoli, 1986) , p.xi.

84   Nature was Wright's most important influence in his architecture. Historians of Wright – including Neil Levine, Robert McCarter, Kenneth Frampton, Kathryn Smith, Jonathan Lipman, and others – have made this observation in their works.

85   Edgar Tafel, interviewed by Jonathan Lipman, 1 October 1979. The quality of introspection in Wright's public buildings is striking, as noted by architectural historian Kenneth Frampton.

86   Frank Lloyd Wright, as quoted in Lipman, p.51. Lipman quotes Wright in one of his early conversations with Herbert Johnson.

87   Wright often wrote about the destruction of the box. His most concise discussion of it can be found in *An Autobiography*, pp 141–2, in the section, 'Building the New House'.

88   Kaufmann and Raeburn, 1960, p.286.

89   E.J. Winship, Corning Glass Works, Architectural Division to Wright, 14 October 1936. Series of letters between 1936 and 1937, The Frank Lloyd Wright Foundation, 1990.

90   'Administration Center, The World's Most Modern Office Building, Johnson Wax; Racine, Wisconsin, Designed by Frank Lloyd Wright', Press Document, courtesy of S.C. Johnson & Son Company.

91   Advertisement for Corning Glass, 'Corning Means Research in Glass', in November 1939 issue of *Fortune*, courtesy S.C. Johnson & Son.

92   Frampton, in Lipman, p.xii.

93   CJ. Caddell, Building Inspector, Industrial Commission of Wisconsin to Wright, 23 March 1937, The Frank Lloyd Wright Foundation 1990.

94   Edgar Tafel remembers Wright kicking and striking the test column with his cane. Cited in Lipman, p.62.

95   Olgivanna Wright interviewed by Jonathan Lipman, 19 January 1980, cited in Lipman.

96   H.F. Johnson Jr to Wright, 4 October 1942, The Frank Lloyd Wright Foundation.

97   Patricia Tice, *Wooton Patent Desks: A Place for Everything and Everything in Its Place* (Indiana State Museum, Indianapolis, 1983).

98   The desk and chair drawing was published in *Architectural Forum* (January 1938).

99   Stanley Abercrombie, 'Office Supplies: Evolving Furniture for the Evolving Workplace', in Donald Albrecht and Chrysanthe B. Broikos (eds), *On the Job: Design and the American Office* (Princeton Architectural Press, New York, 2000), p.85. There were various office systems invented before 1964, like Herman's Miller's 1942 Executive Office Group and the Knoll Planning Unit in 1943. These systems were never successfully mass-produced or fully accepted, however.

100   Frank Lloyd Wright, *The Mike Wallace Interviews* (DVD) (Solomon R. Guggenheim Museum,

New York, 1957). This interview was recorded in two parts, on 1 September 1957 and 28 September 1957.

101   Levine, p.366.

102   Amy Henderson, 'Media and the Rise of Celebrity Culture', *OAH Magazine of History*, vol.6, no.4 (Spring 1992), p.51.

103   William Connolly to Frank Lloyd Wright, 8 October 1936, The Frank Lloyd Wright Foundation.

104   ibid.

105   ibid.

106   ibid. p.2.

107   *Life* magazine, 8 May 1939, p.15.

108   'Office Building Goes Functional', in *Businessweek*, 6 May 1939.

109   *Milwaukee Sentinel*, 24 April 1939.

110   ibid., courtesy S.C. Johnson & Son.

111   ibid.

112   'Office Building Goes Functional'.

113   'The World's Most Modern Office', advertisement by Metal Office Furniture Co., Grand Rapids, Michigan, in *Broadcast Merchandising*, May 1939. 'The Office of the Future', in *American Business*, May 1939, p.41.

114   *Engineering News Record*, 9 December 1937, courtesy S.C. Johnson & Son.

115   *Life* magazine, 8 May 1939.

116   *Spring Valley Democrat* (Illinois), 5 May 1939.

117   'Offices Being Built without Windows; Frank Lloyd Wright Designs Unusual Structure in Racine, Wis', *New York Times*, 10 January 1937. 'Newest Thing Since the Skyscraper', *Spring Valley Democrat*, 5 May 1939. 'Johnson Offices Open to Public', *The Racine Journal-Times*, 21 April 1939.

118   Quoted in both *The Racine Journal-Times*, 21 April 1939 and *Life* magazine, 8 May 1939, in addition to a number of architectural books, journals, and exhibitions.

119   *Broadcast Merchandising*, May 1939.

120   ibid.

121   Henderson, p.52.

122   *Broadcast Merchandising*, May 1939.

123   ibid.

124   *An Autobiography*, p.470.

125   ibid.

126   ibid., p.469.

127   William N. Connolly, Public Relations Vice-President, 'Public Relations by Johnson Wax', *Jonwax Journal, The Anniversary Issue*, March 1961, p.16.

128   'Welcome to the Home of Johnson's Wax', p.5. S.C. Johnson & Son.

129   Memo, Jack Ramsey to William Connolly, 9 November 1936, The Frank Lloyd Wright Foundation 1990.

130   ibid.

131   ibid.

132   ibid.

133   H.F. Johnson, 'Panel Discussion, 'The Place of Advertising in the Marketing Process', 7 May 1957. S.C. Johnson & Son.

134   Meryle Seacrest, *Frank Lloyd Wright, A Biography* (University of Chicago Press, Chicago), p.444. Also in Johnson.

4   FORM Lever House

1   President of Lever Brothers US Operations Charles Luckman told the parent company, Unilever, 'if you let me do what I want, I will get millions and millions of dollars of free advertising for Lever Brothers from all around the world.' Charles Luckman, quoted in his book *Twice in a Lifetime: From Soap to Skyscrapers* (W.W. Norton, New York, 1988), pp 243–4. Note: The scholarship of this study of Lever House was dependent on other archival sources, including the Papers of Nathaniel Owings, the Raymond Loewy Archive, and the Gordon Bunshaft Collection. Unilever is an extant corporation and I was not allowed access to its archives.

2   Carol Herselle Krinsky, *Gordon Bunshaft of Skidmore, Owings & Merrill* (Architectural History Foundation, New York; MIT Press, Cambridge, MA, 1988), p.18. Krinsky points out that the design would become a prototype for countless buildings in US and abroad, with few of them approaching its level of sophistication.

3   Nathaniel Alexander Owings, *The Spaces In Between: An Architect's Journey* (Houghton Mifflin, Boston, 1973), p.109.

4   Jane Jacobs, 'New York's Office Boom', *Architectural Forum*, vol.106 (March 1957), p.105.

5   ibid., p.106.

6   Charles Wilson, *The History of Unilever: A Study in Economic Growth and Social Change* (Praeger, New York, 1968), p.21. Wilson states that in 1844, Friedrich Engels described Bolton as the worst of Lancashire's industrial towns.

7   The Lever family had previously owned a retail grocery store since 1842. Lever shifted to a wholesale enterprise in 1864. Wilson, p.27.

8   ibid.

9   William Lever was one of the earliest members of the Garden City Association, founded by fellow Englishman Ebenezer Howard in 1901. Garden cities complemented social reform by improving the living and working conditions of the industrial proletariat. Margaret Crawford, *Building the Workingman's Paradise: The Design of American Company Towns* (Verso, London, 1995), p.70.

10   Address of W.H. Lever to the Architectural Association in London, 21 March 1902, in *Souvenir of Port Sunlight* (Lever Brothers Limited, Port Sunlight, 1927). For more on Lever Brothers' 'prosperity sharing', see Edward Hubbard and Michael Shippobottom, *A Guide to Port Sunlight Village* (Liverpool University Press, Liverpool, 2005), p.4. Also, the company was an example of 'welfare capitalism', the practice of a corporation providing welfare-like services including health care, housing, and pensions to its employees. Richard Edwards, *Contested Terrain: The Transformation of the Workplace in the Twentieth Century* (Basic Books, New York, 1979).

11   Hubbard and Shippobottom, p.2.

12   Walter L. Creese, *The Search for Environment: The Garden City Before and After*, expanded edition (Johns Hopkins University Press, Baltimore, 1992), p.31, cited in Crawford, p.71.

13   Hubbard and Shippobottom, p.33.

14   Crawford, p.71.

15   Polly Toynbee, *A Working Life* (Macmillan, London, 1971), cited in Crawford, p.71.

16   W.H. Lever to John Cheshire, 13 June 1909, cited in Wilson, p.21.

17   W.J. Reader, *Fifty Years of Unilever, 1930–1980* (Heinemann, London, 1980), p.33.

18   Wilson, p.41. In his diary of an American tour which he made in 1888, Lever recorded the genesis of the slogan 'Why Does a Woman Look Old Sooner than a Man?' which he bought from Frank Siddal, a Philadelphian soap maker. A local trade publication, *The Lancashire Grocer*, teemed with articles and stories reprinted from American newspapers and periodicals.

19   ibid., p.41.

20   ibid., p.44.

21   A multinational is a firm that controls operations or income-generating assets in more than one country. Multinationals are owned in their home economy and invest in host economies. The most straightforward example of multinational investment occurs when a company establishes a wholly owned subsidiary in a foreign country, which the US Lever Brothers is to Unilever. For a detailed definition of a multinational corporation, see Geoffrey Jones, *Multinationals and Global Capitalism: From the Nineteenth to the Twenty-First Century* (Oxford University Press, Oxford, 2005), p.5.

22   Reader, p.6.

23   Geoffrey Jones, 'Control, Performance, and Knowledge Transfers in Large Multinationals: Unilever in the United States, 1945–1980', *Business History Review*, vol.76, no.3 (Autumn 2002), pp 435–78.

24   Wilson, p.52.

25   Charles Luckman quoted a business news article about his role at Lever Brothers; Luckman, p.22.

26   ibid., p.28.

27   ibid.

28   ibid., p.31.

29   Herbert Muschamp, 'Charles Luckman, Architect who Designed Penn Station's Replacement, Dies at 89', *New York Times*, 28 January 1999.

30   ibid.

31   Luckman, p.204.

32   Nathaniel Owings, 'Chapter Three Draft', *The Spaces In Between*, unpublished manuscript, 18 March 1971, p.4. Nathaniel Alexander Owings Papers, Box 50, Library of Congress, Washington, D.C. The full quotation reads, 'I was concerned about what I was: salesman, huckster, manure spreader? I had ideas, yes – boiling over with them. . . . The problem with me was the detail. . . . I had to place my ideas into another's hands for execution.'

33   Owings, *The Spaces In Between*, p.21.

34   ibid., p.36.

35   Nicholas Adams, *Skidmore, Owings & Merrill: SOM since 1936* (Electa, Milan and Phaidon, London, 2007), pp 19–24.

36   Roland Marchand, *Creating the Corporate Soul: The Rise of Public Relations and Corporate Imagery in American Big Business* (University of California Press, Berkeley, CA, 1998), pp 267–8.

37   On the *Century of Progress* exhibition, see Lenox Lohr, *Fair Management: A Story of a Century of Progress* (Cuneo Press, Chicago, 1952), as cited in Adams.

38   Owings, *The Spaces In Between*, p.65.

39   ibid., p.66.

40   ibid.

41   ibid.

42   Adams, p.21.

43   ibid., p.21.

44   ibid.

45   Owings described the occasion of his and George Fry's celebration as getting 'drunk one New Year's Eve'. Owings wrote that it was two years after 1949, but he wrote in the LOC manuscript draft dated 25 May 1971 that it was 1948. Owings, *The Spaces In Between*, p.106.

46   Gordon Bunshaft, 'Oral History of Gordon Bunshaft', interview by Betty J. Blum, manuscript, Chicago Architects Oral History Project, The Art Institute of Chicago, 1990, p.157.

47   Owings published a version of this speech in Nathaniel A. Owings, 'A Radically New Conception of Tomorrow's Office Building', *National Real Estate and Building Journal*, January 1948.

48   ibid.

49   ibid., p.28.

50   ibid.

51   Jacobs, p.106.

52   ibid.

53   Owings, 'A Radically New Conception of Tomorrow's Office Building', pp 28–9.

54   ibid.

55   ibid.

56   Owings, *The Spaces In Between*, p.106.

57   Gordon Bunshaft, SOM partner and designer in charge of the Lever House design, told interviewer Betty Blum, '. . . you know, somebody likes to say Lever House is Corbu. Another guy says it's Mies because it has thin mullions. And they're both full of baloney. It's modern and probably influenced by Corbu's pilotis and things, period. But it's an insult to Le Corbusier. He would do a much more interesting building than Lever.' 'Oral History of Gordon Bunshaft', p.138.

58   Terms used by Jane Jacobs, p.106.

59   Luckman, p.237.

60   Owings, *The Spaces In Between*, p.108. Also cited in Krinsky, p.19. Charles Luckman reiterated the reason for Lever Brothers' move, writing, 'We moved to New York because that's where the advertising was', in his 1988 memoir.

61   'Oral History of Gordon Bunshaft', p.158.

62   Luckman, pp 241–4.

63   George Fry to Nathaniel Owings, p.14, 6 March 1970, NAO papers, Box 49, LOC.

64   'Oral History of Gordon Bunshaft', p.163.

65   Gordon Bunshaft, interviewed by Arthur Drexler, Tape 2, 9 January 1980, sound recording, Gordon Bunshaft, 1909–1990, architectural drawings and papers, Avery Library, Columbia University.

66   'Oral History of Gordon Bunshaft', p.97.

67   ibid., p.95.

68   ibid., p.96.

69   Adams, p.24.

70   'Oral History of Gordon Bunshaft', p.159.

71   ibid., p.171.

72   ibid., p.162.

73   Gordon Bunshaft, quoted by Nathaniel Owings, in Owings, *The Spaces In Between*, p.75.

74   ibid.

75   'Oral History of Gordon Bunshaft', p.171.

76   ibid., p.171.

77   Bill Brown to Nathaniel Owings, October 1970, p.10. Nathaniel Alexander Owings Papers, Box 49, Library of Congress.

78   ibid.

79   'Oral History of Gordon Bunshaft', p.170.

80   Adams, p.11.

81   ibid.

82   Gordon Bunshaft, quoted by Nathaniel Owings, in Owings, *The Spaces In Between*, p.75.

83   ibid.

84   ibid., p.268.

85   ibid.

86   ibid., p.270. In his 2006 history of SOM, Nicholas Adams commented that, 'No one at SOM was ever in closer touch with public taste than Nathaniel Owings.' Adams, p.15.

87   *Time*, 2 August 1968, vol.92, no.5.

88   See the discussion of zoning limits in Adams, p.66 and Krinsky, p.19.

89   Bunshaft, interviewed by Drexler, Tape 2.

90   ibid.

91   Luckman, p.242.

92   ibid., p.339.

93   Bunshaft interviewed by Drexler, Tape 2.

94   'Oral History of Gordon Bunshaft', p.162.

95   ibid.

96   ibid.

97   ibid.

98   ibid.

99   ibid. Bunshaft went on to say that Lever House received the 25th AIA Award and an AIA magazine story.

100   ibid.

101   Nathaniel Owings, 'Chapter Five', *The Spaces In Between*, draft manuscript, p.6. Nathaniel Alexander Owings Papers, Box 50, Library of Congress.

102   ibid.

103   While SOM touted the Lever House scheme as unique, a similar office building design by architect Pietro Belluschi was proposed for 194X, six years before the Lever House design. Designed to promote community development in a city, as opposed to the suburbs, Belluschi's office design featured a 12-storey office slab and a pedestrian plaza intended to develop into an outdoor community space. The two elements comprised a vertical and horizontal massing, bearing resemblance to the Lever House design. However, Belluschi's slab was oriented in a parallel, not perpendicular, relationship to the street. There were other differences between the two projects, including the inclusion of shops on the ground level in Belluschi's scheme, and the lack thereof in Lever House. Yet, it should be noted that Belluschi's unbuilt, yet widely circulated, design predated SOM's by six years. See 'New Buildings for 194X', *Architectural Forum* (May 1943), pp 108–12. Also see Andrew Shanken's excellent book, *194X: Architecture, Planning, and Consumer Culture on the American Home Front* (University of Minnesota Press, Minneapolis, MN, 2009).

104   The Lever House presentation model was made by Ted Conrad, an independent model-maker. Luckman, p.242.

105   ibid.

106   ibid.

107   ibid.

108   ibid.

109   ibid.

110   ibid., p.244.

111   ibid., p.246.

112   One of the youngest executives of a major American company, Charles Luckman appeared on the cover of *Time* magazine's 10 June 1947 issue. ibid., p.247.

113   Bunshaft, interviewed by Drexler, Tape 2.

114   'Oral History of Gordon Bunshaft', p.161.

115   Bunshaft, interviewed by Drexler, Tape 2.

116   Brown to Owings, October 1970, p.10, Box 49, Nathaniel Alexander Owings Papers, Library of Congress.

117   Bunshaft, interviewed by Drexler, Tape 2.

118   ibid.

119   ibid.

120   ibid.

121   ibid.

122   Despite the architect and client's claims, Lever House's window-washing apparatus was not the first one of its kind. The Pietro Belluschi-designed Equitable Building had a mechanical exterior window-washing apparatus suspended from the roof which predated Lever House's.

123   Reinhold Martin, *The Organizational Complex: Architecture, Media and Corporate Space* (MIT Press, Cambridge, MA, 2003), pp 101–5. Martin argues that Lever House's cleaning apparatus is a symbol of modern hygiene.

124   Interior design – designated as Raymond Loewy Associates in Raymond's Loewy's office – did not involve him, but instead was led by architect William Snaith.

125   Charles Luckman, speaking about Raymond Loewy, cited on http://www.raymondloewy.com/about/quotes.html, accessed January 2010. Estate of Raymond Loewy.

126   Raymond Loewy, *Never Leave Well Enough Alone* (Simon & Schuster, New York, 1951), pp 277–8.

127   ibid.

128   ibid.

129   Luckman, p.137.

130   Loewy's reasoning for the colour choice was presented in *Interiors* magazine. 'New York's Blue Glass Tower: An Insider's View', *Interiors* (August 1952), p.152.

131   'Color Can't Be Beaten as a Sales Stimulant', *Paint and Oil Dealer* (March 1944). Raymond Loewy Collection, Hagley Museum and Library.

132   'New York's Blue Glass Tower: An Insider's View', p.153.

133   Lewis Mumford, 'House of Glass', *The New Yorker*, 9 August 1952, pp 51–2.

134   P.K. Thomajan, 'Lever House, A Manhattan Display Attraction', *Advertising Requirements* (September 1954), p.63, Raymond Loewy Collection, HAG.

135   ibid., p.64.

136   ibid.

137   While Jacques Lipchitz was initially considered to design the ground floor plaza, he was rejected by Bunshaft because his work was not modern enough, and Isamu Noguchi was hired. He designed a full scheme for Lever House's plaza, but it was rejected

because of cost. In the end, SOM designed the plaza. Bunshaft, interviewed by Drexler, Tape 2.

138   Vincent Scully, 'The Death of the Street', *Perspecta*, vol.8 (1963), pp 91–6. Scully pointed out that Lever House's architectural success depended to some extent on the traditional heavy materials of the adjacent and surrounding buildings.

139   The architects took advantage of a provision in the zoning law that permitted a tower without setbacks of any height, if it did not occupy more than 25 per cent of its building lot.

140   Owings, *The Spaces In Between*, p.107.

141   ibid.

142   ibid., p.110.

143   'New York's Blue Glass Tower: An Insider's View', p.152.

144   Bunshaft, interviewed by Drexler, Tape 2.

145   Aline B. Louchheim, 'Newest Building in the New Style', *The New York Times*, 27 April 1952, p.9.

146   Ada Louise Huxtable, 'The Park Avenue School of Architecture', *The New York Times Magazine*, 15 December 1957, p.30.

147   'Oral History of Gordon Bunshaft', p.167.

148   Mumford, pp 48–54.

149   ibid.

150   ibid.

151   ibid.

152   ibid.

153   ibid.

154   ibid.

155   Gordon Bunshaft claimed that Lever Brothers believed Lever House to be their monument. Gordon Bunshaft interviewed by Arthur Drexler, Tape 1, 16 January 1980, sound recording, Gordon Bunshaft, 1909–1990, architectural drawings and papers, Avery Library, Columbia University.

156   Bill Brown referenced J.E. Drew in a letter to Nathaniel Owings, October 1970, p.10, Box 49, Nathaniel Alexander Owings Papers, Library of Congress.

157   ibid.

158   J.E. Drew, 'The Economic Value of Design', American Institute of Architects Annual Convention, New Orleans, 25 June 1959, copy in Lever House file, SOM, in Alexandra Lange, 'Tower, Typewriter and Trademark: Architects, Designers and the Corporate Utopia, 1956–1964' (PhD dissertation, New York University, 2005), p.134. My emphasis.

159   Lever Brothers quantified the success rates of the building in terms of employee recruitment and retention; see ibid.

160   Owings, *The Spaces In Between*, p.260.

161   ibid., pp 270–71.

162   ibid.

163   ibid.

164   ibid., p.266.

165   ibid.

166   ibid., p.268.

167   Brown to Owings, October 1970, p.10, Nathaniel Alexander Owings Papers, Box 49, Library of Congress.

168   The Inland Steel Building (Chicago, 1956–1958) possessed SOM's signature form in its two glass and stainless-steel towers, but it was the client's influence, the suggestion of buttresses, that made it unique. Crown Zellerbach's (San Francisco, 1957–1959) massing displayed SOM's formula of two volumes. Yet, a departure from Lever House was that it featured protruding vertical mullions. Union Carbide (New York, 1957–1960) asserted its design difference from Lever House with steel protrusions on its facade, inspired instead by Mies van der Rohe's Seagram Building, built a couple years earlier, from 1954–1958.

5   MATERIAL The Röhm and Haas Building

1   At this time, leading consumer goods companies – including Procter & Gamble, General Foods, and Unilever – developed the concept of brand management. F.H.K. Henrion and A. Parkin, *Design Coordination and Corporate Image* (Studio Vista, London, 1967). Books describing corporate identity in this era include Henrion and Parkin's *Design Coordination and Corporate Image* (1967), and James Pilditch's *Communication by Design: A Study in Corporate Identity* (McGraw-Hill, New York, 1970).

2   Colin Rowe, 'Chicago Frame', reprinted in *The Mathematics of the Ideal Villa, and Other Essays* (MIT Press, Cambridge, MA, 1982), p.108.

3   John F. Bauman, 'Expressways, Public Housing and Renewal: A Blueprint for Postwar Philadelphia, 1945–1960', *Pennsylvania History: A Journal of Mid-Atlantic Studies*, vol.57, no.1 (January 1990), pp 44–65.

4   Gregory L. Heller, *Ed Bacon: Planning, Politics, and the Building of Modern Philadelphia* (University of Pennsylvania Press, Philadelphia, PA, 2013), p.130.

5   For a detailed history of the Bicentennial planning, see Heller, pp 184–90.

6   A 1965 *Architectural Record* article presented a Left-leaning view of urban renewal in Philadelphia, delivering a damning prediction that 'until the shelter needs of our lowest income groups are met, urban renewal will never progress beyond the face lifting of downtown, a few new industrial districts, and the reclamation of isolated residential neighborhoods for upper income families.' Mildred F. Schmertz, 'Philadelphia Report: A Long Wait for the Renaissance', *Architectural Record* (July 1965), p.120.

7   Other urban renewal projects of the time included Vincent Kling's Municipal Services Building, Penn Center office towers, Stonorov and Haws-designed Hopkinson House apartment building, Pei's Society Hill Towers, and Louis Kahn's Mill Creek public housing.

8   The politically active Greater Philadelphia Movement was a volunteer group of corporate leaders who believed the city's scandalous political corruption threatened its economic future. Guian McKee, in Heller, p.53.

9   Martin Anderson discusses the entry of large corporations into the urban renewal field and specifically points to Reynolds Aluminum and Alcoa as deeply involved. Martin Anderson, *The Federal Bulldozer: A Critical Analysis of Urban Renewal, 1942–1962* (MIT Press, Cambridge, MA, 1964), p.109. He notes aluminium companies Alcoa and Reynolds Metals as positive examples of corporate developers. For example, Alcoa, a large manufacturer of aluminium products, became involved in urban renewal when it bought most of Zeckendorf's urban renewal interests. Also, Anderson identifies the Reynolds Aluminum Company as the best example of a corporation-developer. Both are discussed later as exemplary clients of branded architecture.

10   Letter From D.T. Brophy, Plastics Department to Kydex Thermoformers & Fabricators, 5 May 1969, the Röhm and Haas Collection, Science History Institute.

11   Röhm and Haas received an Army-Navy Excellence Award in January 1943, as well as commendations in September 1943, October 1944, and May 1945. Regina Lee Blaszczyk, *Röhm and Haas: A Century of Innovation* (Fenwick Publishing Group, Bainbridge Island, Washington, 2009), p.77.

12   ibid., p.107.

13   *Looking Ahead Through Rohm & Haas Plexiglas* (Jam Handy Organization; Röhm and Haas Company), 1947, film.

14   ibid.

15   ibid.

16   ibid.

17   ibid.

18   ibid.

19   Sheldon Hochheiser, *Röhm and Haas, History of a Chemical Company* (University of Pennsylvania Press, Philadelphia, PA, 1986), p.88.

20   Blaszczyk, p.79. Regina Blaszczyk is a business historian and wrote the most recent Röhm and Haas history based on unfettered access to the company's archives. Before Blaszczyk's book, Sheldon Hochheiser's history of the Röhm and Haas company was published in 1986.

21   Blaszczyk, p.116.

22   ibid., p.124.

23   ibid.

24   Ralph Connor interview, 1983, Series III Research & Reference Materials, p.140, the Röhm and Haas Collection, Science History Institute.

25   The patent department was in the Penn Mutual Building, and a number of employees were across town at 1700 Walnut Street.

26   Ralph Connor interview.

27   Meredith Clausen, who is the authority on architect Pietro Belluschi, points out that corporate clients in the 1950s and 1960s recognised that architecturally distinctive buildings paid off in profits and prestige. Yet at the same time, these clients shied away from 'prize-winning architects' because of their high fees and time-consuming code variances. Meredith Clausen, *Pietro Belluschi: Modern American Architect* (MIT Press, Cambridge, MA, 1994), p.283.

28   Memo, Alexander Ewing to Andrew Jarvis, Re: Röhm and Haas Building, 6 March 2006, p.1, courtesy of EwingCole. Unfortunately, the firm of EwingCole, successor of George Ewing & Co., has not kept records of the design and correspondence of the Röhm and Haas Building. Alexander Ewing's recollections of the Röhm and Haas Building project occurred 40 years later.

29   Memo, Stanley Cole to Andrew Jarvis, March 2006, p.1, courtesy of EwingCole.

30   The search for a new Röhm and Haas headquarters location went beyond the city, with suburban locations being seriously considered. A good number of employees commuted from suburban homes and Trenton, Jenkintown, and the Main Line

were contenders for the new site. After some study, remaining downtown made the most sense because transportation routes converging on suburban locations were uneven. As it turned out commute time to the city remained easiest for most employees, thus the least number of employees would be lost as a result of the impending move. Ralph Connor interview.

31   ibid.

32   The redevelopment area was along 5th and 6th Streets from Chestnut Street northward to Race Street and the access to the Benjamin Franklin Bridge. Memo, Stanley Cole to Andrew Jarvis, March 2006, p.1, courtesy of EwingCole.

33   William McClintock worked closely with Jack Robin, the executive director of the Old Philadelphia Development Corporation, and William Rafsky of the Philadelphia Redevelopment Authority, plus a recent planning school graduate, Walter D'Alessio. They did the heavy lifting, but with essential input from Mayor Dilworth, Ed Bacon, the Haas brothers, and board members of the Old Philadelphia Development Corporation Memo, Alexander Ewing to Andrew Jarvis, Re: Röhm and Haas Building, 6 March 2006, p.2, courtesy of EwingCole.

34   The Calendar of Renewal, Old Philadelphia Development Corporation, 1963, the Röhm and Haas Collection, Science History Institute.

35   ibid.

36   Stanley Cole was the only architect in the company. Nadine Cole (Stanley Cole's widow), telephone call, 3 February 2017.

37   ibid.

38   Walter D'Alessio email to the author, 8 August 2017. While it is fortunate that Walter D'Alessio was still living at the time of writing this book, his recollections of the building project 50 years prior may be distorted.

39   Memo, Alexander Ewing to Andrew Jarvis, Re: Röhm and Haas Building, 6 March 2006, p.2, courtesy of EwingCole.

40   Meeting minutes dated 12 June 1962, design meeting with Dean Pietro Belluschi, Alexander Ewing, Martin Gordon, and Alexander Toland (last three of the George M. Ewing Co.) at MIT, Belluschi Collection, Syracuse University, Special Collections Research Center.

41   ibid.

42   Walter D'Alessio email to the author, 3 August 2017. At the time of the Röhm and Haas project (from 1960 onwards), Walter D'Alessio was the Center City

Project Coordinator for the Redevelopment Authority of the City of Philadelphia. He was with the Authority from 1960 to 1972 and served as the executive director from 1971 to 1972.

43   Walter D'Alessio email to the author, 3 August 2017. Geddes shared modernist ideals with Belluschi as well as a similar dual career in academia and practice. In 1963, he and his firm would complete the expressionist Philadelphia Police Administration Building. By 1965, Geddes would become dean of the architecture department at Princeton University, a post he would hold for the next 17 years.

44   31 May 1962, WT McClintock, Treasurer, Röhm and Haas to Dean Pietro Belluschi, Belluschi Collection, Syracuse University, Special Collections Research Center.

45   Meeting minutes dated 3 August 1962, Belluschi Collection, Syracuse University, Special Collections Research Center.

46   Walter D'Alessio email to the author, 8 August 2017.

47   Jan C. Rowen, 'Wanting to Be: The Philadelphia School', *Progressive Architecture* (April 1961).

48   Attending Louis Kahn's lecture at the University of Pennsylvania architecture school, Alec Ewing sat with his wife, Nance Ewing. While Kahn was passionately speaking, Nance turned to Alec and whispered, 'This is all bullshit, isn't it?' In response, Alec smiled and nodded knowingly. Phone interview with Andrew Jarvis by the author, 8 February 2017.

49   Memo, Stanley Cole to Andy Jarvis, 8 March 2006, p.1, courtesy of EwingCole.

50   Clausen lists these and additional individuals, institutions, and corporations that hired Belluschi to consult. Clausen, p.271.

51   I am indebted to Meredith Clausen's seminal scholarship in *Pietro Belluschi: Modern American Architect* for the details of Pietro Belluschi's background.

52   Clausen, p.20.

53   Belluschi addressed students at the University of Washington, according to an article in *The University of Washington Daily*, Seattle, 14 May 1948, quoted in Clausen, p.188.

54   Belluschi encouraged architects to face 'creatively as free spirits and in deep honesty the complexities of our modern world, never forgetting that man is the measure of all values'. Pietro Belluschi, 'The Meaning of Regionalism', *Architectural Record*

(December 1955), pp 131–9. Cited in Clausen, pp 213–14.

55   Clausen points out that Belluschi and the Equitable Building's acclaim was lessened by a number of factors including his distant West Coast location and geographic distance from MoMA and the tastemakers. Clausen, p.172. Clausen clarified this point with the author, 2 September 2017.

56   Clausen, p.194.

57   ibid.

58   Judith Blau and K.L. Lieben, 'Growth, Decline, and Death: A Panel Study of Architectural Firms', in Judith R. Blau, Mark E. La Gory and John S. Pipkin (eds), *Professionals and Urban Form* (State University of New York Press, Albany, 1983), pp 224–50, cited in Dana Cuff, *Architecture: The Story of Practice* (MIT Press, Cambridge, MA, 1991), p.55.

59   John Morris Dixon, 'Design Quality in the Big Firm', *Progressive Architecture*, vol.63, no.2 (February 1982), pp 23–4, cited in Cuff, p.47.

60   Clausen describes the shying away of corporate clients from 'prize-winning architects' because they were cost- and time-prohibitive. She shows how Belluschi's consultancy was a compromise, a renowned architect but not a prima donna. At the same time, hiring Belluschi as a consultant with a well-priced commercial architecture firm was cheaper. Clausen, pp 283–4.

61   Meredith Clausen points out that Belluschi's design for Röhm and Haas clearly displays modern architectural principles. The formalistic turn of the design, the exposed reinforced concrete, and the muscular columns show Belluschi's desire to keep up with changing developments in architecture at the time. Clausen clarified this point with the author, 2 September 2017.

62   'As private interests continued to clash with those of the public throughout the decade, Belluschi became emblematic of an exploitative establishment.' Clausen, p.267.

63   Jo Stubblebine (ed.), *The Northwest Architecture of Pietro Belluschi* (F.W. Dodge Corporation, New York, 1953), p.30.

64   Memo, Stanley Cole to Andrew Jarvis, March 2006, p.1, courtesy of EwingCole. Like Ewing's, Stanley Cole's recollections of the Röhm and Haas Building project occurred 40 years later, so there is the possibility of distortion.

65   Clausen, p.313.

66   Meeting minutes dated 12 June 1962, design meeting with Dean Pietro Belluschi, Alexander Ewing, Martin Gordon, and Alexander Toland (last three of the George M. Ewing Co.) at MIT, p.1, Belluschi Collection, Syracuse University, Special Collections Research Center.

67   ibid., p.1.

68   ibid., p.2.

69   ibid., p.1.

70   ibid., p.1.

71   ibid., p.2.

72   Alec Ewing recalled, 'The design proceeded in a true association relationship. Stan [Cole] and I would go to Cambridge, Massachusetts for critiques from Pietro or he would come to Philadelphia and work with us "on the board." The process began by my associate Sandy Toland and I developing pre-schematic alternates and Pietro producing his suggested design.' Memo, Alec Ewing to Andy Jarvis, 6 March 2006, p.2, courtesy of EwingCole.

73   At the weekly design and construction meetings, the participants were Richard Lindabury, project coordinator, Otto Haas, sometimes John Haas, a Röhm and Haas attorney, Alec Ewing, and Walter D'Alessio. Walter D'Alessio email to the author, 8 August 2017.

74   Minutes of meeting at George M. Ewing Co. with Dean Pietro Belluschi, 26 July 1962, p.1, Belluschi Collection, Syracuse University, Special Collections Research Center.

75   ibid., p.1.

76   Belluschi recommended Dan Kiley as the landscape architect for the project. 'Information on Röhm and Haas Building', p.1, the Röhm and Haas Collection, Science History Institute.

77   'Glass and Plastic in a Prizewinner', *Glass Digest*, November 1966, p.54, the Röhm and Haas Collection, Science History Institute.

78   Röhm and Haas, 'Information on Röhm and Haas Building', p.3, The Röhm and Haas Collection, Science History Institute.

79   The five-foot overhang of the lattice provides a walkway for window washers responsible for cleaning the upper floor windows.

80   Röhm and Haas, 'Information on Röhm and Haas Building', p.2, the Röhm and Haas Collection, Science History Institute.

81   'Glass and Plastic in a Prizewinner', p.80.

82   Meeting minutes dated 12 June 1962, referring to Pietro Belluschi: 'He said that somehow the scale of Independence Hall should be introduced into the tower.' Design meeting with Dean Pietro Belluschi, Alexander Ewing, Martin Gordon, and Alexander Toland (last three of the George M. Ewing Co.) at MIT, p.1, Belluschi Collection, Syracuse University, Special Collections Research Center.

83   Memo, Alec Ewing to Andy Jarvis, 6 March 2006, p.2, courtesy of EwingCole.

84   *Architectural Record*, vol.139, January 1966, pp 141–8.

85   In the years preceding the Röhm and Haas design, Belluschi had incorporated screening devices in his projects including the Bennington College Library in Vermont (1957–1959) and the Belluschi/SOM project for the Tucker Maxon School for the Deaf, in Portland, Oregon. For more information about these projects, see Clausen, pp 245–9.

86   Douglas Haskell, 'Ornament Rides Again', *Architectural Forum* (April 1958), p.85.

87   ibid.

88   Adolf Loos's lecture on 'Ornament and Crime' was given on 21 January 1908 in Vienna and first published in *Cahiers d'aujourd'hui*, no.5 (1913) under the German title *Ornament und Verbrechen*.

89   Haskell.

90   Alan Colquhoun, *Modernity and the Classical Tradition: Architectural Essays 1980–1987* (MIT Press, Cambridge, MA, 1989), p.187.

91   For further scholarship on IBM's corporate branding work, refer to John Harwood, *The Interface: IBM and the Transformation of Corporate Design, 1945–1976* (University of Minnesota Press, Minneapolis, MN, 2011).

92   A number of photographs of Saarinen's John Deere & Co. headquarters are in the Röhm and Haas Collection at the Science History Institute, in the form of contact sheets.

93   For further study of Eero Saarinen's corporate architecture, see Alexandra Lange, 'Tower, Typewriter and Trademark: Architects, Designers and the Corporate Utopia, 1956–1964' (PhD dissertation, New York University, 2005).

94   In a direct mailing letter to authorized Plexiglas distributors, W.T. Reedy, manager of the plastics department at Röhm and Haas, touted Plexiglas acrylic sheet as a safe alternative to glass doors, using the example that the American Medical Association estimates that 40,000 people try to walk through glass doors, with 6,000 winding up in hospital. Letter dated 15 December 1966, the Röhm and Haas Collection, Science History Institute.

95   A number of interesting examples of architectural applications of Plexiglas appear in paste-ups for publication, prepared by Röhm and Haas's advertising department. The Röhm and Haas Collection, Science History Institute.

96   On a building, fascias form the vertical surface under a roof edge or cornice. In this high position, fascias are highly visible and would be the idea place for signage.

97   Frank Lloyd Wright's V.C. Morris Gift Shop in San Francisco, which featured a large Plexiglas lighting fixture, appeared on the cover of the in-house magazine, *Rohm and Hass Reporter*, April–May 1950, the Röhm and Haas Collection, Science History Institute.

98   'State Capitol Bank in Oklahoma City, Oklahoma', 'Capp Towers Motor Hotel Rooftop Dome in Minneapolis, Minnesota', 'Oak Cliff Savings & Loan, Dallas, Texas', *Paste-Up*, the Röhm and Haas Collection, Science History Institute.

99   'Equitable Life Assurance Society Building, New York City', *Paste-Up*, the Röhm and Haas Collection, Science History Institute.

100   'Parke Davis District Office and Warehouse in Cherry Hill, New Jersey', *Paste-Up*, the Röhm and Haas Collection, Science History Institute.

101   'Montgomery Ward Store in the Apache Plaza Shopping Center in Minneapolis, Minnesota', 'Mansfield Shopping Center, Springfield, Ohio', *Paste-Up*, the Röhm and Haas Collection, Science History Institute.

102   'Welcome to Röhm and Haas' pamphlet, pp 3–4, the Röhm and Haas Collection, CHF.

103   ibid., p.1.

104   ibid.

105   Lighting, reprint, October 1966, 2, the Röhm and Haas Collection, Science History Institute.

106   Memo, C. Van R. Bogert Jr of George M. Ewing Co. to Röhm and Haas Company, CC: Stanley Cole, Richard Lindabury, Alex Ewing, Belluschi Collection, Syracuse University, Special Collections Research Center.

107   ibid.

108   In 1964, György Kepes would collaborate with Pietro Belluschi again on St Mary's Cathedral in San Francisco, completed in 1969.

109   *Röhm and Haas Reporter*, March–April 1966, 'New Art Forms in Plexiglas', pp 4–9, the Röhm and Haas Collection, Science History Institute.

110   ibid.

111   Memo, Alec Ewing to Andy Jarvis, 6 March 2006, p.2, courtesy of EwingCole.

112   ibid.

113   Ewing and Cole would remain partners until Cole's death in 2013. The firm EwingCole still exists, located across the street from the Röhm and Haas Building, in the Federal Reserve Bank Building, which the firm designed.

114   Good collaborations were a rare occurrence, as Belluschi's short-lived collaboration with SOM and Ewing's frustrating work with Vincent Kling on Lankenau Hospital proved. Andy Jarvis described Ewing's frustrating collaboration with Vincent Kling as a counterpoint to the good collaboration with Belluschi. Andy Jarvis of EwingCole, phone conversation with the author, 8 February 2017.

115   Robert Gutman, *Architectural Practice: A Critical View* (Princeton Architectural Press, New York, 1988), p.42.

116   News release, Röhm and Haas wins 'Office of the Year' Award, 2-66-69, Röhm and Haas Company News Release, David S. Marston, 17 May 1966, the Röhm and Haas Collection, Science History Institute.

117   In the mid-1960s, due to hysteria over relations with Russia, 'fall-out' shelters were fairly common, but 'blast' shelter constructions were rare. Walter D'Alessio emails to the author, 3 August 2017, 8 August 2017. D'Alessio said that the Röhm and Haas blast shelter was the only one that he knows was designed and built as part of an urban renewal project in this area.

118   News release, Röhm and Haas wins 'Office of the Year' Award.

119   *Architectural Record*, vol.139, January 1966, pp 141–8.

120   Liz Moor, *The Rise of Brands* (Oxford, Berg, 2007), p.30.

121   ibid.

122   Henrion and Parkin.

123   ibid., p.7.

124   Corporate identity includes trademarks and logos. Trademarks identify a company's goods. Trademarks include names, logos, slogans, and designs. Logos are a graphic element – a graphic mark, emblem, symbol, that is part of a trademark.

125   Henrion and Parkin, p.7.

126   Open House for the Röhm and Haas Family, 23–24 October 1965, the Röhm and Haas Collection, Science History Institute.

127   The original logo was a vertically oriented triangle with a composition of Röhm and Haas on the top half and rows of a wave pattern on the bottom half.

128   Henrion and Parkin, p.162.

129   ibid., p.163.

130   See Lange.

131   Henrion and Parkin, p.6.

132   Architect Stanley Cole, the client's representative, served as a de facto design coordinator of the various designers of the Röhm and Haas Building.

133   Michael Saphier, 'Office Design as a Public Relations Medium', *The Office* (March 1966).

134   For further scholarship on the Reynolds Metals headquarters by Minoru Yamasaki, see Grace Ong Yan, 'Architecture, Advertising and Corporations, 1929–1959' (PhD dissertation, University of Pennsylvania, 2010), and 'Wrapping Aluminum at the Reynolds Metals Company: From Cold War Consumerism to the Age of Sustainability', *Design and Culture*, vol.4, no.3 (November 2012), pp 299–324.

135   Röhm and Haas created a number of paste-up layouts illustrating architectural applications of Plexiglas and providing product specifications. A booklet was being planned to promote Plexiglas applications in architecture. The Röhm and Haas Collection, Science History Institute.

136   Plexiglas Sales Letter (Distributors), vol.8, no.2, Box 80, Advertising Materials, Folder 4, the Röhm and Haas Collection, Science History Institute.

137   In addition to Plexiglas, Kydex 5000, an opaque acrylic material, was also applied to building products markets.

6   CONCLUSION Connecting with Society and the Future of Architectural Branding

1   The negative aspect of top-down businesses is shown in Naomi Klein's discussion of the jarring contrast of transcendent with dehumanising labour practices. I make an analogous point that architectural branding of the 1970s, 1980s, and 1990s served a similar function of heightened idealism that was unfulfilled, and ultimately rejected. Naomi Klein, 'No Logo at 10', *The Baffler*, no.18 (December 2009), pp 30–39.

2   Hal Foster quotes Guy Debord's 1967 book *Society of the Spectacle* in making his point about the untenable exclusivity of Frank Gehry's work. Hal Foster, *Design and Crime (and Other Diatribes)* (Verso, London, 2002), p.41.

3   Robert Venturi, *Complexity and Contradiction in Architecture: With an Introduction by Vincent Scully* (The Museum of Modern Art, New York, distributed by Doubleday, Garden City, NY, 1966), p.30.

4   See Charles Jencks's book, *The Iconic Building* (Rizzoli, New York, 2005). Herbert Muschamp's 7 September 1997 essay, 'The Miracle in Bilbao', in *The New York Times Magazine*, was the earliest popular media piece to detail the Frank Gehry-designed Bilbao Guggenheim and its role as an architectural catalyst for urban regeneration.

5   Branding expert Douglas Holt discusses crowd culture in 'Branding in the Age of Social Media', *Harvard Business Review*, March (2016), pp 40–48, 50. Also see, Douglas B. Holt, *How Brands become Icons: The Principles of Cultural Branding* (Harvard Business Review Press, Boston, MA, 2004).

6   Holt explains how a countercultural rise against brands has created a need for authenticity, or 'postmodern branding paradigm', meaning that brands must be perceived as invented and disseminated by parties without an instrumental economic agenda. Douglas B. Holt, 'Why Do Brands Cause Trouble? A Dialectical Theory of Consumer Culture and Branding', *Journal of Consumer Research*, vol.29, no.1 (2002), p.83.

BIBLIOGRAPHY

'A New Shelter for Savings: George Howe and William Lescaze, Architects', *Architectural Forum*, vol.57 (December 1932), pp 483–98.

Abramson, Daniel M. *Skyscraper Rivals: The AIG Building and the Architecture of Wall Street* (Princeton Architectural Press, New York, 2001).

Adams, Nicholas. *Skidmore, Owings & Merrill: SOM since 1936* (Electa Architecture, Milan; Phaidon Press, London, 2007).

Albrecht, Donald, and Chrysanthe B. Broikos (eds). *On the Job: Design and the American Office* (Princeton Architectural Press, New York, 2000).

Alter, George, Claudia Goldin, and Elyce Rotella. 'The Savings of Ordinary Americans: The Philadelphia Saving Fund Society in the Mid-Nineteenth Century', *Journal of Economic History*, vol.54, no.4 (December 1994), pp 735–67.

Anderson, Martin. *The Federal Bulldozer: A Critical Analysis of Urban Renewal, 1942–1962* (MIT Press, Cambridge, MA, 1964).

Balmer, John M.T., and Stephen A. Greyser (eds). *Revealing the Corporation: Perspectives on Identity, Image, Reputation, Corporate Branding, and Corporate-level Marketing* (Routledge, London, 2003).

Banham, Reyner. 'Machine Aesthetic', *Architectural Review*, vol.117 (April 1955), pp 225–8.

Banham, Reyner, and Penny Sparke (eds). *Design by Choice* (Rizzoli, New York, 1981).

Barboza, David. 'At Johnson Wax, A Family Passes on its Heirloom; Father Divides a Business to Keep the Children United', *The New York Times*, 22 August 1999.

Bass, Sam Warner, Jr. *The Private City: Philadelphia in Three Periods of Its Growth* (University of Pennsylvania Press, Philadelphia, PA, 1968).

Bauman, John F. 'Expressways, Public Housing and Renewal: A Blueprint for Postwar Philadelphia, 1945–1960', *Pennsylvania History: A Journal of Mid-Atlantic Studies*, vol.57, no.1 (January 1990), pp 44–65.

Bayer, Herbert. 'On Typography', in Arthur Cohen and Herbert Bayer (eds), *Herbert Bayer: The Complete Work* (MIT Press, Cambridge, MA, 1984).

Bayer, Herbert, Walter Gropius and Ise Gropius. *Bauhaus 1919–1928* (Museum of Modern Art, New York, 1952).

Belfoure, Charles. *Monuments to Money: The Architecture of American Banks* (McFarland & Co., Jefferson, NC, 2005).

Belluschi, Pietro. 'The Meaning of Regionalism', *Architectural Record* (December 1955), pp 131–9.

Bergdoll, Barry, et al. *Bauhaus 1919–1933: Workshops for Modernity* (Museum of Modern Art, New York, 2009).

Bernays, Edward L. *Propaganda* (H. Liveright, New York, 1928).

Bertelli, Patrizio, Rem Koolhaas, Jens Hommert and Michael Kubo. *Projects for Prada, Part 1* (Fondazione Prada Edizioni, Milan, 2001).

Blaszczyk, Regina Lee. *Röhm and Haas: A Century of Innovation* (Fenwick Publishing Group, Bainbridge Island, Washington, 2009).

Blau, Judith R., Mark E. La Gory and John S. Pipkin (eds). *Professionals and Urban Form* (State University of New York Press, Albany, 1983).

Brooks, H. Allen. 'Frank Lloyd Wright and the Destruction of the Box', *Journal of the Society of Architectural Historians*, vol.38, no.1 (March 1979), pp 7–14.

Brownell, Baker, and Frank Lloyd Wright. *Architecture and Modern Life* (Harper & Brothers, New York and London, 1937).

Brownlee, David Bruce. *Building the City Beautiful: The Benjamin Franklin Parkway and the Philadelphia Museum of Art* (Philadelphia Museum of Art, Philadelphia, PA, 1989).

Brownlee, David Bruce, and David Gilson De Long. *Louis I. Kahn: In the Realm of Architecture* (Rizzoli, New York, 1991).

Brownlee, David Bruce, David Gilson De Long, Kathryn B. Hiesinger, Robert Venturi and Denise Scott Brown. *Out of the Ordinary: Robert Venturi, Denise*

Scott Brown and Associates: Architecture, Urbanism, Design (Philadelphia Museum of Art, Philadelphia, PA, 2001).

Bunshaft, Gordon. 'Oral History of Gordon Bunshaft'. Interview by Betty J. Blum, manuscript, 1990. *The Chicago Architects Oral History Project*, The Art Institute of Chicago.

Bush, Donald J. The Streamlined Decade (George Braziller, New York, 1975).

Campbell, Barbara. 'H.F. Johnson Dies; Led Wax Company', *The New York Times*, 14 December 1978.

Carter, Brian. *Johnson Wax Administration Building and Research Tower: Frank Lloyd Wright* (London, Phaidon Press, 1998).

Chandler, Alfred Dupont. *Strategy and Structure: Chapters in the History of the Industrial Enterprise* (MIT Press, Cambridge, MA, 1969).

Cheney, Sheldon, and Martha Cheney. *Art and the Machine: An Account of Industrial Design in 20th-Century America* (McGraw Hill, New York, 1936).

Clausen, Meredith L. 'The Department Store: Development of the Type', *Journal of Architectural Education*, vol.39, no.1 (1985), pp 20–29.

Clausen, Meredith L. *Spiritual Space: The Religious Architecture of Pietro Belluschi* (University of Washington Press, Seattle, 1992).

Clausen, Meredith. *Pietro Belluschi: Modern American Architect* (MIT Press, Cambridge, MA, 1994).

Clausen, Meredith L. *The Pan Am Building and the Shattering of the Modernist Dream* (MIT Press, Cambridge, MA, 2005).

Cohen, Lizabeth. *A Consumers' Republic: The Politics of Mass Consumption in Postwar America* (Vintage Books, New York, 2003).

Colomina, Beatriz. *Privacy and Publicity: Modern Architecture as Mass Media* (MIT Press, Cambridge, MA, 1994).

Colquhoun, Alan. *Modernity and the Classical Tradition: Architectural Essays, 1980–1987* (MIT Press, Cambridge, MA, 1989).

Colquhoun, Alan. *Modern Architecture*. Oxford History of Art (Oxford University Press, Oxford and New York, 2002).

'Corporation: Old Empire, New Prince', *Time*, 10 June 1946.

Crawford, Margaret. *Building the Workingman's Paradise: The Design of American Company Towns* (Verso, London and New York, 1995).

Creese, Walter L. *The Search for Environment: The Garden City Before and After*. Expanded edition (Johns Hopkins University Press, Baltimore, 1992).

Cuff, Dana. *Architecture: The Story of Practice* (MIT Press, Cambridge, MA, 1991).

Danz, Ernst, and Skidmore Owings & Merrill. *Architecture of Skidmore, Owings & Merrill, 1950–1962* (Praeger, New York, 1963).

deBlois, Natalie. 'Oral History of Natalie deBlois'. Interview by Betty J. Blum, manuscript, 2004. *The Chicago Architects Oral History Project*, The Art Institute of Chicago.

Debord, Guy. *Society of the Spectacle* (Zone Books, New York 1994[1967]).

Dichter, Ernest. *The Strategy of Desire* (Facsimiles-Garl, New York, 1960).

Dixon, John Morris. 'Design Quality in the Big Firm', *Progressive Architecture*, vol.63, no.2 (February 1982).

'Does Modern Architecture Pay?' *Architectural Forum*, vol.83, no.9 (September 1943), pp 69–75.

Doordan, Dennis. *Design History: An Anthology* (MIT Press, Cambridge, MA, 1996).

Dunlop, Beth, Robert McCarter, James Steele and Brian Carter. *Frank Lloyd Wright: Unity Temple, Barnsdall (Hollyhock) House, Johnson Wax Administration Building and Research Tower*, Architecture 3S (Phaidon Press, London, 1999).

Edwards, Richard. *Contested Terrain: The Transformation of the Workplace in the Twentieth Century* (Basic Books, New York, 1979).

'Fair Atmosphere as Wright Building Opens', *Milwaukee Sentinel*, 24 April 1939.

Fenske, Gail. *The Skyscraper and the City: The Woolworth Building and the Making of Modern New York* (University of Chicago Press, Chicago, 2008).

Flowers, Benjamin. *The Politics and Power of Building New York City in the Twentieth Century* (University of Pennsylvania Press, Philadelphia, PA, 2009).

Foster, Hal. *Design and Crime (and Other Diatribes)* (Verso, London, 2002).

Frampton, Kenneth. *Modern Architecture: A Critical History* (Thames & Hudson, London, 1980).

Friedman, Donald. 'Hidden Intricacies: The Development of Modern Building Skeletons', *APT Bulletin: The Journal of Preservation Technology*, vol.43, no.4 (2012), pp 13–21.

Garth, John. 'The Office of the Future for S.C. Johnson and Son, Incorporated', *American Business*, May 1939.

Gill, Brendan. *Many Masks: A Life of Frank Lloyd Wright* (G.P. Putnam's Sons, New York, 1987).

Gray, Nicolete. *Lettering on Buildings: 270 Illustrations* (Architectural Press, London, 1960).

Gudis, Catherine. *Buyways: Billboards, Automobiles, and the American Landscape* (London, Routledge, 2004)

Gutman, Robert. *Architectural Practice: A Critical View* (Princeton Architectural Press, New York, 1988).

Harrington, Burton. *The Essentials of Poster Design* (Poster Advertising Association Inc., Chicago, 1925).

Harwood, John. *The Interface: IBM and the Transformation of Corporate Design, 1945–1976* (University of Minnesota Press, Minneapolis, MN, 2011).

Haskell, Douglas. 'Building or Sculpture? The Architecture of "Mass"', *Architectural Record* (April 1930).

Haskell, Douglas. 'The Filing-Cabinet Building', *Creative Art*, vol.10 (June 1932), pp 446–8.

Haskell, Douglas. 'Ornament Rides Again', *Architectural Forum* (April 1958), pp 85–6.

Heller, Gregory L. *Ed Bacon: Planning, Politics, and the Building of Modern Philadelphia* (University of Pennsylvania Press, Philadelphia, PA, 2013).

Heller, Steven. 'Commercial Modern: American Design Style, 1925–1933', *Print*, vol.49, no.5 (September–October, 1995), pp 58–122.

Henderson, Amy. 'Media and the Rise of Celebrity Culture', *OAH Magazine of History*, vol.6, no.4 (Spring 1992).

Henrion, F.H.K., and Alan Parkin. *Design Coordination and Corporate Image* (Studio Vista, London, 1967).

Hertzberg, Mark. *Wright in Racine: The Architect's Vision for One American City* (Pomegranate, Petaluma, CA, 2004).

Hitchcock, Henry-Russell, *Modern Architecture: Romanticism and Reintegration* (Payson & Clarke Ltd, New York, 1929).

Hitchcock, Henry-Russell. 'The Architecture of Bureaucracy and the Architecture of Genius', *Architectural Review*, vol.101 (January 1947), pp 3–6.

Hitchcock, Henry-Russell. *Architecture: Nineteenth and Twentieth Centuries* (Penguin Books, Harmondsworth, 1958).

Hitchcock, Henry-Russell and Philip Johnson. *The International Style: Architecture since 1922* (W.W. Norton, New York, 1932).

Hochheiser, Sheldon. *Röhm and Haas: History of a Chemical Company* (University of Pennsylvania Press, Philadelphia, PA, 1986).

Holt, Douglas B. 'Why Do Brands Cause Trouble? A Dialectical Theory of Consumer Culture and Branding', *Journal of Consumer Research*, vol.29, no.1 (2002), pp 70–90.

Holt, Douglas, B. *How Brands Become Icons: The Principles of Cultural Branding* (Harvard Business Review Press, Boston, MA, 2004).

Holt, Douglas, B. 'Branding in the Age of Social Media', *Harvard Business Review* (March 2016), pp 40–48, 50.

Houndshell, David A. *From the American System to Mass Production, 1800–1932: The Development of Manufacturing Technology in the United States* (Johns Hopkins University Press, Baltimore, 1984).

Howe, George. 'Philadelphia Savings Fund Society Branch Offices', *Architectural Forum,* vol.48 (June 1928), pp 881–6.

Hubbard, Edward, and Michael Shippobottom. *A Guide to Port Sunlight Village* (Liverpool University Press, Liverpool, 2005).

Huxtable, Ada Louise. 'The Park Avenue School of Architecture', *The New York Times Magazine*, 15 December 1957.

Jacobs, Jane. 'New York's Office Boom', *Architectural Forum*, vol.106 (March 1957), pp 104–13.

Jakle, John A. *Signs in America's Auto Age: Signatures of Landscape and Place* (University of Iowa Press, Iowa City, 2004).

Jam Handy Organization. *Looking Ahead Through Rohm & Haas Plexiglas*. Röhm and Haas Company, 1947, film.

James, Kathleen. *Erich Mendelsohn and the Architecture of German Modernism: Modern Architecture and Cultural Identity* (Cambridge University Press, Cambridge, 1997).

Jencks, Charles. *The Iconic Building* (Rizzoli, New York, 2005).

Johnson, Philip. 'Is Sullivan the Father of Functionalism?' *Art News*, no.55 (December 1956), pp 44–6, 56–7.

Johnson, Samuel C. *The Essence of a Family Enterprise: Doing Business the Johnson Way* (The Curtis Publishing Company, Indianapolis, 1988).

'Johnson's Wax Program Smoothes Sales Approach to Dealers and Consumers', *Broadcast Merchandising* (May 1939), pp 4–5.

Jones, Geoffrey. 'Control, Performance, and Knowledge Transfers in Large Multinationals: Unilever in the United States, 1945–1980', *Business History Review*, vol.76, no.3 (Autumn 2002), pp 435–78.

Jones, Geoffrey. *Multinationals and Global Capitalism: From the Nineteenth to the Twenty-First Century* (Oxford University Press, Oxford and New York, 2005).

Jordy, William H. 'PSFS: Its Development and Its Significance in Modern Architecture', *The Journal of the Society of Architectural Historians*, vol.21, no.2 (May 1962), pp 47–83.

Kaufmann, Edgar, and Ben Raeburn (eds). *Frank Lloyd Wright: Writings & Buildings* (New American Library, New York, 1960).

Kiesler, Frederick. *Contemporary Art Applied to the Store and Its Display* (Brentano's, New York, 1930).

King, Stephen. 'Brand-Building in the 1990s', *Journal of Marketing Management*, vol.7, no.1 (1991), pp 3–13.

Kinross, Robin. *Modern Typography: An Essay in Critical History* (Hyphen Press, London, 2004).

Klein, Naomi. *No Logo* (Picador, New York, 2000).

Klein, Naomi. 'No Logo at 10', *The Baffler*, no.18 (December 2009), pp 30–39.

Krinsky, Carol Herselle. *Gordon Bunshaft of Skidmore, Owings & Merrill* (Architectural History Foundation, New York; MIT Press, Cambridge, MA, 1988).

Lambert, Phyllis. *Building Seagram* (Yale University Press, New Haven, CT, 2013).

Lange, Alexandra. 'Tower, Typewriter and Trademark: Architects, Designers and the Corporate Utopia, 1956–1964' (PhD dissertation, New York University, 2005).

Lanmon, Lorraine Welling. *William Lescaze, Architect* (Art Alliance Press, Philadelphia, PA; Associated University Presses, London, 1987).

Leach, William. *Land of Desire: Merchants, Power, and the Rise of a New American Culture* (Vintage, New York, 1994).

Lears, Jackson T. *Fables of Abundance: A Cultural History of Advertising in America* (Basic Books, New York, 1995).

Leatherbarrow, David. *Architecture Otherwise Oriented* (Princeton Architectural Press, New York, 2009).

Leatherbarrow, David, and Mohsen Mostafavi. *Surface Architecture* (MIT Press, Cambridge, MA, 2002).

Le Corbusier. *Almanach d'architecture moderne*, Collection de 'L'Esprit Nouveau' (G. Cráes et Cie, Paris, 1925).

Lescaze, William. *On Being an Architect* (New York, G.P. Putnam's Sons, 1942).

Levine, Neil. *The Architecture of Frank Lloyd Wright* (Princeton University Press, Princeton, NJ, 1996).

Levine, Neil. *The Urbanism of Frank Lloyd Wright* (Princeton University Press, Princeton, NJ, 2015).

Licht, Walter. *Industrializing America: The Nineteenth Century* (Johns Hopkins University Press, Baltimore and London, 1995).

Lipman, Jonathan. *Frank Lloyd Wright and the Johnson Wax Buildings* (Rizzoli, New York, 1986).

Loewy, Raymond. *Never Leave Well Enough Alone* (Simon & Schuster, New York, 1951).

Lohr, Lenox. *Fair Management: A Story of a Century of Progress* (Cuneo Press, Chicago, 1952).

Longstreth, Richard. *The American Department Store Transformed, 1920–1960* (Yale University Press, New Haven, CT, 2010).

Louchheim, Aline B. 'Newest Building in the New Style', *The New York Times*, 27 April 1952.

Luckman, Charles. *Twice in a Lifetime: From Soap to Skyscrapers* (W.W. Norton, New York, 1988).

Lupton, Ellen, and J. Abbott Miller. *The ABC's of [triangle] [circle] [square]: The Bauhaus and Design Theory* (Princeton Architectural Press, New York, 1991).

McCarter, Robert. *Frank Lloyd Wright* (London, Phaidon, 1999).

McMurtrie, Douglas C. *Modern Typography & Layout* (Eyncourt Press, Chicago, 1929).

Marchand, Roland. *Advertising the American Dream: Making Way for Modernity, 1920–1940* (University of California Press, Berkeley, CA, 1986).

Marchand, Roland. *Creating the Corporate Soul: The Rise of Public Relations and Corporate Imagery in American Big Business* (University of California Press, Berkeley, CA, 1998).

Martin, Reinhold. *The Organizational Complex: Architecture, Media and Corporate Space* (MIT Press, Cambridge, MA, 2003).

May, Elaine Tyler. *Homeward Bound: American Families in the Cold War Era* (Basic Books, New York, 1988).

'Merchandising in a Modern Manner', *Buildings: The Magazine of Building Management* (October 1947).

Merwood-Salisbury, Joanna. *Chicago 1890: The Skyscraper and the Modern City* (University of Chicago Press, Chicago, 2009)

Mies van der Rohe, Ludwig, Detlef Mertins and George Baird. *The Presence of Mies* (Princeton Architectural Press, New York, 1994).

'Modern Living: To Cherish Rather than Destroy', *Time*, 2 August 1968.

Moor, Liz. *The Rise of Brands* (Oxford, Berg, 2007).

Morshed, Adnan. *Impossible Heights: Skyscrapers, Flight, and the Master Builder* (University of Minnesota, Minneapolis, MN, 2015).

Moudry, Roberta (ed.). *The American Skyscraper: Cultural Histories* (Cambridge University Press, Cambridge, 2005).

Mozingo, Louise. *Pastoral Capitalism: A History of Suburban Corporate Landscapes* (MIT Press, Cambridge, MA, 2014).

Mumford, Lewis. 'House of Glass', *The New Yorker*, 9 August 1952, pp 48–54.

Mumford, Lewis, and Robert Wojtowicz (eds). *Sidewalk Critic: Lewis Mumford's Writings on New York* (Princeton Architectural Press, New York, 1998).

Muschamp, Herbert. *Man About Town* (MIT Press, Cambridge, MA, 1973).

Muschamp, Herbert. 'The Miracle in Bilbao', *The New York Times Magazine*, 7 September 1997.

Muschamp, Herbert. 'Charles Luckman, Architect who Designed Penn Station's Replacement, Dies at 89', *New York Times*, 28 January 1999.

Neuhaus, Jessamyn. *Housework and Housewives in American Advertising: Married to the Mop* (Palgrave Macmillan, New York, 2011).

Neumeier, Marty. *Brand Gap: How to Bridge the Distance Between Business Strategy and Design* (New Riders, Berkeley, CA, 2006).

'New Buildings for 194X', *Architectural Forum* (May 1943), pp 108–12.

'New Frank Lloyd Wright Office Building Shows Shape of Things to Come', *Life*, 8 May 1939.

'New York's Blue Glass Tower: An Insider's View', *Interiors* (August 1952), pp 58–65, 152–4.

Newhouse, Victoria. *Wallace K. Harrison, Architect* (Rizzoli, New York, 1989).

Ong Yan, Grace. 'Architecture, Advertising and Corporations, 1929–1959' (PhD dissertation, University of Pennsylvania, 2010).

Ong Yan, Grace. 'Wrapping Aluminum at the Reynolds Metals Company: From Cold War Consumerism to the Age of Sustainability', *Design and Culture*, vol.4, no.3 (November 2012), pp 299–324.

Owings, Nathaniel A. 'A Radically New Conception of Tomorrow's Office Building', *National Real Estate and Building Journal* (January 1948).

Owings, Nathaniel Alexander. *The Spaces In Between: An Architect's Journey* (Houghton Mifflin, Boston, 1973).

Pfeiffer, Bruce Brooks. *Frank Lloyd Wright: The Heroic Years: 1920–1932* (Rizzoli, New York, 2009).

Pilditch, James. *Communication by Design: A Study in Corporate Identity* (McGraw-Hill, New York, 1970).

Pine, B. Joseph, II, and James H. Gilmore. *The Experience Economy: Work Is Theatre & Every Business a Stage* (Harvard Business Review Press, Boston, 1999).

Pope, Daniel. *The Making of Modern Advertising* (Basic Books, New York, 1983).

Quinan, Jack. *Frank Lloyd Wright's Larkin Building: Myth and Fact* (University of Chicago Press, Chicago, 1987).

Reader, W.J. *Fifty Years of Unilever, 1930–1980* (Heinemann, London, 1980).

Ribbat, Christoph. *Flickering Light: A History of Neon* (Reaktion Books, London, 2011).

Rohan, Timothy M. 'Challenging the Curtain Wall: Paul Rudolph's Blue Cross and Blue Shield Building', *Journal of the Society of Architectural Historians*, vol.66, no.1 (March 2007), pp 84–109.

Rowe, Colin. *The Mathematics of the Ideal Villa, and Other Essays* (MIT Press, Cambridge, MA, 1982).

Rowen, Jan C. 'Wanting to Be: The Philadelphia School', *Progressive Architecture* (April 1961), pp 130–69.

Rudolph, Paul, and Sibyl Moholy-Nagy. *The Architecture of Paul Rudolph* (Praeger, New York, 1970).

Rudolph, Paul, and Yukio Futagawa. *Paul Rudolph: Drawings* (A.D.A. EDITA, Tokyo, 1972).

Saphier, Michael. 'Office Design as a Public Relations Medium', *The Office* (March 1966), pp 71–5.

Schmertz, Mildred F. 'Philadelphia Report: A Long Wait for the Renaissance', *Architectural Record* (July 1965), pp 119–32.

Scully, Vincent. 'Louis Sullivan's Architectural Ornament: A Brief Note Concerning Humanist Design in the Age of Force', *Perspecta*, vol.5 (1959), pp 73–80.

Scully, Vincent. 'The Death of the Street', *Perspecta*, vol.8 (1963), pp 91–102.

Seacrest, Meryle. *Frank Lloyd Wright: A Biography* (University of Chicago Press, Chicago, 1998).

Shanken, Andrew. *194X: Architecture, Planning, and Consumer Culture on the American Home Front* (University of Minnesota Press, Minneapolis, MN, 2009).

Sivulka, Juliann. *Soap, Sex, and Cigarettes: A Cultural History of American Advertising* (Wadsworth Publishing, Belmont, CA, 1998).

Smith, Kathryn. *Frank Lloyd Wright: America's Master Architect* (Abbeville Press, New York, 1998).

Solomonson, Katherine. *The Chicago Tribune Tower Competition: Skyscraper Design and Cultural Change in the 1920s* (Cambridge University Press, New York, 2001).

Sparke, Penny. *The Modern Interior* (Reaktion Books, London, 2008).

Stern, Robert A.M. 'PSFS: Beaux-Arts Theory and Rational Expressionism', *Journal of the Society of Architectural Historians*, vol.21 (May 1962), pp 84–102.

Stern, Robert A.M. *George Howe: Towards a Modern American Architecture* (Yale University Press, New Haven, CT, 1975).

Stern, Robert A.M., Thomas Mellins and David Fishman. *New York 1960: Architecture and Urbanism between the Second World War and the Bicentennial* (Monacelli Press, New York, 1995).

Stone, Edward Durell. *The Evolution of an Architect* (Horizon Press, New York, 1962).

Strasser, Susan. *Satisfaction Guaranteed: The Making of the American Mass Market* (Smithsonian Books, Washington, DC, 2004).

Stubblebine, Jo (ed.). *The Northwest Architecture of Pietro Belluschi* (F.W. Dodge Corporation, New York, 1953).

Sullivan, Louis. 'The Tall Office Building Artistically Considered', *Lippincott's Monthly Magazine*, vol.339 (March 1896), pp 403–9.

Summerson, John. 'The Case for a Theory of Modern Architecture', *RIBA Journal* (June 1957), pp 307–10.

Tafuri, Manfredo, and Francesco dal Co. *Modern Architecture* (Harry Abrams, New York, 1980).

Taverne, Ed, Cor Wagenaar and Martien de Vletter. *J.J.P. Oud: Poetic Functionalist, 1890–1963: The Complete Works* (NAi Publishers, Rotterdam, 2001).

'The Case of Charles Luckman: What Happened to Lever Brothers' "Wonder Boy"', *Fortune* (April 1950), pp 81–3, 167–8, 172.

Tice, Patricia. *Wooton Patent Desks: A Place for Everything and Everything in Its Place* (Indiana State Museum, Indianapolis, 1983).

Toynbee, Polly. *A Working Life* (Macmillan, London, 1971).

Tschichold, Jan. *The New Typography: A Handbook for Modern Designers. Weimar and Now: German Cultural Criticism* (University of California Press, Berkeley, CA, 1995).

Venturi, Robert. *Complexity and Contradiction in Architecture: With an Introduction by Vincent Scully* (Museum of Modern Art, New York, distributed by Doubleday, Garden City, NY, 1966).

Venturi, Robert, Denise Scott Brown and Steven Izenour. *Learning from Las Vegas* (MIT Press, Cambridge, MA, 1972).

Veronesi, Giulia. 'Yamasaki and Edward Durell Stone', *Zodiac*, vol.8 (1961), pp 128–31.

Wadhwani, R. Daniel. 'Soothing the People's Panic: The Banking Crisis of the 1930s in Philadelphia', *Pennsylvania Legacies*, vol.11, no.1 (May 2011), pp 24–31.

Ward, Janet. *Weimar Surfaces: Urban Visual Culture in 1920s Germany* (University of California Press, Berkeley, CA, 2001).

'Wellesley's Alternative to "Collegiate Gothic"', *Architectural Forum*, vol.111 (July 1959), pp 88–95.

West, Helen Howe. *George Howe, Architect, 1886–1955: Recollections of My Beloved Father* (W. Nunn Co., Philadelphia, PA, 1973).

Wharton, Annabel Jane. *Building the Cold War: Hilton International Hotels and Modern Architecture* (University of Chicago Press, Chicago, 2001).

Willcox, James M. *A History of the Philadelphia Saving Fund Society, 1816–1916* (J.B. Lippincott Co., Philadelphia, PA, 1916).

Willis, Carol. *Form Follows Finance: Skyscrapers and Skylines in New York and Chicago* (Princeton Architectural Press, New York, 1995).

Wilson, Charles. *The History of Unilever: A Study in Economic Growth and Social Change* (Praeger, New York, 1968).

Woodham, Jonathan. *Twentieth-Century Design* (Oxford University Press, Oxford, 1997).

Wright, Frank Lloyd. Wright Special Issue, *Architectural Forum* (January 1938).

Wright, Frank Lloyd. *An Autobiography* (Pomegranate, San Francisco, 2005; first published by Duell, Sloan and Pearce, New York, 1943).

Wright, Frank Lloyd, Edgar Kaufmann and Ben Raeburn (eds). *Writings and Buildings* (World Pub. Co., Cleveland, 1960).

Yamasaki, Minoru. 'Toward an Architecture for Enjoyment', *Architectural Record*, vol.118 (August 1955), p.144.

'Yamasaki's Ode to Aluminum', *Architectural Forum*, vol.111 (November 1959), pp 140–45.

Yamasaki, Minoru. *A Life in Architecture*. First edition (Weatherhill, New York, 1979).

Yellen, Samuel. *American Labor Struggles* (Amo, New York, 1969).

Zucker, Paul. *New Architecture and City Planning: A Symposium* (Philosophical Library, New York, 1944).

INDEX

Note: *italic* page numbers indicate figures; numbers containing n. refer to notes.

ILLUSTRATION CREDITS